LATIN COURSE

Part

by the same author
LATIN COURSE FOR SCHOOLS, PART I
LATIN COURSE FOR SCHOOLS, PART II
LATIN COURSE FOR SCHOOLS, PART III
GREEK FOR BEGINNERS

LATIN COURSE FOR SCHOOLS
Part II

by
L. A. WILDING, M.A.
Senior Classical Master, Dragon School, Oxford
Formerly Scholar of Oriel College, Oxford

SECOND EDITION

DUCKWORTH

This impression 2004
This edition published in 1995 by
Gerald Duckworth & Co. Ltd.
90-93 Cowcross Street, London EC1M 6BF
Tel: 020 7490 7300
Fax: 020 7490 0080
inquiries@duckworth-publishers.co.uk
www.ducknet.co.uk

First published by Faber & Faber Ltd. in 1950
© 1950 by L.A. Wilding

A catalogue record for this book is available
from the British Library

ISBN 0 7156 2675 2

Printed and bound in Great Britain by
CPI Antony Rowe, Chippenham and Eastbourne

Preface to the Second Edition

The bringing out of a second edition has enabled me to make some corrections and to put some additional exercises at the end of the book; it has been suggested that these will be useful for further practice in some of the main constructions.

Oxford, 1952

Preface to the First Edition

The scheme of this book follows that of Part I. The emphasis is on the Latin-English approach, with translation as the basis of the lesson. Elementary Latin Grammar is continued from the point to which it was taken in Part I; for convenience all the Grammar covered by both Parts is set out in a summary at the end of the book; it is not exhaustive, but should provide a good basis for more advanced work. A short summary of some of the usages and constructions covered by Part I is also included.

The question of pace has constantly been kept in mind: for the sake of thoroughness, the first few chapters, which introduce the Passive Voice, proceed fairly slowly; similarly, the pupil's experience of the uses of the Participles grows from a simple acquaintance with them at an earlier stage.

The passages for translation are taken from Livy and Caesar, the original being followed more and more closely, as the pupil's range of grammar and syntax is increased. Pieces of continuous English, based on the translation, have again been included; these perform a double function: the pupil, as in Part I, learns to put into Latin something more worthwhile than an isolated sentence, and so becomes familiar with the

7

elements of Prose composition; secondly, the pieces provide scope for revision of ground already covered, and are preferable to hundreds of sentences of a drill nature.

The Syntax includes the use of the Passive Voice, Deponent Verbs, Relative and Interrogative Pronouns, Participles, Indirect Statement, the Independent Subjunctive, Consecutive and Final Clauses, Indirect Commands, and Indirect Questions. It has not been thought necessary to include derivation tests in this book, as the pupil's interest in this side of the language will already have been stimulated and will continue to grow in his further study. The vocabulary may be slightly larger than that found in some 'readers', but it will be found that this is mostly accounted for by the translation being kept fairly near to the original; this has meant, for example, the use of several compounds of simple verbs.

The ground covered is common ground for anyone learning Latin, whether he or she is afterwards going to pursue the study to an advanced stage or not. All that the author can attempt to do is to present this ground to pupil and teacher. The length of time to be taken over Parts I and II must depend not only upon the ability and age of the pupil, but also on the number of periods a week which are allotted to the subject. The author believes that the 'common ground' here presented will be found by teachers to be readily adaptable to the courses either of secondary or of preparatory schools, and that even if a boy or girl never goes beyond Part II, something will have been mastered that has a value in itself.

I am most grateful for the helpful suggestions of my colleagues, especially Mr. R. St. J. Yates; to Mr. J. B. Poynton for corrections in the manuscript and proofs; to my publishers for their care and patience.

Oxford, 1950

Introduction to the Pupil

There is not a great deal to add to what I said in my Introduction to the Beginner in Part I. All that you learnt in the first book will be needed again in this book, but having mastered the first book, you will find this one a good deal easier. In case some things are forgotten from time to time, all the Grammar that came in Part I is printed at the end of the exercises, together with the new Grammar that comes in this book. Some of the important earlier rules will be found there too.

I will not spoil the stories told in this book by repeating them here. You will find that the men of the ancient world were very much like ourselves, whether they were Romans, Carthaginians or Britons; you will find that they were faced with the same sort of problems, even though the circumstances were different; our interest today lies in finding out how they tackled their problems. I will leave you to find out, among other things, that camouflage, secret weapons, under-water defences, and even what corresponded to clothes rationing and petrol rationing were just as real difficulties more than two thousand years ago as they have been in the twentieth century!

Contents

Every chapter contains exercises from Latin into English and from English into Latin. The following is a summary of the Grammar and Syntax covered by each chapter, with the titles of the pieces of continuous Latin Translation.

11

12 *Contents*

Contents

MAPS

Chapter 1

1st Conjugation: Present, Future, and Imperfect Indicative Passive

	Present Tense		Future Tense		Imperfect Tense	
S.	amor	*I am*	amābor	*I shall*	amābar	*I was*
	amāris	*(being)*	amāberis	*be*	amābāris	*(being)*
	amātur	*loved,*	amābitur	*loved,*	amābātur	*loved,*
Pl.	amāmur	etc.	amābimur	etc.	amābāmur	etc.
	amāminī		amābiminī		amābāminī	
	amantur		amābuntur		amābantur	

So far, we have met Verbs only in the Active Voice, when the Subject of the Verb *affects* someone or something by its action:

Manlius Gallum oppugnat.
Manlius attacks the Gaul.

Manlius certainly *affected* the Gaul by his action (*attacking*); in fact, we know from Livy's account that he hurled him head-long down from the Capitol!

Transitive Verbs are also fully conjugated in the **Passive** Voice, when the Subject of the Verb *is* itself *affected* (*Passive* comes from a Latin Verb meaning *I suffer*, which will be met later: the Subject *suffers* an action). In Latin, as in English, we can consider the above incident from the Gaul's point of view:

Gallus ā Manliō oppugnātur.
The Gaul is attacked by Manlius.

The Gaul (now the Subject) certainly *was affected*; he *suffered* the attacking. Therefore the Verb is in the Passive Voice.

When the Verb is Passive and the *doer* or **Agent** is a *person* or other *living being,* the Agent is expressed, as in the last example, by the Ablative with the Preposition **ā** or **ab.**

If the cause of an action is a *thing* and not a *person*, then the plain Ablative of the Instrument is used:

Tarpēia aurō superātur.
Tarpeia is won over by gold.

(*It has not been thought necessary, in presenting the Passive Voice, to mark the Verb-Stem with a hyphen. It will be seen that* **amā-** *appears throughout the Indicative Tenses, except in* **amor,** *where it has been absorbed.*)

1st Conjugation: Present Infinitive Passive

The Present Infinitive Passive of a 1st Conjugation Verb ends in **-ārī**, e.g. **amārī,** *to be loved*:

Līberī cūrārī dēbent.
Children ought to be looked after.

1st Conjugation: Imperative Passive

The Imperative Passive of **amō**: **amāre** (s.), **amāminī** (pl.), *be loved*.

EXERCISE 1.

1. Bellum a Boudicca contra Romanos paratur.
2. Et pedites et equites a Caesare transportantur.
3. Coloniae Romanae a Britannis vastantur.
4. Sole calido cruciamur.
5. Agricola propter Domitiani invidiam e Britannia revocatur.
6. Opere difficili non superaris.
7. Gratum erat Horatio a Romanis laudari.
8. Manlius et comites ab anseribus conservantur.
9. Nonne fabulis antiquis delectamini?
10. Cloaca maxima a Tarquinio Prisco[1] Romae aedificatur.

[1] Tarquin the Elder, one of the Roman kings, 616-579 B.C.

EXERCISE 2.
1. Cacus is being attacked by Hercules.
2. Many hostages are being set free through Cloelia's bold-
    ness.
3. Wine and oil are imported into Britain.
4. We are delighted by Boadicea's victory.
5. It will be pleasant to be invited to the show.
6. Why are you (s.) being blamed by the master?
7. Androclus and the lion are always greeted in the streets.
8. The wood is being reconnoitred by the Roman cavalry.
9. The lion is not wounded by Hercules's club.
10. The Britons are being routed by our army.

EXERCISE 3.
1. Multae insidiae a Britannis parabantur.
2. Num a Druidis superabimur, o milites?
3. Provincia multos annos ab Agricola administrabatur.
4. Signum ante vigiliam tertiam dabitur.
5. Cloelia propter audaciam a rege laudatur.
6. Turpe est, o Britanni, a Romanis superari.
7. Si Romanos hodie superaveritis, tandem liberabimini.
8. Spectaculum populo Romano in Circo dabatur.
9. Epistola tua delector.
10. Obsides a rege Porsenna exspectabantur.

EXERCISE 4.

THE CAUDINE FORKS (1)

From 343 *to* 290 B.C. *the Romans were continually fighting
against the Samnites. Gāius Pontius, the Samnite general, took
the field in* 321.

Pontius exercitum educit et circa Caudium castra clam
locat. Inde Calatiam, ubi iam consules Romani sunt et castra,
milites decem mittit. Ei iussu Pontii habitum pastoralem
induerant nec procul a Romanis praesidiis hinc et illinc
pecora pascunt; mox praedae causa a Romanis oppugnantur;
superantur et inde in castris interrogantur. 'Legiones Samni-

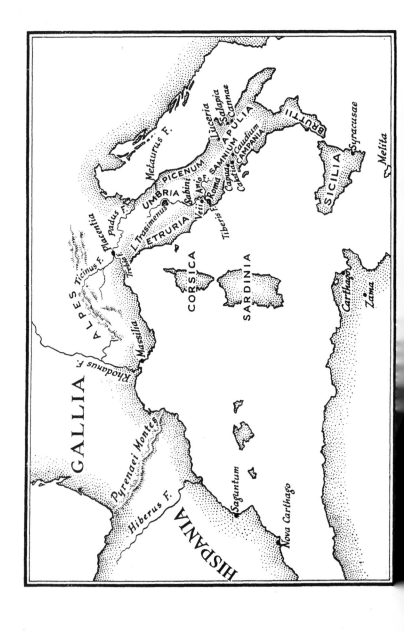

tium', inquiunt, 'sunt in Apulia, Luceriam omnibus copiis obsident; brevi tempore ea urbs occupabitur.' Ea res ab omnibus captivis confirmatur. Samnites iam eum rumorem apud Romanos de industria vulgaverant; fidem auxerunt captivi. Res statim a Romanis deliberatur, quod Lucerini sunt boni ac fideles socii. Sine mora Romani Luceriam cum toto exercitu contendere properant.

EXERCISE 5.
1. Beautiful country-houses were being built in Britain.
2. Unless our allies hurry, we shall not be freed.
3. Great power was wont to be entrusted to the consuls.
4. If we resist, Caledonia will not be conquered.
5. Sometimes the Romans were helped by the natives of Britain.
6. Surely you will not be blamed, if you do not reach home today?
7. By order of Camillus, the city of Veii was being attacked on all sides.
8. The Sabines are being invited by the Romans to the games.
9. We were delayed for a long time by the deep river.
10. Never will our fields be laid waste by the Roman army.

EXERCISE 6.
For five years the Samnites are everywhere defeated. At length they beg for peace. Peace, however, is refused by the Romans. Then the fortune of the Samnites is changed. Pontius, their general, sent a message to the Roman consuls by means of prisoners. 'The town of Luceria', they say, 'is being attacked by the whole army of the Samnites, and unless you hurry, it will soon fall into their hands.'

Because the inhabitants of Luceria were allies of the Romans, the consuls determined to lead their army into Apulia. At once everything was being got ready for[1] a long march; the soldiers collected their arms and baggage and struck camp. Then, when the signal is given, the column advances towards Luceria.

[1] ad.

Chapter 2

1st Conjugation: Perfect, Future Perfect, and Pluperfect Indicative Passive

The Perfect, Future Perfect, and Pluperfect Tenses of the Indicative Passive of all Conjugations are formed in the same way: by joining the Perfect Participle Passive with Tenses of **sum**.

A Participle is a Verbal Adjective; it agrees like an Adjective, but it also has the nature of a Verb. The Perfect Participle Passive of **amō** is **amātus, -a, -um** (declined like **bonus**), and means *loved* or *having been loved*.

Amātus sum is *I was loved* or *have been loved*; if *I* is feminine, the Latin is **amāta sum:** so **oppidum aedificātum est,** *the town was built.*

Similarly, **amātus erō,** *I shall have been loved*; **amātus eram,** *I had been loved.*

The Perfect Participle Passive is formed from the Supine-Base by changing the **-um** of the Supine into **-us.** The Supine (the use of which will be learnt later) of a regular 1st Conjugation Verb ends in **-ātum,** e.g. **amātum;** hence the Perfect Participle Passive **amātus.**

(*Supines of Verbs which are not conjugated regularly are given in the Vocabularies.*)

	Perfect Tense		*Future Perfect Tense*		*Pluperfect Tense*	
S.	**amātus sum,**	*I was*	**amātus erō,**	*I shall*	**amātus eram,**	*I had*
	amātus es	*loved,*	**amātus eris**	*have*	**amātus erās**	*been*
	amātus est	or	**amātus erit**	*been*	**amātus erat**	*loved,*
Pl.	**amātī sumus**	*have*	**amātī erimus**	*loved,*	**amātī erāmus**	etc.
	amātī estis	*been*	**amātī eritis**	etc.	**amātī erātis**	
	amātī sunt	*loved,*	**amātī erunt**		**amātī erant**	
		etc.				

22

Rōma in septem montibus aedificāta est.
Rome was built on seven hills.

Sometimes, for the sake of variety, the order is reversed, e.g.
est aedificāta.

EXERCISE 7.
1. Leo ab Hercule tandem superatus est.
2. Insidiae a Britannis in silva paratae sunt.
3. Victoria magna Atheniensibus nuntiata erat.
4. Verbis imperatoris omnes confirmati sumus.
5. Brevi tempore hostes fugati erunt.
6. Duae coloniae a Britannis erant vastatae.
7. Tribus annis aedificatum erit theatrum magnum.
8. Androclus a Caesare post spectaculum liberatus est.
9. Cur hodie a leone non oppugnatus es?
10. Tres Albani a Romano necati sunt.

EXERCISE 8.

THE CAUDINE FORKS (2)

Romani Luceriam brevi via per Furculas Caudinas[1] pete-
bant; ibi sunt saltus duo alti, angusti silvosique; montes
perpetui utrinque impendent. Iacet inter eos in medio campus
herbidus. Non ad campum pervenies, nisi primum saltum
intraveris; inde nullus est exitus, nisi aut viam repetes aut per
secundum saltum perangustum evades.

In eum campum consules per primum saltum agmen
demittunt et ad secundum saltum pergunt. Tum fraus hostium
apparet. Romani enim hic erant exspectati. Samnites arboribus et saxis ingentibus saltum saepserant et praesidio locum
occupaverant. Statim agmen viam repetit; eam quoque hostibus armatis iam plenam invenit. Animi omnium stupore
superati sunt; quod nulla eis spes salutis manebat, diu im-
mobiles silebant. Tandem sine imperio centurionum milites
castra muniunt et vallo circumdant.

[1] **furcula,** *a fork*. The passes were fork-shaped, and near Caudium,
a small city in Samnium.

EXERCISE 9.

1. The prisoners were questioned in the Roman camp.
2. Rumours had been published by the Samnites among the Romans.
3. Soon the Romans will have been overcome by an ambush.
4. Manlius had been awoken by the geese.
5. 'The lion and I', said he, 'were transported to Rome.'
6. Many stories have been told about Hercules.
7. The matter was at once deliberated by the consuls.
8. Human footprints had been noted by the Gauls.
9. Soon you (pl.) will have been freed from the danger.
10. Sabine maidens were invited with their parents to the games.

EXERCISE 10.

The consuls did not hesitate to lead the column by a short route. First they penetrated a deep and narrow pass and reached a grassy plain; from there they began to enter a second pass. Around the two passes and the plain lie mountains and woods. But the march was renewed in vain, because the second pass had already been seized by the Samnites. Meanwhile the enemy had been placed in the rear too; there was no hope of escape left for the column. So by means of a false message and a trap the Roman armies had been surrounded on every side. In vain did the soldiers blame the treachery of the enemy.

Chapter 3
2nd Conjugation: Present, Future, and Imperfect Indicative Passive

	Present Tense		*Future Tense*		*Imperfect Tense*	
S.	**moneor**	*I am*	**monēbor**	*I shall*	**monēbar**	*I was*
	monēris	*(being)*	**monēberis**	*be*	**monēbāris**	*being*
	monētur	*advised,*	**monēbitur**	*advised,*	**monēbātur**	*advised,*
Pl.	**monēmur**	etc.	**monēbimur**	etc.	**monēbāmur**	etc.
	monēminī		**monēbiminī**		**monēbāminī**	
	monentur		**monēbuntur**		**monēbantur**	

Videor can mean *I seem*, besides *I am seen*. It is often used with an Infinitive:

Captīvī vēra dīcere vidēbantur.
The prisoners seemed to be speaking the truth.

When **videor** is followed by an Adjective, **esse** (the Infinitive of **sum**), *to be*, is often left out; the Adjective must be in the same Case as the Subject, because it *completes* the sense, i.e. is its **Complement**:

Tyrannī beātī videntur, non tamen sunt.
Tyrants seem (to be) happy, but are not.

2nd Conjugation: Present Infinitive Passive

The Present Infinitive Passive of a 2nd Conjugation Verb ends in **-ērī**, e.g. **monērī**, *to be advised*:

Līberī ā parentibus monērī solent.
Children are wont to be advised by their parents.

2nd Conjugation: Imperative Passive

The Imperative Passive of **moneō**: **monēre** (s.), **monēminī** (pl.), *be advised.*

EXERCISE 11.

1. Pons ab Horatio diu tenebatur.
2. Neque a Druidis neque a feminis nos terremur.
3. Circus Maximus turba virorum feminarumque impletur.
4. Movebiturne Caesar clamoribus populi?
5. Fines Romanorum semper bellis augebantur.
6. A me monere: disce linguam Latinam.
7. Leo Androclo non infestus videbatur.
8. Romulus in numero deorum haberi solebat.
9. Urbs Luceria a Samnitibus non obsidebatur.
10. Exemplis bonorum omnes monemur.

EXERCISE 12.

THE CAUDINE FORKS (3)

Castra Romana fremitu militum implentur, terror nocte augetur. Ne Samnitibus quidem erat consilium in tam laetis rebus; itaque Herennium Pontium, patrem ducis, per litteras consulere constituerunt. Is iam senex erat; in corpore tamen invalido vigebat vis animi. Ubi filii nuntius pervenit, 'Omnes', inquit, 'dimitte inviolatos'. Ea sententia filio non placet; iterum patrem consulit. 'Occide omnes ad unum[1]; tertium consilium non est.' Neque ea sententia bona esse videtur; interim Romani legatos ad Pontium mittunt et aut pacem aequam aut pugnam petunt. Respondit Pontius 'Quanquam superati estis, fortunae belli vos dedere nescitis; inermes igitur cum singulis vestimentis sub iugum[2] vos mittam. Si ab agro Samnitium decedetis, Romani et Samnites secundum suas leges vivent.' Ubi condiciones pacis consulibus renuntiatae sunt, nemo non magna maestitia commovebatur.

[1] *to a man.*

[2] This was a symbol of humiliating defeat; the 'yoke' consisted of two upright spears, with a third laid horizontally across the top, under which a conquered army was required to pass.

EXERCISE 13.

1. The city of Veii was besieged for many years.
2. Surely you (pl.) are not frightened by such an enemy?
3. A levy of the army is being held throughout Italy.

4. The message of the prisoners seemed true.
5. Unless you destroy the bridge, an easy victory will be afforded to the enemy.
6. Why are we not being taught Greek?
7. Androclus does not seem to be frightened by the lion.
8. Camp will be struck at once owing to the news of the prisoners.
9. Many young men were being trained for war.
10. Be (s.) taught even by the examples of the Romans.

EXERCISE 14.

When he had[1] surrounded the Roman armies in the pass, Pontius sent a messenger to his father. His advice, however, did not seem to Pontius to be useful. He therefore summoned his father to the camp. When he had[1] entered the meeting, Herennius explained his reasons. 'If you let the Romans go,' said he, 'everlasting peace will be established through a great kindness; if you destroy two armies, war will be renewed after many years.' Then the son replied: 'Does it not seem to you to be expedient to let the armies go and impose severe conditions by the right of war?' 'If you impose severe conditions, hatred will be increased; the Roman people does not know how to remain inactive[2] after such a disaster.'

[1] See note below.

[2] *I remain inactive*, **quiescō** (3).

Reminder about the use of **ubi,** *when*

It is important to remember that Latin uses the Perfect Tense with **ubi,** *when*, where in English we use the Pluperfect, e.g. **ubi vēnit,** *when he had come*.

Chapter 4

2nd Conjugation: Perfect, Future Perfect and Pluperfect Indicative Passive

The Supine of a regular 2nd Conjugation Verb ends in **-itum,** e.g. **monitum,** but many do not follow the regular form, and the vocabularies should be consulted.

	Perfect Tense	*Future Perfect Tense*	*Pluperfect Tense*
S.	**monitus sum,** *I was advised* or *have been advised.*	**monitus erō,** *I shall have been advised.*	**monitus eram,** *I had been advised.*
	monitus es, etc.	**monitus eris,** etc.	**monitus erās,** etc.

EXERCISE 15.
1. Multi elephanti ad bellum a Pyrrho exerciti erant.
2. Consules ab exploratoribus de periculo non moniti sunt.
3. Insidiis Samnitium ab itinere prohibiti sumus.
4. Interdum Romani essedis Britannorum perterriti sunt.
5. Consilium perfugae non honestum esse visum erat.
6. Tota urbs praeter arcem erat deleta.
7. Mox lacus aqua impletus erit.
8. Romulus non iterum apud homines visus est.
9. Nonne exemplo Tarpeiae monitus es?
10. Multae Persarum naves magna tempestate deletae sunt.

EXERCISE 16.

THE CAUDINE FORKS (4)

Omnes diu silebant. Tandem Lucius Lentulus, princeps legatorum, 'Mihi quidem', inquit, 'mortem pro patria petere praeclarum esse videtur: aut me devovere pro populo Romano legionibusque aut in hostes me immittere paratus sum. Sed hic patriam nostram video, ubi sunt Romanae legiones. Si exercitus deletus erit, non servabitur urbs Roma. Hodie non morte, sed ignominia nostra eam servare debemus.' Inde consules castra Pontii intraverunt et ei cesserunt. Iam aderat hora fatalis ignominiae.

Primos sub iugum consules prope seminudos miserunt Samnites; tum quaestores[1] et tribunos militum[2]; tum omnes milites. Circumstabant armati hostes; multi gladii sunt intentati; nonnulli etiam sunt vulnerati necatique ob superbiam vultus. Ubi e saltu evaserunt, ab inferis evadere sibi videbantur et tum primum lucem spectare; lux tamen foedo agmini erat tristis, reditus in patriam ad parentes miserabilis.

[1] A quaestor was an officer especially responsible for the payment and provisioning of troops.

[2] There were six military tribunes to each legion (at this time, about 4,200 men); they took it in turn to command it.

EXERCISE 17.
1. The inhabitants of Veii were terrified by the sudden attack.
2. The road had been filled with huge rocks and trees.
3. Why had Tarpeia not been warned by her father?
4. You (pl.) will not have been taught in vain.
5. Armed forces of the enemy were seen on all the hills.
6. A levy has been recently held in Italy.
7. The prisoners gave a false message, as they had been ordered.
8. Halt (pl.): the vanguard seems to be held back.
9. How many legions have been trained for war?
10. The Samnites had not yet been seen by the Romans.

EXERCISE 18.
Lentulus, the chief of the ambassadors, made a speech: 'It is useless to resist, because Rome will not be safe without an army. Here are all our hopes and riches; if these are saved, then we shall save our country.' The consuls, when they had [1] been thus advised, handed over hostages to the Samnites and

[1] See note on **ubi** on p. 27.

waited for the fatal hour. The soldiers were not frightened, but were moved by the disgrace of the surrender. Never before had Romans been overcome by so great a disaster; they had surrendered without a battle, without a wound. With difficulty did they keep their hands off the consuls, because through their rashness they had marched into the ambush. They looked at each other and seemed already to see the yoke before their eyes.

Chapter 5
Comparison of Adjectives (1)

Adjectives in Latin, as in English, have three **Degrees of Comparison**:

(1) Positive **mons altus,** *a high mountain.*

(2) Comparative **mons altior,** *a higher mountain* (when **compared** with another mountain).

Note. **Mons altior** might also mean *a too high mountain* (no special idea of comparison being intended) or *a rather high mountain.*

(3) Superlative **mons altissimus,** *the highest mountain* (of a number of mountains) or *a very high mountain.*

The Comparative and Superlative are usually formed by adding **-ior** and **-issimus** to the last consonant of the Stem:

densus, *thick*	**densior**	**densissimus**
fortis, *brave*	**fortior**	**fortissimus**
ingens, *huge*	**ingentior**	**ingentissimus**
audax, *bold*	**audācior**	**audācissimus**

The Comparative of Adjectives in **-er** is quite regular, but their Superlative is formed by adding **-rimus** to the Nom. masc. sing. of the Positive:

pulcher, *beautiful*	**pulchrior**	**pulcherrimus**
miser, *wretched*	**miserior**	**miserrimus**
ācer, *keen*	**ācrior**	**ācerrimus**

Six Adjectives in **-ilis** have a regular Comparative, but add **-limus** to the l of the Stem, to form the Superlative:

facilis, *easy*	**facilior**	**facillimus**
difficilis, *difficult*	**difficilior**	**difficillimus**
similis,[1] *like*	**similior**	**simillimus**
dissimilis,[1] *unlike*	**dissimilior**	**dissimillimus**

[1] Followed by Gen. or Dat.

31

gracilis, *slender*	gracilior	gracillimus
humilis, *low*	humilior	humillimus

The Comparative is declined as a Consonant Stem Adjective:

Stem   **altiōr-,** *higher, deeper.*

Sing.	M. and F.	N.	*Plur.* M. and F.	N.
N.V.	altior	altius	altiōrēs	altiōra
Acc.	altiōrem	altius	altiōrēs	altiōra
Gen.	altiōris		altiōrum	
Dat.	altiōrī		altiōribus	
Abl.	altiōre		altiōribus	

The Superlative is declined like **bonus.**

To express *than*

Quam can always be used to express *than* after a Comparative; the things compared are then in the same Case:

(a) **Gallia est lātior quam Britannia.**
Gaul is wider than Britain.

(b) **Opus est facilius tibi quam mihi.**
The work is easier for you than for me.

When two things in the Nom. or Acc. are directly compared, then the **Ablative of Comparison** is often used: so (a) could be written:

(c) **Gallia est lātior Britanniā.**
Gaul is wider than (differing from) Britain.

(d) **Vīdit formam ampliōrem hūmānā.**
He saw a figure bigger than a human figure.

EXERCISE 19.

1. Silvae Britanniae erant densissimae.
2. Noctes sunt breviores in Britannia quam in Italia.
3. Porsenna Cloeliam, virginem audacissimam, laudavit.
4. Pauci fuerunt fortiores Horatio.
5. Romani via breviore contendebant.
6. Audaciusne fuit Cloeliae factum quam Horatii?
7. Propter vitrum Britanni horridiores in pugna esse videntur.

8. Nihil est iucundius amicitia.
9. Imperare et parere sunt res dissimillimae.
10. Quod locus Britannis erat notissimus, facilius eis erat
    pugnare quam Romanis.

EXERCISE 20.

TWO METHODS OF TAKING ELEPHANTS ACROSS THE RHONE

Carthage had held command of the Mediterranean for a long time, and declared war on Rome, who had now completed the conquest of Italy, in 264 B.C. Rome gained Sicily as a result of the First Carthaginian (or Punic) War, but also the hatred of Hamilcar and his son Hannibal. In 218 Rome declared war on Carthage, after Hannibal had captured the Spanish town of Saguntum. Hannibal then made Spain his base for his famous march on Rome. One of his first tasks was the transport of 37 elephants across the Rhone.

Elephanti ad ripam Rhodani congregantur; ferocissimus ex eis a rectore suo irritatur; tum rector in aquam se praecipitat et trans flumen natat; elephantus statim pone eum se in flumen immittit et ita gregem trahit; aquam altiorem omnes timent, impetus tamen aquae trans flumen eos transmittit.

Variat tamen memoria eius rei. Secundum nonnullos scriptores ratem longam a terra Poeni in flumen porrigunt; tum eam ad ripam religant et iam similem[1] pontis humo consternunt. Deinde ratis brevior longiori vinculis copulatur. Sex tum elephanti una cum feminis per stabilem ratem velut per viam incedunt; ubi ratem breviorem intraverunt, homines vincula resolvunt et ratem navigiis trahunt. Excidunt ob trepidationem aliquot ex elephantis in flumen; nihilominus sine rectoribus, propter pondus suum stabiles, vada quaerunt et in terram evadunt.

[1] Supply **eam** with **similem**.

EXERCISE 21.

1. Few things are more beautiful than the spring.
2. The longer road was safer.
3. The Roman army awaited a most miserable disgrace.

4. If the work is rather difficult, ask the master for help.
5. The country is more well-known to you (pl.) than to the Romans.
6. The Romans drove out Tarquinius, because he was too violent.
7. Larcius and Herminius were braver than the rest.
8. Tarquinius Priscus built a very huge circus.
9. The ears of the geese were sharper than those of the dogs.
10. Why did we not have a more cautious general?

EXERCISE 22.

Hannibal had trained many elephants for war. It was very difficult to transport them across the river Rhone, because it was very wide and very deep. Writers hand down various accounts[1] about this matter. Perhaps the elephants entered the water, when they had been goaded by their drivers. But if we believe some writers, the Carthaginians stretched a long raft into the river; this raft was very like a bridge; when they had covered it with soil, they joined a shorter raft to it by chains; when the elephants had entered the shorter raft, they loosened the chains and so carried the elephants across.

[1] Put *various things* (neut. pl.).

Chapter 6
Comparison of Adjectives (2)

Some Adjectives form their Comparative and Superlative from different Stems:

Positive	Comparative	Superlative
bonus, *good*	**melior**	**optimus**
malus, *bad*	**pēior**	**pessimus**
magnus, *great*	**māior**	**maximus**
parvus, *small*	**minor**	**minimus**
multus, *much*	**plūs** (neut.)	**plūrimus**

Note. **Māiōrēs, -um,** is often used as a masc. Noun for *ancestors.*

Plūs is declined as follows:

Sing.	N.	*Plur.*	M. and F.	N.
N.V.A.	**plūs**		**plūrēs**	**plūra**
Gen.	**plūris**		**plūrium**	
Dat.	—		**plūribus**	
Abl.	**plūre**		**plūribus**	

Plūs in the sing. is a neuter Noun and is followed by the Partitive Genitive (used after numbers and words expressing a Part of something), e.g. **plūs audāciae,** *more boldness.* In the plural it is used as an Adjective, e.g. **plūrēs mīlitēs,** *more soldiers.*

Some Comparatives and Superlatives have no normal Positive, but are derived from Prepositions:

infrā, *below*	**inferior**, *lower,*	**infimus, īmus,** *lowest*
prae, *before*	**prior**, *earlier, former*	**prīmus,** *first*
suprā, *above*	**superior**, *higher, earlier*	**suprēmus, summus,** *highest*
prope, *near*	**propior**, *nearer*	**proximus,** *nearest, next*
ultrā, *beyond*	**ulterior**, *further*	**ultimus,** *last*

A few other Irregular Comparisons are given in the Summary of Grammar.

By now it will often have been noticed how economical Latin is in its use of words; here are some examples, which include the use of the Superlative:

(*a*) **Prīmus vēnit,** *he was the first to come* (*he came first*).

(*b*) **Ad summum (īmum) montem pervēnimus.**
We reached the top (*the bottom*) *of the hill.*

Like the idiomatic agreement of the Superlative with the Noun in (*b*) is that of **medius,** *middle*, and **reliquus,** *remaining, rest*:

Reliquae cōpiae mediam silvam penetrāvērunt.
The rest of the troops penetrated the middle of the wood.

EXERCISE 23.
1. Britannia est minor Gallia.
2. Maior pars elephantorum in rate manebat.
3. Praesidium Samnitium in summo saltu videtur.
4. Hodie melius est patriam servare quam ignominiam vitare.
5. Magister Camillo consilium pessimum proposuit.
6. Plus virorum quam feminarum Romae quondam erat.
7. Romani saltum ulteriorem non intraverunt.
8. Lentulus in medios hostes se immittere erat paratus.
9. Sicilia in bello superiore a Romanis comparata erat.
10. Romani Iovi Optimo Maximo sacrificare solebant.

EXERCISE 24.

THE PASSAGE OF THE ALPS:
(1) HANNIBAL'S ENCOURAGEMENT

Hannibal, ubi[1] exercitum trans Rhodanum transmisit, Romam trans Alpes contendere parabat. Plurimi tamen e militibus, adhuc memores superioris belli, hostes timebant; iter quoque immensum atque Alpes metuebant. Hannibal

[1] See important note at the end of this chapter.

igitur contionem advocat et militum animos confirmat. 'Per tot annos', inquit, 'hostes semper vicistis; omnes gentes Hispaniae sunt in potestate Poenorum; nunc superest minor pars itineris; iam in conspectu Alpes habetis. Cur montium altitudines timetis? Pyrenaeos montes superavistis; fingite montes Pyrenaeis altiores; at nullae terrae caelum tangunt neque insuperabiles sunt. Multi antea cum liberis ac coniugibus Alpes ascenderunt; num militibus armatis inviae sunt Alpes? Si nomen Romanum delere constituistis, nihil asperum, nihil difficile vobis videbitur. Aut cedite genti meliori aut itineris finem petite.'

EXERCISE 25.

1. Horatius had very great courage.
2. The yoke seemed to the Romans to be worse than death.
3. 'It is better', said he, 'to let the army go.'
4. The Britons were hurling spears from higher ground.
5. One of the Gauls had reached the top of the Capitol.
6. The biggest things are not always the best.
7. The Romans killed more of the enemy in flight than in the battle.
8. Be (pl.) worthy of your ancestors.
9. Soon the first elephant had reached the middle of the river.
10. Horatius was the last to leave the bridge.

EXERCISE 26.

The Carthaginians had been defeated in the previous war and were still afraid of the Romans. They had indeed crossed the Pyrenees and had marched to the Rhone from New Carthage[1]; but now they dreaded both higher mountains and a bigger journey. Hannibal, however, had determined to lead his army to Italy and conquer the Roman people. He therefore called his troops together and made a speech. 'You have already been in many dangers; to no one did the journey seem too long before; the Alps are indeed higher than the Pyrenees, but if they are not impassable for the Gauls, surely they are not impassable for

[1] This was Hannibal's base in Spain.

our army? The ancestors of the Gauls sent across their wives and children; you will carry on your journey only the instruments of war. The Gauls once conquered Rome; is it too difficult for you to approach it?'

Note on Translating

Adverbial Clauses, introduced by words meaning *when, because, although,* etc., generally come before the Main Clause in Latin. When they have the same Subject, the tendency is to put the Subject first, i.e. in front of the Adverbial Clause, with a comma after it. Latin says 'Caesar, when he had landed, built a camp'. But in English we find this awkward and unnatural, and would rather say either 'When Caesar had landed, he built a camp', or 'When he had landed, Caesar built a camp'. The Latin way of putting things should, however, be remembered in translating from English.

Chapter 7
Adverbs and their Comparison

An **Adverb** is so called because its meaning is added *to the Verb* (**ad verbum**); it generally gives some information about *how*, *when*, or *where*, e.g. *he ran quickly, he will come often, he lived there.*

The following is a simple working rule for the regular formation of Latin Adverbs:

(1) For Adjectives of the 1st and 2nd Declension, add -ē (sometimes -ō) to the last consonant of the Stem, e.g. **dignē,** *worthily*; **tūtō,** *safely*;

(2) For Adjectives of the 3rd Declension, add **-iter** to the last consonant of the Stem (but only **-er** to **-nt**), e.g. **fortiter,** *bravely*; **sapienter,** *wisely*.

The Comparative of an Adverb is the neuter Acc. sing. of the Comparative Adjective; the Superlative of an Adverb is formed by changing the **-us** of the Superlative Adjective into -ē (rarely **-um**):

Adjective	Adverb	Comparative	Superlative
dignus	**dignē,** *worthily*	**dignius**	**dignissimē**
miser	**miserē,** *wretchedly*	**miserius**	**miserrimē**
pulcher	**pulchrē,** *beautifully*	**pulchrius**	**pulcherrimē**
ācer	**ācriter,** *keenly*	**ācrius**	**ācerrimē**
celer	**celeriter,** *swiftly*	**celerius**	**celerrimē**
fortis	**fortiter,** *bravely*	**fortius**	**fortissimē**
constans	**constanter,** *firmly*	**constantius**	**constantissimē**

But note:

audax	**audacter,** *boldly*	**audācius**	**audācissimē**
facilis	**facile,** *easily*	**facilius**	**facillimē**

39

Some Irregular Comparisons of Adverbs

Adjective	Adverb	Comparative	Superlative
bonus	bene, *well*	melius	optimē
malus	male, *badly*	pēius	pessimē
magnus	magnopere, *greatly*	magis	maximē
parvus	paulum, *little*	minus	minimē
multus	multum, *much*	plūs	plūrimum

Magis is *more*, of degree; **plūs** is *more*, of quantity:

Alpēs magis quam Rōmānōs timēbant.
They feared the Alps more than the Romans.

Plūs quam trīgintā aderant.
More than thirty were there.

Note also:

diū, *for a long time*	diūtius	diūtissimē
nūper, *lately*	—	nūperrimē
—	potius, *rather*	potissimum, *especially*
saepe, *often*	saepius	saepissimē

Quam is often used to strengthen a Superlative, e.g. **quam plūrimī,** *as many men as possible*; **quam celerrimē,** *as quickly as possible*.

Exercise 27.

1. Poeni adversus Hispanos acriter pugnabant.
2. Nonne Graeci templa pulchrius quam Romani aedificaverunt?
3. Horatius multitudini Etruscorum constanter resistebat.
4. Consules deditione turpi maxime perturbati sunt.
5. Milites iter longum per Alpes magis quam hostes timebant.
6. Exercitus Luceriam quam celerrime festinabat.
7. Si magister verba lentius recitabit, melius intellegemus
8. Samnites Romanos insidiis facillime circumvenerant.
9. Imperator, nisi locum bene explorat, male suos ducit.
10. Hodie nos dedere potius quam resistere debemus.

EXERCISE 28.

THE PASSAGE OF THE ALPS:
(2) FALSE GUIDES

Ubi Poeni propius ad Alpes appropinquaverunt, tum montium altitudo et nivium moles terrorem renovaverunt. Mox tamen principes populi montani ad Hannibalem veniunt. 'Amicitia Poenorum', inquiunt, 'gratior est nobis quam vis; commeatum vobis itinerisque duces praebebimus et obsides trademus.' Hannibal non temere eis credit neque eos repudiat, sed benigne respondet et duces praemittit. Primum agmen elephanti et equites erant; Hannibal post cum peditibus sollicitus incedit et omnia circumspectat. Subito ubi in angustiorem viam venerunt, undique ex insidiis barbari a fronte et a tergo surgunt et Poenos petunt, saxa ingentia in agmen devolvunt. Tum vero Poeni in summum periculum venerunt. Nam dum dubitat Hannibal in angustias agmen ducere, montani a lateribus quoque oppugnant; agmen interrumpunt viamque obstruunt. Ita Hannibal noctem unam sine equitibus et impedimentis egit.

EXERCISE 29.

1. The elephants were not easily transported by the Carthaginians.
2. The enemy were less afraid of the Pyrenees than of the Alps.
3. The elephants boldly advanced on to the long raft.
4. Cicero used to write to his friends very often.
5. Because the Romans built their roads well, very many remain today.
6. Resist (pl.) the enemy very firmly.
7. On that day the Romans surrendered themselves most miserably to the Samnites.
8. Your country-house was most beautifully built.
9. If we march more quickly, we shall reach the bottom of the hill before night.
10. Don't (pl.) stay longer on the top of the tree.

EXERCISE 30.

The Carthaginians were greatly terrified both by the snows and by the mountains. When they had advanced a little, the chiefs of a mountain tribe came to Hannibal and promised him provisions and guides. It seemed foolish to Hannibal to reject these gifts, but more foolish to trust the chiefs rashly; they therefore gave him hostages. Hannibal, however, was nearly overcome by his own tricks, treachery and ambush. He sent forward the guides with the cavalry and elephants, and then advanced slowly with the infantry. Suddenly in a narrow place the foreigners attacked in front and in rear, and rolled down stones from the mountain. Nor was Hannibal safe on the flanks. From there, too, the enemy attacked the column and blocked the way. Meanwhile the cavalry had advanced safely and spent that night without their commander.

Chapter 8
3rd Conjugation: Indicative Passive

	Present Tense	Future Tense	Imperfect Tense
S.	regor, *I am*	regar, *I shall be*	regēbar, *I was*
	regeris *(being)*	regēris *ruled.*	regēbāris *(being)*
	regitur *ruled.*	regētur	regēbātur *ruled.*
Pl.	regimur	regēmur	regēbāmur
	regiminī	regēminī	regēbāminī
	reguntur	regentur	regēbantur

3rd Conjugation: Present Infinitive Passive

The Present Infinitive Passive of a 3rd Conjugation Verb ends in -ī, e.g. regī:

Turpe erat sub iugum mittī.
It was disgraceful to be sent under the yoke.

3rd Conjugation: Imperative Passive

The Imperative Passive of **regō: regere** (s.), **regiminī** (pl.), *be ruled.*

3rd Conjugation: Perfect, Future Perfect, and Pluperfect Passive

The Supine of **regō** is **rectum**; many 3rd Conjugation Supines end in **-tum**, many in **-sum**, e.g. **missum** from **mittō**; others have a Supine like that of a 2nd Conjug. Verb, e.g. **positum** from **pōnō**; or like that of a 4th Conjug. Verb, e.g. **petītum** from **petō**.

The principal parts of Verbs should be learnt by heart, in the Summary of Grammar at the end of the book. Supines of Verbs used in the exercises will be found in the Vocabularies.

Perfect Tense	Future Perfect Tense	Pluperfect Tense
rectus sum, *I was*	**rectus erō,** *I shall*	**rectus eram,** *I had*
rectus es, *ruled*	**rectus eris,** *have*	**rectus erās,** *been*
etc. or *have*	etc. *been*	etc. *ruled.*
been	*ruled.*	
ruled.		

EXERCISE 31.
1. Exercitus in saltum temere ducitur.
2. Nonne exploratores a consulibus mittentur?
3. Verba sapientia patris a Pontio non intelleguntur.
4. Poeni a Gallis in insidias ducebantur.
5. Tota via nive alta tecta erat.
6. Cur consilium viri sapientis neglectum est?
7. Roma non conservabitur, si tot milites occisi erunt.
8. Castra a Romanis in campo posita erant.
9. Nolite, o milites, talibus periculis vinci.
10. Tarpeia scutis ingentibus Sabinorum oppressa est.

EXERCISE 32.

THE PASSAGE OF THE ALPS:
(3) THE SUMMIT AND DIFFICULT DESCENT

Nono die in summum montem pervenerunt. Militibus, fessis et labore et proelio, quies per duos dies concessa est. Ingens tamen terror casu nivis eis additus est. Prima luce iter lente redintegratum est, sed, quod multi iam desperabant, Hannibal agmen cohibuit. Ex tumulo omnibus Italiae campos ostentat. 'Moenia videtis', inquit, 'non modo Italiae sed etiam urbis Romanae; cetera erunt plana et facilia; paucis proeliis arcem Romanorum in potestate vestra habebitis.'

Inde agmen processit; ex Alpibus tamen in campos via maxime angusta et lubrica descendebant. In uno quidem loco rupes abrupta erat. Viam igitur novam Poeni ita muniverunt: quod saxa caedere difficillimum erat, milites cumulum ingentem lignorum congerunt et igni incendunt; deinde acetum infundunt et saxa iam putria ferro frangunt. Inde per novam viam non solum homines et iumenta, sed etiam elephanti deducti sunt.

EXERCISE 33.

1. Many books are written, not all are read.
2. Surely the army will not be led without scouts?
3. Fair terms were being sought by the consuls.
4. All the Spanish tribes had been easily defeated by the Carthaginians.
5. One night was spent by Hannibal without his cavalry.
6. After a few battles the Romans will have been conquered.
7. Good books are often wont to be neglected.
8. The poems of Homer were often learned by Roman boys.
9. A very small part of the bridge had now been left.
10. Many examples of bravery have been handed down to us by the Romans.

EXERCISE 34.

The Carthaginians were losing hope, because many dangers were hindering them; it was even more difficult to descend from the Alps than to climb up. Hannibal therefore made a speech from the top of a mound. 'The Alps', said he, 'are the walls of Rome; the plains of Italy will soon be in your power; within a few days the citizens of Rome will have been conquered.' The soldiers were encouraged by Hannibal's words, and slowly the column was led down towards the plains. In one place, however, the road had been broken away by a recent fall of earth. The column halted and pitched camp. Hannibal examined the spot and decided to build a new road. Logs were piled together and set on fire; then vinegar was poured on to the hot rocks; finally the rocks were broken by iron. Four days were taken up[1] in this work.

[1] *I take up*, in this sense, **consūmō.**

Chapter 9
4th Conjugation: Indicative Passive

	Present Tense	*Future Tense*	*Imperfect Tense*
S.	audior, *I am*	audiar, *I shall*	audiēbar, *I was*
	audīris (*being*)	audiēris *be*	audiēbāris (*being*)
	audītur *heard.*	audiētur . *heard.*	audiēbātur *heard.*
Pl.	audīmur	audiēmur	audiēbāmur
	audīminī	audiēminī	audiēbāminī
	audiuntur	audientur	audiēbantur

4th Conjugation: Present Infinitive Passive

The Present Infinitive of a 4th Conjugation Verb ends in -īrī, e.g. audīrī:

Britannia mūrō custōdīrī vidēbātur.
Britain seemed to be guarded by the wall.

4th Conjugation: Imperative Passive

The Imperative Passive of **audiō: audīre** (s.), **audīminī** (pl.), *be heard.*

4th Conjugation: Perfect, Future Perfect, Pluperfect Passive

The Supine of a regular 4th Conjugation Verb ends in **-ītum,** but some are not regular.

	Perfect Tense		*Future Perfect Tense*		*Pluperfect Tense*	
S.	audītus sum,	*I was*	audītus erō,	*I shall*	audītus eram,	*I*
	audītus es,	*heard*	audītus eris,	*have*	audītus erās,	*had*
	etc.	or	etc.	*been*	etc.	*been*
		have		*heard.*		*heard.*
		been				
		heard.				

EXERCISE 35.

1. Verba Hannibalis a militibus fessis audiuntur.
2. Poeni saepe in itinere impediebantur.
3. Per duces via facilior vobis aperietur.
4. Arx Romana melius ab anseribus quam a militibus custodita est.
5. Via nova per quattuor dies a Poenis muniebatur.
6. Fragor pontis ab omnibus auditur.
7. Nolite impediri montium altitudine.
8. Si via munita erit, mox in campos Italiae descendemus.
9. Ratis longa ad ripam Rhodani vincta erat.
10. Etrusci ab Horatio solo diu impediti erant.

EXERCISE 36.

THE BATTLE OF THE TREBIA:
FIGHTING BEFORE BREAKFAST

After crossing the Alps, Hannibal had 26,000 men left, about a quarter of the force that had set out from Nova Carthāgō. He easily defeated the Romans on the river Tīcīnus. Publius Cornēlius Scīpiō, the Roman consul, who was in command, retired to Placentia, and then to a strong position on the river Trebia. Here he was joined by Tiberius Semprōnius, the other consul, who, flushed with success over a Carthaginian fleet, was over eager to do battle with Hannibal himself. The battles of the Tīcīnus and Trebia both took place in 218 B.C.

Hannibal prima luce equites trans Trebiam flumen transmisit. Appropinquabant, ut iussi erant, ad portas castrorum Romanorum, hostes telis lacessebant, deinde sensim ad ulteriorem ripam fluminis pertrahebant. Sempronius temere atque improvide omnes copias eduxit. Erat forte hiemis tempus; milites non pranderant[1]; sentiebatur acerrima vis frigoris. Ubi Romani aquam pectoribus tenus intraverunt, corpora rigebant, manus vix arma tenebant. Ut dies procedebat, omnes et lassitudine et fame impediebantur.

Hannibalis interim milites ante tabernacula corpora cibo et ignibus curant et oleo membra molliunt. Ubi adventus

---

[1] The first meal in the day for a Roman was bread dipped in wine.

hostium nuntiatur, alacres in aciem procedunt. Fessi Romani Poenis integris fortiter sed frustra restiterunt. Non solum cum equitibus et peditibus, sed etiam cum elephantis pugnaverunt. Insidias quoque Hannibal a tergo locaverat. Plurimi aciem hostium perruperunt, quod ab reditu flumine impediti sunt. Pars reliquorum flumen petiverunt et aut aquis absumpti sunt aut ab hostibus occisi. Apud Poenos autem propter imbrem et maximam vim frigoris laetitia victoriae vix sensa est.

EXERCISE 37.

1. False rumours are heard by the consuls.
2. The Carthaginians were hindered by snow and ice.
3. Where shall wisdom be found?
4. We shouted often, but we were not heard.
5. A way had been found across the Alps by the Gauls.
6. It was not easy for Hannibal to be heard by the whole army.
7. Britain was fortified by a very long wall.
8. In vain will Italy be guarded by the Alps.
9. Britain was discovered, not conquered, by Caesar.
10. The hands of the prisoners had been bound.

EXERCISE 38.

At dawn the Roman sentries were being provoked by the enemy's cavalry. Without delay, although they had not had breakfast, first the Roman cavalry, then the infantry were led out; soon, because the enemy seemed to be yielding, they were being drawn towards the river Trebia. Here they were hindered both by the cold and by the depth of the water. Meanwhile the Carthaginians eagerly awaited their arrival, because they had already breakfasted in front of fires; also their bodies had been softened with oil. Although they were tired, the Romans fought bravely for a long time, and resisted even the elephants, contrary to the expectation of the enemy. At length with much toil a way was opened up through the ranks of the Carthaginians. Thus very many of the Romans escaped to a neighbouring town; of the rest many made for the river, but were overwhelmed by the enemy.

Chapter 10
Demonstrative Pronouns: **hīc** and **ille**

hīc, *this (near me)*

Sing.	M.	F.	N.	Plur.	M.	F.	N.
Nom.	hīc	haec	hōc		hī	hae	haec
Acc.	hunc	hanc	hōc		hōs	hās	haec
Gen.	hūius	hūius	hūius		hōrum	hārum	hōrum
Dat.	huīc	huīc	huīc		hīs	hīs	hīs
Abl.	hōc	hāc	hōc		hīs	hīs	hīs

ille, *that (over there)*

Sing.	M.	F.	N.	Plur.	M.	F.	N.
Nom.	ille	illa	illud		illī	illae	illa
Acc.	illum	illam	illud		illōs	illās	illa
Gen.	illĭus	illĭus	illĭus		illōrum	illārum	illōrum
Dat.	illī	illī	illī		illīs	illīs	illīs
Abl.	illō	illā	illō		illīs	illīs	illīs

Hīc and ille are used either (1) as Adjectives with Nouns, e.g. hīc ager, *this territory,* illud oppidum, *that town,* or (2) as true Pronouns, e.g. hīc, *he, this man,* illa, *she* (more emphatic than ea).

Hīc often refers to the latter of two persons or things already mentioned, and ille to the former:

> **Duo comitēs cum Horātiō in ponte manēbant; hīc diū, illī parumper impetum hostium sustinuērunt.**
>
> *Two companions stayed with Horatius on the bridge; the latter long resisted the enemy's attack, the former only for a short time.*

Ille is sometimes used with a Noun (generally following it) to express *the well-known, the famous (so and so)*:

> **Alexander ille multās urbēs condidit.**
>
> *The famous Alexander founded many cities.*

49

Iste, ista, istud is declined like **ille,** and means *that* or *that man (near you)*; it sometimes carries with it an idea of contempt or ridicule:

Liber iste nōn mihi placet.
I do not like that book of yours.

EXERCISE 39.

1. Galli hos montes antea ascenderunt.
2. Haec verba Pontio displicebant.
3. Hi montes sunt altiores illis.
4. Hic locus erat insidiis aptissimus.
5. Hannibal ille Romanos in Italia saepe superavit.
6. Romulus et Remus fratres erant: hic ab illo necatus est.
7. Poeni ratem longam in flumen porrigunt et minorem huic copulant.
8. In illa pugna Romani victi sunt, quod defessi erant.
9. Romani de hac re statim deliberant.
10. Murus iste est humilior.

EXERCISE 40.

THE SIEGE OF SYRACUSE:
(1) GENIUS OF ARCHIMEDES

Hannibal had gained northern Italy by his victory on the Trebia. He then gained a complete victory at Lake Trasimene (217 B.C.) and marched through Umbria, Pīcēnum, and Āpūlia, turning from there to ravage Campānia. Quintus Fabius Maximus, who was appointed dictator, gave the Romans a chance to recover through his delaying tactics, but in 216 B.C. the consuls engaged Hannibal in the disastrous battle of Cannae. Hannibal was now joined by the city of Capua and most of southern Italy. The war continues in southern Italy, in Spain, and in Sicily, where Syracuse had declared for Carthage. Marcellus, one of the consuls, begins the siege of Syracuse in 214 B.C.

Romani terra marique simul Syracusas oppugnabant. Unus homo eo tempore Syracusanos maxime adiuvabat. Archimedes ille erat, non solum caeli praeclarus spectator, sed etiam mirabilior inventor[1] bellicorum tormentorum. Hic murum urbis omni genere tormentorum instruxit. Murum Achradinae (haec pars urbis ad mare spectat) sexaginta quinqueremibus Marcellus oppugnabat; in his portabantur turres; ceteras naves, plenas sagittariis et funditoribus, longius a muro tenebat. Adversus has Archimedes tormenta in muris disposuit: in naves ulteriores saxa ingentia emittebat; propiores levioribus petebat telis; postremo murum ab imo ad summum parvis cavernis aperuit; ita Syracusani tuti tela in hostes clam fundebant. Proximae tamen naves erant intra coniectum tormentorum; in harum proram de tollenone[2] demittebatur ferrea manus; primo hac puppis subito ex aqua erigebatur; deinde, ubi manus est remissa, nautae magnopere trepidabant, quia undae in navem infundebantur.

[1] He was the inventor also of the famous screw that bears his name.
[2] **tollēnō, -ōnis** (m.), *swing-beam, crane.* The **manus** (*grappling hook*) was fastened to it by a strong chain; there was a counterweight of lead attached to the other end.

EXERCISE 41.
1. These soldiers have not had breakfast.
2. That road has been broken away by a fall of earth.
3. The Romans were almost overcome by this disaster.
4. From this place you will descend into the plains of Italy.
5. These men made for Placentia, those men for the river.
6. The army was encouraged by those words of Hannibal.
7. A statue was given to the famous Horatius.
8. On the Capitol there were both dogs and geese; the latter were more alert than the former.
9. That plan of yours is very bad.
10. Why did Scipio leave this strong position?

EXERCISE 42.
Syracuse was attacked for a long time both by land and sea. The inhabitants, however, were helped by the skill of the famous Archimedes. In peace this man had watched the sky and the stars; now he turned his mind to arms and artillery. By his advice the walls of Achradina were everywhere equipped with

artillery; by this large stones were hurled forth against the further ships of the enemy; against the nearer ships the soldiers poured their javelins by hand. The Romans then brought some of their ships right up to the walls; on to these the Syracusans let down an iron grappling-hook; by means of this they suddenly raised a ship out of the sea and then let it go again. The Roman sailors were greatly frightened, because the ship seemed to them to be falling from the wall into the waves.

Chapter 11
Ipse and īdem

---

ipse, *self.*

Sing.	M.	F.	N.	*Plur.*	M.	F.	N.
Nom.	ipse	ipsa	ipsum		ipsī	ipsae	ipsa
Acc.	ipsum	ipsam	ipsum		ipsōs	ipsās	ipsa
Gen.	ipsĭus	ipsĭus	ipsĭus		ipsōrum	ipsārum	ipsōrum
Dat.	ipsī	ipsī	ipsī		ipsīs	ipsīs	ipsīs
Abl.	ipsō	ipsā	ipsō		ipsīs	ipsīs	ipsīs

īdem, *the same.*

Sing.	M.	F.	N.
Nom.	īdem	eadem	idem
Acc.	eundem	eandem	idem
Gen.	ēiusdem	ēiusdem	ēiusdem
Dat.	eīdem	eīdem	eīdem
Abl.	eōdem	eādem	eōdem

Plur.	M.	F.	N.
Nom.	eīdem *or* īdem	eaedem	eadem
Acc.	eōsdem	eāsdem	eadem
Gen.	eōrundem	eārundem	eōrundem
Dat.		eīsdem *or* īsdem	
Abl.		eīsdem *or* īsdem	

Both these Pronouns are used either (1) as Adjectives with Nouns, e.g. **Rōmulus ipse,** *Romulus himself,* **eadem verba,** *the same words,* or (2) as true Pronouns, **ipsa,** *she herself,* **īdem,** *the same (man).*

Ipse can be used to emphasize any Pronoun, in any Case, e.g. **ego ipse,** *I myself;* **vōbīs ipsīs,** *you yourselves.* But often the Person is not expressed apart from the Verb, e.g. **ipsī appropinquant,** *they are themselves approaching.*

53

Ipse must never be confused with the Reflexive Pronoun, **sē, suī, sibi, sē.** If **ipse** is removed from a Latin sentence, the sentence will still make good sense; compare **ipse vēnī** with **vēnī.** Wherever **sē** is used, it is vital to the sense, e.g. in **stultī sē laudant,** *foolish men praise themselves;* **laudō** is a Transitive Verb which requires a Direct Object, and without **sē** the sense would be incomplete.

Sometimes **ipse** can be translated by *very*:

> **Nāvēs ad ipsōs mūrōs vēnērunt.**
> *The ships came up to the very walls.*

EXERCISE 43.

1. Romani Romulum ipsum in numero deorum habebant.
2. Poeni Hannibalis ipsius verba audiverunt.
3. Idem magister pueros linguas et Latinam et Graecam docet.
4. Porsenna Cloeliam ipsam inter obsides postulavit.
5. Si eadem magister saepe recitaverit, tandem pueri ea discent.
6. Ipsi pugnate; nolite socios exspectare.
7. Hannibal ipse suis artibus paene superatus est.
8. Non semper nobis ipsis laboramus.
9. Archimedes caelum spectare solebat; idem tormenta invenit.
10. Aedificia ipsa dormire videntur.

EXERCISE 44.

THE SIEGE OF SYRACUSE:
(2) OPPORTUNITY WELL SEIZED

Romani, quia mari Syracusas frustra expugnabant, totis viribus impetum terra redintegrabant. Sed ea pars quoque eodem genere tormentorum per artem Archimedis instructa erat. Natura ipsa loci etiam iuvabat; saxa enim de altis rupibus non solum a militibus tormento mittebantur, sed etiam ipso pondere provolvebantur et graviter in hostes incidebant. Constituit igitur Marcellus oppugnationem omittere et Syracusanos terra marique obsidere. Longissimi tamen erant

muri neque difficile erat navibus Poenorum portum intrare.
Itaque diu obsidio erat vana.

Tandem duos post annos unus ex Romanis ex propinquo
loco murum exploravit, lapides numeravit, ipse secum altitudinem aestimavit; tum, quod murus satis humilis et vel
mediocribus scalis superabilis esse videbatur, Marcello rem
nuntiat. Mox forte celebrabatur a Syracusanis dies festus
Dianae; ea nocte magna pars militum in turribus epulis se
dederant et iam vino sopiti erant. Interea iussu Marcelli fere
mille milites se somno curaverant, et iam armati ad locum
deducti sunt. Sine strepitu primi murum scalis ascenderunt;
mox mille armati eodem modo partem urbis occupaverant.

EXERCISE 45.
1. Hannibal himself advanced with the infantry.
2. Soon you (pl.) will approach Rome itself.
3. The very height of the Alps frightened the Carthaginians.
4. Many Gauls had crossed the Alps by the same route
    before.
5. The Romans fought well by land; they did not always
    show the same skill by sea.
6. The consuls themselves were blamed for this disaster.
7. We schoolmasters often say the same thing.
8. Read the book yourselves.
9. On that very day Hannibal fell into an ambush.
10. I blame myself, not you.

EXERCISE 46.
The Romans determined to renew their attack by land. But
on this side, too, both the very nature of the place and the same
skill of Archimedes helped the Syracusans, nor was it easy,
owing to the length of the walls, to besiege so large a city. At
last by chance one of the Roman soldiers prepared a plan. He
secretly approached the wall and counted the stones; thus he
reckoned the height of the wall. He then announced his plan to
Marcellus. Because the wall was rather low and on account of
this very fact was carefully guarded, the latter waited for an
opportunity; he meanwhile got ready ladders of the same

height. By chance the Syracusans were soon celebrating the festival day of Diana; on that same night, when they had been overcome by wine and sleep, Marcellus himself led his men, together with their ladders, to the wall; after a short time a thousand men had noiselessly entered the city.

Chapter 12
Pronominal Adjectives: **alius, alter; ullus**

alius, *other, another (of any number).*

Sing.	M.	F.	N.	Plur.	M.	F.	N.
Nom.	alius	alia	aliud		aliī	aliae	alia
Acc.	alium	aliam	aliud		aliōs	aliās	alia
Gen.	alīus	alīus	alīus		aliōrum	aliārum	aliōrum
Dat.	aliī	aliī	aliī		aliīs	aliīs	aliīs
Abl.	aliō	aliā	aliō		aliīs	aliīs	aliīs

Alius is used in several ways; only two need be noticed for the moment:

(1) **Alius,** *other, another,* (a) used singly, and (b) sometimes followed by **quam,** *than:*

> **Fīlius Aenēae aliam urbem sub Albānō monte condidit.**
> *Aeneas's son founded another city under the Alban Mount.*

> **Nihil aliud quam domicilium petimus.**
> *We seek nothing else (other) than a home.*

(2) **Alius** is sometimes repeated in the same Case in two or more clauses; **alius . . ., alius . . .,** *one . . ., another . . .;* **aliī . . ., aliī . . .,** *some . . ., others . . .:*

> **Aliud est audīre, aliud intellegere.**
> *It is one thing to hear, another to understand.*

> **Aliī fossās complent, aliī dēfensōrēs vallō dēpellunt.**
> *Some (soldiers) fill in the ditches, others drive the defenders down from the rampart.*

alter, *the one* or *the other* (*of two*).

Sing	M.	F.	N.
Nom.	alter	altera	alterum
Acc.	alterum	alteram	alterum
Gen.	alterĭus	alterĭus	alterĭus
Dat.	alterī	alterī	alterī
Abl.	alterō	alterā	alterō

Plur.	M.	F.	N.
Nom.	alterī	alterae	altera
Acc.	alterōs	alterās	altera
Gen.	alterōrum	alterārum	alterōrum
Dat.	alterīs	alterīs	alterīs
Abl.	alterīs	alterīs	alterīs

Like **alter** is declined **neuter,** *neither,* except that e is dropped before **r,** after the Nom. sing. masc.

Alter is used of *the one* or *the other* of a pair, e.g. *eyes, hands, consuls;* so is **neuter:**

> **Alterō oculō vulnerātus est.**
> *He was wounded in one eye.*

> **Neuter consul aderat.**
> *Neither consul* (or *of the two consuls*) *was present.*

At this point, one more Pronominal Adjective should be noticed, **ullus, -a, -um** (declined like **ūnus**), *any;* it is used after a negative or a word that contains a negative idea, e.g. **vix** and **aegrē,** *scarcely, hardly;* **sine,** *without:*

> **Nostrī in perīculō erant, neque ullum erat subsidium.**
> *Our men were in danger, and there was no support.*

N.B.—Latin always uses **neque ullus,** never **et nullus.**

> **Sine ullō imperiō mīlitēs consistunt.**
> *The soldiers halt without any order.*

EXERCISE 47.

1. Ubi prīmī elephantī expositī sunt, aliī trānsmissī sunt.
2. Elephantī ad alteram rīpam trānsmittuntur.
3. Aliī Placentiam, aliī flūmen petīvērunt.

4. Altera via brevior, altera tutior erat.
5. Quid aliud sunt Alpes quam montes alti?
6. Alter frater ab altero necatus est.
7. Aliud est rem orare, aliud impetrare.
8. Romani in saltum sine ullo duce contenderunt.
9. Neutrum consilium Pontio placebat.
10. Altera ratis alteri copulata est.

EXERCISE 48.

THE SIEGE OF SYRACUSE: (3) FINAL CAPTURE AND A TRAGIC MISTAKE

Mox tuba signum datum est et undique non furtim, sed vi aperta pugnabant Romani; custodes hoc subito impetu perterrebantur; alii de muro saliebant, alii per murum se fugae mandabant; magna pars tamen ignara tanti mali erat, quia vino somnoque superata erat. Prima luce Marcellus reliquis cum copiis muros intravit et e loco superiore urbem, omnium illo tempore fere pulcherrimam, diu spectabat; etiam, ut nobis traditum est, partim ob gaudium, partim ob antiquae urbis[1] misericordiam, flebat.

Inde Achradinam, ubi plurimi Poeni et Syracusani adhuc resistebant, obsidere instituit. Hanc multas propter causas tandem in potestatem suam redegit: plures ex hostibus quam e Romanis pestilentia et vi aestus absumpti erant; Romani exercitum Punicum deleverant; Poeni aliam classem frustra exspectaverant; postremo praefectus Hispanus, nomine Moericus, praesidium prodiderat et Romanos per portam admiserat.

Syracusani nihil aliud quam salutem sibi liberisque petunt; haec promittitur, sed urbs ad praedam militibus datur. Forte etiam in medio tumultu Archimedes ille, operi intentus, formas in pulvere describebat; invenit eum miles ignarus atque necat. Mortem eius Marcellus maxime deploravit et sepulturam honestam curavit.

[1] Objective Genitive.

EXERCISE 49.

1. Some feared the enemy, others the long journey.
2. For four days the Carthaginians were building another road.
3. Others have climbed these mountains before.
4. Hannibal was now blind in one eye.
5. Cloelia swam from the enemy's camp to the other bank of the Tiber.
6. Some made for the walls, others opened the gates.
7. The one consul led out the army, the other remained in Rome.
8. For a long time neither army yielded.
9. It is one thing to conquer, it is another to rule.
10. The Romans had been surrounded, and there was no hope of flight.

EXERCISE 50.

Quickly the Romans put the guards to flight, some along the wall, others down from the wall into the city. After a few hours Marcellus himself entered this part of the city with his other troops. He climbed up to a high place and from here looked at one of the fairest cities. Many things came into his mind, the disaster of the Athenians,[1] the wealth of so many Syracusan kings,[2] the recent victory of the Romans.

Then when he had seized other parts of the city, he decided to besiege Achradina. Both armies were oppressed by a serious pestilence. Because the soldiers themselves looked after the sick, the pestilence quickly grew and many were destroyed, more, however, of the enemy than of the Romans. Finally after many months Achradina was betrayed by a Spanish officer. Except for the royal treasure, the booty was handed over to the soldiers; safety was promised to the Syracusans themselves and their children, but one of the soldiers in ignorance killed the famous Archimedes, busy on his work.

[1] The failure in 413 B.C. of the Athenian expedition against Syracuse was one of the main causes of the downfall of the Athenian empire.

[2] Especially Gelo and Hiero, two famous tyrants of Syracuse in the fifth century.

Chapter 13

Verbs requiring a Complement and Revision Exercises

(1) **Rōmānī Fabium Maximum dictātōrem creāvērunt.**
The Romans made Fabius Maximus dictator.

In this example the Verb **creāvērunt** governs the Accusative **Fabium Maximum** as the Direct Object, but needs an additional Accusative to complete the sense, i.e. as the **Complement.**

There are several Transitive Verbs in Latin which, when used in the Active Voice, often need this additional Accusative:

appellō, vocō, *I call (by name).*   **habeō,** *I think, consider.*
creō, *I appoint, elect.*   **praestō,** *I show.*
dēclārō, *I declare.*   **salūtō,** *I greet, hail.*

The additional Accusative may be a Noun or an Adjective:

Rōmānī Fabium parem Hannibalī habuērunt.
The Romans considered Fabius (as) equal to Hannibal.

(2) When these Verbs of *calling, appointing,* etc., are used in the Passive Voice, then the Complement is in the same Case as the Subject, as after the Verb **sum,** *I am*:

Hannibal dux dēclārātus est.
Hannibal was declared general.

Compare the similar use with **videor,** *I seem,* as explained in Chapter 3; here is another example:

Cicerōnī senectūs nōn misera vidēbātur.
Old age did not appear unhappy to Cicero.

EXERCISE 51.
1. Leo Androclum amicum salutavit.
2. Circus ille Maximus appellatur.
3. Romani Camillum dictatorem creaverant.

4. Cur Alpes difficiliores quam alii montes videntur?
5. Ubi Tarquinius Superbus expulsus est, Brutus et Collatinus consules creati sunt.
6. Nova urbs Alba Longa appellata est.
7. Porsennae Cloelia fortior Horatio videbatur.
8. Omnes amicitiam iucundissimam habemus.
9. Hannibal diu se hostem obstinatum praestitit.
10. Romani Syracusas fere omnium pulcherrimam urbem habebant.

EXERCISE 52.

1. The Romans called Tarquinius the Proud.
2. Fabius Maximus was appointed dictator.
3. The citizens hailed Romulus as a god and father of the city.
4. On account of the walls and the Tiber, the city of Rome seemed safe.
5. The Roman senators were called fathers.
6. Caesar did not disembark his troops at once, because he did not consider the place suitable.
7. Agricola showed himself moderate towards the Britons.
8. The Roman citadel was called the Capitol.
9. To hand over their arms to the Samnites seemed very disgraceful to the Romans.
10. Hannibal had always considered the Romans as the enemies of his country.

Sentences for Revision

EXERCISE 53.

1. Naves ad imum murum appropinquabant.
2. Romulus a Romanis deus habebatur.
3. Melius est amari quam timeri.
4. Aliud est consulere, aliud consilio parere.
5. Romani fortunae belli se dedere nesciebant.
6. Interdum melius est cedere quam resistere.
7. Tela a loco superiore in Romanos incidebant.
8. Horatius salutem ultimus petivit.
9. Nonnullis est plus pecuniae quam sapientiae.
10. Primo Romani saepius victi sunt quam vicerunt.

EXERCISE 54.

1. This hill is higher than that.
2. The other pass had already been seized by the enemy.
3. The inhabitants of Luceria were considered faithful allies of the Romans.
4. Without any order the soldiers began to fortify the camp.
5. Why had you (s.) not been asked your opinion?
6. The elephants were quickly sent across the river by the rush of the water.
7. The Carthaginians were not the first to climb the Alps.
8. Few cities were more beautiful than Syracuse.
9. The Carthaginians were suddenly attacked in front and in rear.
10. A huge pile of logs was heaped together.

EXERCISE 55.

1. Cur sine ullis exploratoribus exercitus ducebatur?
2. Romani arte Archimedis diu impediti erant.
3. Propter vim frigoris difficile erat arma tenere.
4. Archimedes ille ab ignaro milite occisus est.
5. Remus murum humiliorem Romuli contempsit.
6. Arx Atheniensium Acropolis appellata est.
7. Illa nocte canes ipsi dormiebant.
8. Hannibal ipso adventu suo Romanos terruit.
9. Audire et intellegere non sunt eadem.
10. Archimedes terra marique Syracusanos eadem arte iuvabat.

EXERCISE 56.

1. In vain was another fleet awaited.
2. The soldiers had entered the city without any noise.
3. Some were killed by the plague, others by the heat.
4. Marcellus himself entered the city at dawn.
5. We seek nothing but safety for the citizens.
6. That ground is not suitable for cavalry.
7. The very walls seemed to be falling on to the ships.
8. The Romans had conquered the Carthaginians in the former war.
9. Stones were rolled down from the top of the wall.
10. The further ships were safer than the nearer ones.

Chapter 14
Perfect Infinitives, Active and Passive

	Perfect Infinitive Active	*Perfect Infinitive Passive*
1st Conj.	**amāvisse** *to have loved*	**amātus (-a, -um) esse** *to have been loved*
2nd Conj.	**monuisse** *to have advised*	**monitus (-a, -um) esse** *to have been advised*
3rd Conj.	**rexisse** *to have ruled*	**rectus (-a, -um) esse** *to have been ruled*
4th Conj.	**audīvisse** *to have heard*	**audītus (-a, -um) esse** *to have been heard*
sum	**fuisse** *to have been*	

It will be seen that the **Perf. Infin. Active** is formed by adding -isse to the Perfect Base, and the **Perf. Infin. Passive** by using the Perfect Participle Passive with **esse**.

Perfect Infinitives, like Present Infinitives, are sometimes used as **Nouns**:

Tam diū domō abfuisse Poenīs ingrātum erat.
To have been away from home so long was displeasing to the Carthaginians.

Both Present and Perfect Infinitives are often used **Prolatively** after the Passives of Verbs of *saying* and *thinking*; **videor,** *I seem*, is also often used with a Perfect Infinitive, as well as with a Present Infinitive:

Agricola prōvinciam bene administrāvisse dīcitur.
Agricola is said to have governed the province well.

Prōvincia ab Agricolā bene administrāta esse putātur.
The province is thought to have been well governed by Agricola.

In the last example **administrāta** is part of the Complement and therefore agrees with the subject **prōvincia** in **Case, Number, and Gender.**

Pater Pontium bene monuisse vidētur.

His father seems to have advised Pontius well.

Extent of Space

Space, measurement, and **distance** are expressed in the **Accusative** Case:

Mūrus erat decem pedēs altus.

The wall was ten feet high.

Hannibal sex mīlia passuum Rōmā aberat.

Hannibal was six miles from Rome.

Note.—**Mille,** *a thousand,* is an indeclinable Adjective; **mille passūs,** 1000 *paces,* is a Roman *mile* (1618 English yards).

The plural of **mille, mīlia (-ium, -ibus),** is a Noun, always followed by the Genitive, e.g. **quattuor mīlia equitum,** *four thousand cavalry;* **duo mīlia passuum,** *two miles.*

EXERCISE 57.

1. Ascanius Albam Longam condidisse putatur.
2. Mille armati murum nocte ascenderunt.
3. Lupa narratur Romulum et Remum curavisse.
4. Hannibal carissimus militibus suis fuisse videtur.
5. Urbs Veii fere duodecim milia passuum Roma abest.
6. Tarpeia aurum pro deditione postulavisse narratur.
7. Galli murum sex pedes altum aedificaverant.
8. Multa genera tormentorum ab Archimede inventa esse dicuntur.
9. Castra fossa octo pedes alta muniebantur.
10. Capitolium ab anseribus conservatum esse narratur.

EXERCISE 58.

HANNIBAL IN SIGHT OF ROME

In 211 B.C. *Hannibal tried to relieve Capua, which was being besieged by three Roman armies. Not being successful in this, he made a sudden dash northwards and for a moment was in sight of Rome.*

Hannibal ad Anienem fluvium castra admoverat et iam modo tria milia passuum ab urbe aberat. Ipse cum duobus milibus equitum paene ad ipsa moenia venit. Hoc imperatori Romano indignum visum est; itaque Poenos in castra reppulit. Postero die Hannibal in aciem omnes copias eduxit; suum quoque exercitum consules instruxerunt. Sed hoc ipso tempore imber ingens et Poenos et Romanos perturbavit; milites vix arma retinuerunt et statim castra petiverunt. Eadem res postero die eodem loco accidit. Fortunam suam Hannibal magna voce deploravisse dicitur.

Alia res, quanquam minima erat, spem eius minuit: forte possessor eius agri, ubi Hannibal ipse castra habebat, eum pretio solito nihilominus venditabat; emptor tamen Romae inventus esse nuntiatus est. Hoc Hannibali superbum atque indignum videbatur: statim iussu eius tabernas argentarias[1] Romanorum (multae enim circa forum tunc erant) praeco venditabat. Nihilominus Hannibal sine certamine exercitum statim abduxit.

[1] *of silver money* (**argentum**); **taberna argentāria**, *a bank*.

EXERCISE 59.
1. Remus is related to have leapt over the new wall.
2. Romulus was believed to have been carried to heaven by a storm.
3. How many miles is Capua from Rome?
4. The ditch was ten feet wide and seven feet deep.
5. I seem to have heard that story before.
6. Hercules is said to have been the strongest of men.
7. Fifteen thousand Romans were killed in that battle.
8. Hannibal's army was many miles from Carthage.

9. The Romans seemed to have been saved by Fortune[1] herself on that day.
10. Socrates was thought to have been a very wise man.

[1] **Fortūna,** *goddess of luck*.

EXERCISE 60.

It was pleasing to Hannibal to be only three miles from Rome. Joyfully he at last looked at the walls of the city. After a short time both the Romans and the Carthaginians were ready for battle, but at that very moment they were scattered by a huge rainstorm. To have defeated the enemy so often and then to be defeated by nature seemed to Hannibal to be most unfair. Another thing, although it was very small, is said to have greatly moved him : a Roman citizen was reported to be offering for sale at the usual price the very place where Hannibal had pitched his camp. Hannibal, angry at this, at once summoned an auctioneer. At his bidding the auctioneer was soon offering Roman shops for sale. Hannibal, however, struck camp without delay and led his troops towards Samnium.

Chapter 15

Relative Pronoun

Quī, *who, which.*

Sing.	M.	F.	N.	*Plur.*	M.	F.	N.
Nom.	quī	quae	quod		quī	quae	quae
Acc.	quem	quam	quod		quōs	quās	quae
Gen.	cūius	cūius	cūius		quōrum	quārum	quōrum
Dat.	cūī	cūī	cūī		quibus or quīs		
Abl.	quō	quā	quō		quibus or quīs		

When **cum,** *with,* is used with the Abl., it is written **quōcum,** etc.

This is the house which Jack built contains a Main Clause, *this is the house,* and a **Relative Clause,** *which Jack built.* The second clause is called Relative, because it is *related to* or connected with *the house.* The *house* is a *Jack-built house* (a Relative Clause is sometimes called an Adjectival Clause).

The connecting link is the word *which,* a **Relative Pronoun.** This link connects *house* with *Jack built.*

In Latin *which* must agree like an Adjective with *house* in **Gender** and **Number,** because it is connected with *house.* But *which* is also connected with *built* (*Jack built it*); it is the Direct Object of *built* and in Latin must be in the Accusative **Case.**

So the Latin is:

Haec est domus, quam Iōannēs aedificāvit.

Two links backwards ——————— One link forwards
    Gender, Fem.   **Case,** Acc.
    Number, Sing.

The word in the Main Clause with which the Relative Pronoun is connected may be a Noun, as in the above example, or a Pronoun; it is known as the **Antecedent** (the *going-before* word):

> **Eī, quī missī erant, Hannibalem reppulērunt.**
> *Those who had been sent drove Hannibal back.*

Here **eī** is the Antecedent of **quī**.

We may sum up the rule as follows: the **Relative Pronoun, quī, quae, quod,** agrees in **Gender** and **Number** with its **Antecedent,** but the **Case** of the Relative Pronoun must follow the rule of its **own clause.**

Here are some more Relative Clauses; they should be carefully studied with the above rule in mind:

(1) **Gallī semper bellum gerunt cum Germānīs, quī trans Rhēnum incolunt.**

> *The Gauls are always waging war with the Germans, who live across the Rhine.*

(2) **Gallia est dīvīsa in partēs trēs, quārum ūna ā Belgīs incolitur.**

> *Gaul is divided into three parts, of which one is inhabited by the Belgae.*

(3) **Marcellus, cūi imperium mandātum erat, Syrācūsānōs nōn facile superāvit.**

> *Marcellus, to whom the command had been entrusted, did not defeat the Syracusans easily.*

(4) **Cārī sunt illī, quibuscum mihi est amīcitia.**

> *Dear are those with whom I have friendship.*

Notes.—(i) In English the Relative Pronoun is sometimes expressed by *that*; in fact the story was about *the house **that** Jack built.*

(ii) Sometimes the Relative Pronoun is omitted in English, e.g. *Archimedes was busy with the figures he had drawn.* In Latin it must always be expressed.

(iii) The Main Verb is often placed at the end of the whole sentence, i.e. after the Relative Clause, e.g. **Hannibal obsidēs, quōs Gallī dabant, nōn repudiāvit,** *Hannibal did not refuse the hostages which the Gauls offered.*

Numerals and their Order

Latin Numerals will be found in the Summary of Grammar at the end of the book. In Compound Numbers from 20 to 99, either the English order is followed, or the smaller comes first with **et**, e.g. **vīgintī trēs** or **trēs et vīgintī**, but **ūnus** generally comes first. After 100, the larger number comes first, with or without **et**, e.g. **ducentī et quīnque** or **ducentī quīnque**.

EXERCISE 61.

1. Delector libro quem ad me misisti.
2. Poeni montibus, qui altiores erant Pyrenaeis, terrebantur.
3. Androclus leonem, cuius vitam conservaverat, cognovit.
4. Multae e viis, quas Romani muniverunt, hodie supersunt.
5. Romani ad saltum pervenerunt, in quo Samnites eos exspectabant.
6. Duces, quibuscum procedebant, Romanos in insidias duxerunt.
7. Milites consules, quibus salutem suam mandaverant, culpabant.
8. Etiam ei elephanti, qui in flumen ceciderant, in ripam evaserunt.
9. Pontius patrem, qui iam senex erat, consulere constituit.
10. Romani consilio, quod Lentulus proposuit, paruerunt.

EXERCISE 62.

THE BATTLE OF WITS:
(1) MARCELLUS KILLED IN AMBUSH

The events of the next three chapters occurred in Āpūlia in the south of Italy in 208 B.C. Hannibal continued fighting in southern Italy with less and less success until he was recalled to Carthage in 203 (see Exercise 98).

Tumulus erat silvestris inter Punica et Romana castra, quem neuter exercitus occupaverat. Hic locus Hannibali aptior videbatur insidiis quam castris. Itaque nocte ad eam rem aliquot

Numidarum turmas miserat et in media silva abdiderat, quorum interdiu nemo a loco movebatur. Consul Marcellus, ignarus Poenorum consilii, ipse quoque hunc eundem tumulum explorare constituit; tum aperta via cum equitibus ducentis viginti et Crispino, altero consule, ad collem contendit. Speculator signum dat Numidis, et pars eorum qui in silva se abdiderant ad tergum Romanorum taciti procedunt. Tum subito omnes undique ex insidiis consurgunt et magno clamore Romanos petunt. Romani, qui iam circumventi erant, frustra restiterunt; ambo consules ceteros confirmant et ipsi aliquamdiu pugnant. Marcellus tamen lancea configitur et ex equo cadit moribundus. Equitum tres et quadraginta aut in proelio aut in fuga ceciderunt.

EXERCISE 63.

1. The guides led the Romans into the ambush which the Gauls had prepared.
2. Hannibal did not reject the guides who had been given to him.
3. Archimedes was looking at the figures he had drawn.
4. The advice which his father had given did not please Pontius.
5. Cloelia, who had been handed over to the Etruscans, was very brave.
6. The soldiers with whom the Carthaginians were fighting had not had breakfast.
7. Even elephants were led down by the new road which the Carthaginians had made.
8. Those to whom the signal had been given climbed the walls.
9. The city that the Romans were attacking was called Syracuse.
10. Hannibal, whose cavalry were in sight, was now near Rome.

EXERCISE 64.

Hannibal seized a woody hillock which lay between his own camp and the enemy's: for this seemed very suitable for an ambush. The Numidians whom he had hidden there did not wander, but silently remained in their position. The consul Marcellus, who also had determined to seize this hillock, advanced incautiously towards it with some squadrons of cavalry. A signal was given to the Numidians by a scout who was not expecting so many troops, and at once some of them were secretly sent past the enemy's flanks. Suddenly both those who were in the front and those who were in the rear attacked the Romans. The latter had no hope of safety, as they had been surrounded on all sides. In this fight many cavalry were killed, among these Marcellus himself; Crispinus, the other consul, was wounded.

Chapter 16
Relative Pronoun: Further Exercises

1. Hannibal tabernas, quae circa forum tunc erant, venditabat.
2. Milites ad murum scalas, quas paraverant, secum portabant.
3. Muri 'instructi erant tormentis, quae Archimedes invenerat.
4. Dies, quo Diana celebrabatur, iam aderat.
5. Romam ipsam, ad quam tandem pervenerat, Hannibal spectabat.
6. Ei, quibus consules credebant, falsa narraverant.
7. Bellum, quod Romani cum Hannibale gerebant, longissimum erat.
8. Poeni ad locum, qui modo tria milia passuum Roma abest, pervenerunt.
9. Classis, quam Poeni exspectabant, Syracusas non pervenit.
10. Archimedes, cuius consilio Syracusae defensae erant, a milite Romano occisus est.

EXERCISE 66.

THE BATTLE OF WITS:
(2) FORGERY OF A DESPATCH

Tum Hannibal in tumulo, in quo fuerat proelium equestre, castra ponit. Ibi Marcelli corpus invenit et sepelit. Crispinus, propter mortem collegae et suum vulnus pavidus, castra Romana ponit in monte alto et undique tuto, quem nocte occupaverat. Duorum ducum iam alter alacrem, alter cautum se praestabat. Anulum Marcelli simul cum corpore Hannibal invenerat. Huius rei non ignarus, Crispinus ad civitates, quae ei erant proximae, nuntios miserat. 'Marcellus', inquiunt, 'occisus est; si Hannibal litteras nomine Marcelli miserit, nolite eis credere.' Venit Salapiam a Poenis nuntius cum litteris, quas Hannibal nomine Marcelli composuerat. 'Cras veniam noctu Salapiam: parate milites, qui in praesidio sunt.' Forte tamen praecesserat Salapiam nuntius consulis. Salapitani fraudem senserunt et nuntium alterum statim remiserunt. Oppidanos per muros locant, custodes diligentius instruunt, circa portam, quae ad Hannibalis castra spectabat, fortissimos ponunt.

EXERCISE 67.
1. Marcellus, who had fought very bravely, was killed in this battle.
2. The wall which Romulus had built was despised by Remus.
3. The soldiers, to whom the scout gave the signal, soon surrounded the Romans.
4. The Syracusans, who had come to Marcellus, sought safety for their children.
5. The one road, which was longer, was safer.
6. The Romans were attacked by troops whom Hannibal had placed in the rear.
7. The Gauls Hannibal had won over were not always faithful.
8. You (pl.), who have overcome the Pyrenees, will not be hindered by the Alps.
9. Marcellus was looking at Syracuse, than which few cities were more beautiful.
10. That which is useful is not always good.

EXERCISE 68.
Crispinus, who had himself been wounded and was lamenting the death of his colleague, hastened by night to the nearest hills and pitched camp in a safer position. Meanwhile Hannibal had moved his camp to the very hillock on which he had lately fought, and had found not only the body of Marcellus, but also his signet-ring. Because he was afraid of a trick, Crispinus at

once announced this to the neighbouring states. When the consul's messenger had warned the inhabitants of Salapia and had departed, a letter which had been composed by Hannibal in the name of Marcellus reached Salapia. In this letter Marcellus was said to be advancing towards Salapia and to be demanding help. The Salapitani, who at once perceived the trick, prepared themselves against[1] the danger.

[1] **contrā**.

Additional Exercises on the Relative Pronoun will be found on *p.* 249.

Chapter 17
Verbs of the 3rd Conjugation in -iō

Capiō, capere, cēpī, captum, *I take, capture.*

In Tenses and forms arising from the Present Stem, Verbs of the **capiō** type are of **mixed Conjugation**. In the Present Indicative, Active and Passive, the 1st pers. sing. and the 3rd pers. plur. follow **audiō**; the rest of these Tenses drop the -i of the Stem and follow **regō**. The Future and Imperfect Tenses, Active and Passive, follow **audiō** :

Active

Present	*Future*	*Imperfect*
capiō	**capiam**	**capiēbam**
capis	**capiēs**	**capiēbās**
capit	**capiet**	**capiēbat**
capimus	**capiēmus**	**capiēbāmus**
capitis	**capiētis**	**capiēbātis**
capiunt	**capient**	**capiēbant**

Passive

capior	**capiar**	**capiēbar**
caperis	**capiēris**	**capiēbāris**
capitur	**capiētur**	**capiēbātur**
capimur	**capiēmur**	**capiēbāmur**
capiminī	**capiēminī**	**capiēbāminī**
capiuntur	**capientur**	**capiēbantur**

Imperative Active, **cape, capite**; Passive, **capere, capiminī.**
Present Infinitive Active, **capere**; Passive, **capī.**

Perfect Tenses and Infinitives follow the 3rd Conjugation :
Perfect Active, **cēpī,** etc. ; Passive, **captus sum,** etc.
Perfect Infinitive Active, **cēpisse**; Passive, **captus esse.**

Compounds of **capiō** are conjugated in the same way:

> **accipiō   accipere   accēpī   acceptum**   _I receive_
>
> so also: **dēcipiō,** _I deceive_; **incipiō,** _I begin_; **recipiō,**
> _I accept_; **suscipiō,** _I undertake._
>
>   **mē recipiō,** _I retreat._

Other Verbs and their compounds conjugated like **capiō** in
Present Stem Tenses, Present Infinitives, and Imperatives are:

cupiō	**cupere**	**cupīvī**	**cupītum**	_I desire_
faciō[1]	**facere**	**fēcī**	**factum**	_I do, make_
conficiō	**conficere**	**confēcī**	**confectum**	_I finish_

> so also: **dēficiō,** _I revolt_; **interficiō,** _I kill_; **praeficiō,**[2]
> _I put in command_; **reficiō,** _I repair._

fodiō	**fodere**	**fōdī**	**fossum**	_I dig_
fugiō	**fugere**	**fūgī**	**fugitum**	_I flee_

> so also: **aufugiō,** _I flee away_; **confugiō,** _I flee for
> refuge_; **effugiō,** _I escape_ (trans. and intrans.).

iaciō	**iacere**	**iēcī**	**iactum**	_I throw_
abiciō	**abicere**	**abiēcī**	**abiectum**	_I throw away_

> so also: **cōniciō,** _I throw_; **dēiciō,** _I throw down_; **prōiciō,**
> _I throw forward_; **rēiciō,** _I reject._

percutiō	**percutere**	**percussī**	**percussum**	_I strike_
rapiō	**rapere**	**rapuī**	**raptum**	_I seize_
corripiō	**corripere**	**corripuī**	**correptum**	_I snatch_

> so also: **dīripiō,** _I plunder._

aspiciō	**aspicere**	**aspexī**	**aspectum**	_I look at_

> so also: **conspiciō,** _I catch sight of._

---

[1] 2nd pers. sing. Imperative Active, **fac,** but compounds follow
capiō, e.g. **confice.**

[2] With Acc. of Direct Object, followed by a Dat., e.g. **Hannibal
frātrem exercituī praefēcit,** _Hannibal put his brother in command of
an army_; **Hasdrubal exercituī praefectus est,** _Hasdrubal was put in
command of an army._

Passive of faciō (Present Stem Forms)

Tenses and forms of the Perfect are quite regular, **factus sum, factus esse**, etc.

Tenses and forms for the Present Stem are supplied by **fīō**, *I become* or *I am made*; Present Infinitive **fierī**:

Present	Future	Imperfect
fīō	fīam	fīēbam
fīs	fīēs	fīēbās
fit	fīet	fīēbat
(fīmus)	fīēmus	fīēbāmus
(fītis)	fīētis	fīēbātis
fīunt	fīent	fīēbant

Notes.—(1) **Conficiō, interficiō, praeficiō, reficiō** all have a regular Passive, **conficior**, Infin. **conficī, confectus sum**, etc.

(2) After **fīō** the Complement is in the same Case as the Subject, e.g. **terra fit fēcundior**, *the land is made more fertile.* So also **Camillus factus est dictātor**, *Camillus was made (or became) dictator (see Chapter 13, 2).*

EXERCISE 69.
1. Samnites ambos consules insidiis capiunt.
2. Romani Luceriam via breviore iter faciebant.
3. Labores difficiles Hercules suscipere solebat.
4. Marcellus pulchritudine Syracusarum capiebatur.
5. Hannibal Romam, caput Italiae, capere cupiebat.
6. Consules dolo Samnitium facile decepti erant.
7. Senectus fit levior eis, quibus sunt amici.
8. Romani Syracusis multa diripiebant.
9. Speculator equites Romanos subito e silva conspexit.
10. Magister ille pueros iustissimos aliis praeficit.

EXERCISE 70.

THE BATTLE OF WITS:
(3) A HOT RECEPTION

Hannibal quarta ferme vigilia ad urbem appropinquavit. Primum agmen erat perfugae Romanorum, qui arma Romana habebant; ei, ubi ad portam venerunt, Latine exclamant et vigiles excitare incipiunt: 'Portam aperite; consul adest.' Vigiles, qui deditionem simulant, circa portam trepidant. Cataracta deiecta erat; eam partim vectibus, partim funibus levant; vixdum satis patet iter, cum perfugae celeriter ruunt per portam; et ubi sescenti ferme intraverunt, Salapitani funem quo cataracta suspensa erat remiserunt; cataracta magno sonitu cecidit. Alii in perfugas, qui arma neglegenter ex umeris gerebant, impetum faciunt, alii e turri portae saxa et pila in hostes coniciunt. Ita inde Hannibal, quod sua fraude ipse captus erat, se recepit.

Exercise 71.

1. The Romans desired to finish the war.
2. The Gauls begin to throw down rocks from the mountain.
3. The soldiers caught sight of the enemy who had been placed in the pass.
4. Some were killed, others escaped with the consul.
5. Suddenly the Numidians made an attack on the cavalry from all sides.
6. Hannibal was put in command of the Carthaginian army.
7. Finish (s.) the work you have undertaken.
8. Many Gauls revolted from the Romans.
9. The work will become lighter, if many help.
10. Do not (pl.) throw away hope; you will soon be looking at the walls of Rome.

Exercise 72.

Hannibal marched by night and reached Salapia before dawn. Many Romans had deserted to[1] the Carthaginians and had been placed in the vanguard. When they reached the gate, they began to cry out in Latin and to rouse the sentries. The latter were not deceived by their voices, because Crispinus had warned the Salapitani. They pretended friendship and hurried to raise the portcullis, which they had let down[2] at the first watch. When the portcullis had been raised only a little, the

[1] ad.   [2] dēiciō.

deserters hurled themselves forward into the city. Then the Salapitani suddenly let down the portcullis, and not only attacked the unwary deserters, but also began to hurl weapons from the walls on to the Carthaginians who remained outside the gate.

Chapter 18
Deponent Verbs

There is a large class of Verbs called **Deponent Verbs,** which are **Passive** in nearly every **form,** but **Active** in **meaning;** they are called Deponent, because they have laid aside **(dēpōnō)** a Passive meaning.

They are found in each of the four Conjugations; here are examples of one from each Conjugation:

	Pres. Infin.	Perfect	
1st Conjug. **moror**	**morārī**	**morātus sum**	*I delay*
2nd Conjug. **vereor**	**verērī**	**veritus sum**	*I fear, reverence*
3rd Conjug. **ūtor**	**ūtī**	**ūsus sum**	*I use*
4th Conjug. **mentior**	**mentīrī**	**mentītus sum**	*I tell a lie*

The Supines—**morātum, veritum, ūsum, mentītum**—are Active in form and meaning. There are one or two other Active forms which will be met later.

The scheme of Deponent Verbs is set out in the Summary of Grammar at the end of the book. It is enough, therefore, to set out here, by way of example, the following parts of **moror,** *I delay*, conjugated like **amor:**

Tense		Tense	
Present	**moror,** *I delay.*	Perfect	**morātus sum,** *I (have) delayed.*
Future	**morābor,** *I shall delay.*	Fut. Perf.	**morātus erō,** *I shall have delayed.*
Imperf.	**morābar,** *I was delaying.*	Pluperf.	**morātus eram,** *I had delayed.*

Imperative, **morāre, morāminī,** *delay.*
Perfect Infinitive, **morātus esse,** *to have delayed.*

Some Deponent Verbs are Transitive, e.g. **hortor** (1st Conjug.), *I encourage*; some are Intransitive, e.g. **vagor** (1st Conjug.), *I wander*.

Among the most common of Deponent Verbs are the following:

1st Conjug. (all regular):

cōnor (with Infin.), *I try*	**mīror,** *I wonder at*
conspicor, *I catch sight of, see*	**moror,** *I delay*
	populor, *I ravage*
cunctor, *I delay*	**precor** (with Acc.), *I pray to*
hortor, *I encourage, exhort*	**vagor,** *I wander*

2nd Conjug. (regular):

mereor, *I deserve*	**polliceor,** *I promise*
misereor (with Gen.), *I pity*	**vereor,** *I fear, reverence*

(irregular):

confiteor	**confitērī**	**confessus sum**	*I confess*
tueor	**tuērī**	——	*I defend, protect*

EXERCISE 73.

1. Speculator Romanos subito conspicatus est.
2. Equites effugere frustra conabantur.
3. Multis verbis Hannibal suos hortatus est.
4. Illa nocte Syracusani murum non diligenter tuebantur.
5. Pontius captivorum non miseritus est.
6. Horatius summam laudem meritus erat.
7. Propter lapsum terrae Poeni quattuor dies morati sunt.
8 Pueri Romani parentes verentur.
9. Marcellus praedam suis pollicitus erat.
10. Galli paucos dies urbem Romam populabantur.

EXERCISE 74. (*Deponent Verbs to be used where possible.*)

1. The Roman soldiers wondered at the skill of Archimedes.
2. The general promises safety to the citizens.

3. The Samnites were wandering with their flock near the Roman camp.
4. Horatius prayed to the god and leaped down from the bridge.
5. Many tried to reach the river Trebia.
6. Never had the soldiers ravaged so many temples before.
7. The Romans suddenly caught sight of the Samnites.
8. Why do the consuls not confess their folly?
9. The Carthaginians renewed their march, when Hannibal had encouraged them.
10. The Gauls did not reverence even the senators.

Deponent Verbs of 3rd and 4th Conjugations

3rd Conjug. type:

fruor (with Abl.)	fruī	fructus sum	*I enjoy*
īrascor	īrascī	īrātus sum	*I am angry*
lābor	lābī	lapsus sum	*I slip, fall*
loquor	loquī	locūtus sum	*I speak*
nanciscor	nanciscī	nactus sum	*I obtain*
nascor	nascī	nātus sum	*I am born*
oblīviscor (with Gen.)	oblīviscī	oblītus sum	*I forget*
proficiscor	proficiscī	profectus sum	*I set out, start*
queror (dē)	querī	questus sum	*I complain (about)*
sequor	sequī	secūtus sum	*I follow*
ūtor (with Abl.)	ūtī	ūsus sum	*I use*

With present Stem Tenses conjugated like **capior**:

gradior	gradī	gressus sum	*I step, walk*

so also: **aggredior**, *I attack;* **ēgredior**, *I go out;* **prōgredior**, *I advance.*

morior	morī	mortuus sum	*I die*
patior	patī	passus sum	*I suffer, allow*

4th Conjug. type (regular):

mentior, *I tell a lie*

(irregular):

experior	experīrī	expertus sum	*I try, make trial of*
orior	orīrī	ortus sum	*I rise*

so also: **exorior,** *I spring up.*

Semi-Deponent Verbs

A few Verbs with Active meaning have a Passive form in the Perfect Tenses:

2nd Conjug.

soleō	solēre	solitus sum	*I am accustomed*
audeō	audēre	ausus sum	*I dare*
gaudeō	gaudēre	gāvīsus sum	*I rejoice*

3rd Conjug.

(con)fīdō (with Dat.) fīdere	fīsus sum	*I trust*

EXERCISE 75.
1. Consules sine mora Luceriam profecti sunt.
2. Nunquam diu Romani pace fruebantur.
3. Uterisne gladio, quem tibi dedi?
4. Stultum est sine causa irasci.
5. Post breve tempus pedites Romani equites secuti sunt.
6. Perfugae Romani Latine loquebantur.
7. Vincere scis, Hannibal; victoria uti nescis.
8. Num obliti estis victoriarum vestrarum priorum?
9. Subito magna tempestas orta erat.
10. Pueri non cunctantur, ubi e ludo egrediuntur.

EXERCISE 76. (*Deponent Verbs to be used where possible.*)
1. When the schoolmaster had spoken, Camillus was angry.
2. Hannibal obtained a place suitable for a camp.
3. A new fleet had set out from Carthage.
4. The Roman line, tired through hunger, began to fall.
5. I will set out at once to Rome; follow (s.) as quickly as possible.

6. The guides had lied to Hannibal.
7. Many beasts of burden followed the tracks of the Carthaginian column.
8. The tired animals had fallen on the rocks.
9. Hannibal advanced with the infantry.
10. The Carthaginians were complaining, because the war was so long.

EXERCISE 77.
1. Marcellus ex equo lapsus est et mox mortuus est.
2. Saepe res magnae e causis parvis nascuntur.
3. Fabius proelium non commisit; semper cunctari solebat.
4. Inutile erat de consulum stultitia queri.
5. Omnes Numidae undique ab insidiis exorti sunt.
6. Post hanc victoriam Romani maxime gavisi erant.
7. Num Hannibal Alpes ascendere ausus est?
8. Quamdiu tantas iniurias patiemur, o cives?
9. Cunctabimur potius quam talem hostem aggrediemur.
10. Nunc facile per Italiam progrediemini.

EXERCISE 78. (*Use Deponent or Semi-Deponent Verbs where possible.*)
1. The Carthaginians, tired with much toil, were at last enjoying a rest.
2. Do (pl.) not forget your former courage.
3. Pity (s.) the women and children.
4. Hannibal had not entirely trusted the guides.
5. The Britons complained to Boadicea about their wrongs.
6. Those who deserve rewards do not always obtain them.
7. Quickly the cavalry advanced as far as the Trebia.
8. When Marcellus had died, Hannibal used his signet-ring.
9. Make (s.) use of this victory, and advance at once.
10. The Gauls had suddenly risen up from an ambush.

Chapter 19
Possum

Possum, posse (Pres. Infin.), **potuī** (no Supine), *I am able, can.*
Possum is a contracted form of **potis,** *able,* and **sum.**

Present	*Future*	*Imperfect*
possum	**poterō**	**poteram**
potes	**poteris**	**poterās**
potest	**poterit**	**poterat**
possumus	**poterimus**	**poterāmus**
potestis	**poteritis**	**poterātis**
possunt	**poterunt**	**poterant**

The Tenses formed from the Perfect Base, **potu-,** are conjugated regularly, **potuī, potuerō, potueram;** Perfect Infinitive, **potuisse.**

Possum is followed by a Prolative Infinitive:

Sine benevolentiā nulla urbs stāre potest.
No city can stand without goodwill.

Dēlērī tōtus exercitus potuit (or **poterat**).
The whole army could have (or *might have*) *been destroyed.*

In the last example, it should be noticed that the idea of a past tense, *could have,* is expressed by the past tense of **possum** and not by the past tense of the Infinitive. In the same way, the Imperfect or Perfect of **dēbeō** with a Present Infinitive expresses our *ought to have, should have:*

Exercitus sine explōrātōribus non dēbuit dūcī.
The army should not have been led without scouts.

Iubeō, vetō, cōgō, sinō, prohibeō

Iubeō, *I order,* **vetō,** *I forbid,* **cōgō,** *I compel,* **sinō,** *I allow,* **prohibeō,** *I prevent,* are followed by an Infinitive:

Marcellus mīlitēs portāre scālās iussit.
Marcellus ordered the soldiers to carry ladders.

Iubeō is never followed by a negative; **vetō** is often used instead for *order . . . not:*

Caesar lēgātōs ab opere discēdere vetuerat.
Caesar had ordered his lieutenants not to leave the work.

Imperātor cīvēs obsidēs sibi dare coēgit.
The general compelled the citizens to give him hostages.

Germānī vīnum importārī non sinunt.
The Germans do not allow wine to be imported.

Syrācūsānī Rōmānōs urbem intrāre diū prohibēbant.
The Syracusans for a long time prevented the Romans from entering the city.

EXERCISE 79.
1. Hannibal Salapitanos decipere non poterat.
2. Milites propter lapsum terrae non longius progredi possunt.
3. Romani vix arma tenere poterant.
4. Hannibal omnes prandere iusserat.
5. Romani a Poenis se recipere coacti sunt.
6. Lex consules in urbem Romam exercitum ducere vetat.
7. Equites Romanos lacessere iussi erant.
8. Sine me hoc opus conficere.
9. Hoc heri fieri debuit.
10. Nemo melius hoc facere potuit.

EXERCISE 80.

ROMAN LADIES AND THEIR ADORNMENT (1)

In 215 B.C., the year after the disaster at Cannae, the Lex Oppia had limited extravagance in the personal adornment and dress of Roman women. In 195, more than five years after the peace treaty, there was a strong movement for the abandonment of this war-time control.

Lex Oppia mulieres Romanas vetuerat plus quam semunciam[1] auri habere, purpuram induere, carpento[2] in urbe, nisi

[1] *half an ounce.*   [2] **carpentum,** *two-wheeled covered carriage.*

sacrorum publicorum causa, vehi. Mulieres hanc legem abro-
gari cupiebant. Capitolium turba hominum, et qui legi
favebant et qui non favebant, complebatur. Matronae neque
auctoritate neque imperio virorum domi contineri poterant:
omnes vias urbis aditusque in forum obsidebant; viros, dum ad
forum descendunt, orabant. 'Nunc floret respublica', inquiunt; 'crescit omnium privata fortuna; matronis quoque
pristinum ornatum reddite.' Iam et consules ipsos rogare
audebant. Non tamen poterant persuadere consuli, M.[1] Porcio
Catoni, qui pro lege ita contionem habuit: 'Non sine rubore
per medium agmen mulierum in forum hodie perveni; paene
eis dixi: "Cur in publicum procurritis et vias obsidetis et viros
mulierum aliarum rogatis? Cur vestros viros domi rogare non
potuistis? Blandioresne in publico quam in privato, et viris
alienis quam vestris, estis?" '

[1] Abbrev. for *Marcus*.

EXERCISE 81.

1. You (pl.) can easily climb these mountains.
2. The Romans were able to ascend the walls by ladders.
3. The Syracusans were at last compelled to surrender.
4. Hannibal ordered his men to refresh themselves with
   sleep.
5. That soldier ought not to have killed Archimedes.
6. The Romans were able to conquer by land more easily
   than by sea.
7. Why could not Hannibal have captured Rome?
8. Why do you (s.) not forbid the boy to use this sword?
9. Surely we shall not be compelled to fight before breakfast?
10. The Romans were prevented by the river from returning
    to their camp.

EXERCISE 82.

Roman women had been forbidden by the Oppian Law to
put on purple and gold, or to drive through the streets of the
city. This law greatly displeased them, because the war had
been ended and the state was again flourishing. Husbands and

brothers ordered the ladies to stay at home; they did not obey them, but filled the roads and compelled even Marcus Cato, the consul, to hear them. 'Repeal the law', they cried, 'and allow us to put on our adornment again.' The consul could have replied, 'It is disgraceful for women to besiege the forum. Why can you not ask your husbands and brothers at home? It is better to beg for such things in private than in public.'

Chapter 20
Volō, nōlō, mālō

Volō, velle (Pres. Infin.),   volui, *I am willing, wish.*
Nōlō, nolle,   nōlui, *I am unwilling, do not wish.*
Mālō, malle,   mālui, *I prefer.*

Present Tenses

volō	nōlō	mālō
vīs	nōnvīs	māvīs
vult	nōnvult	māvult
volumus	nōlumus	mālumus
vultis	nōnvultis	māvultis
volunt	nōlunt	mālunt

Future Tenses

volam	nōlam	mālam
volēs	nōlēs	mālēs
etc.	etc.	etc.

Imperfect Tenses

volēbam	nōlēbam	mālēbam
volēbās	nōlēbās	mālēbās
etc.	etc.	etc.

The Tenses formed from the Perfect Bases are regular: volui, nōlui, mālui, etc.; Perfect Infinitives, voluisse, nōluisse, māluisse. The Imperative of nōlō,—nōlī, nōlīte, has been met already in Negative Commands, e.g. nōlī hōc facere, *do not do this.* Volō and mālō have no Imperative.

All three Verbs are followed by a Prolative Infinitive:

Rōmānī Samnītibus cēdere nōlēbant.
The Romans were unwilling to yield to the Samnites.

90

EXERCISE 83.

1. Pontius consilio patris parere nolebat.
2. Marcellus Archimedi parcere voluerat.
3. Visne linguam Latinam discere?
4. Lentulus hostibus cedere quam patriam deserere maluit.
5. Hannibal auxilium Gallorum repudiare nolebat.
6. Romani tumulum silvestrem occupare voluerunt.
7. Nolite spem abicere, o milites.
8. Matronae Romanae purpuram iterum induere volebant.
9. Sapientes esse quam divites malle debemus.
10. Consul adest: urbem intrare volumus.

EXERCISE 84.

ROMAN LADIES AND THEIR ADORNMENT (2)

'Olim feminae Romanae solebant esse omnino in manu parentum, fratrum, virorum. Si nunc pares nobis esse incipient, mox superiores esse volent. Crescent etiam duo vitia, avaritia et luxuria; hae pestes omnia magna imperia deleverunt. Melior quidem laetiorque hodie fit fortuna reipublicae, imperiumque crescit, et iam in Graecia Asiaque vicimus. At spectate spolia, quae inde comparavimus; nonne illa magis nos ceperunt, quam nos illa? Spectate signa, quae ab urbe Syracusis Romam transportata sunt. Audite eos, qui talia laudant, et penates nostros contemnunt. Ego hos malo patrios deos. Praeterea, si haec lex abrogata erit, magnum erit certamen inter mulieres. Divites id habere volent, quod nulla alia habere poterit; pauperes idem cupient et supra vires certabunt. Omnia quae feminae sua pecunia comparare poterunt, comparabunt: ea quae non poterunt, viros orabunt. O miseros viros![1] Nisi lex sumptus uxorum vestrarum minuerit, vos nunquam eos minuetis. Ego feminis cedere nolo.'

[1] This is an Accusative of Exclamation; compare in English *Poor me!*

EXERCISE 85.

1. We wish to be friends and allies of the Romans.
2. The Romans preferred to be ruled by consuls than by kings.

3. Hannibal wished to deceive the Salapitani.
4. Do (s.) not run too quickly.
5. Hannibal did not want to depart from Italy.
6. The Roman ladies wished to ride in the city again.
7. Often we would rather play than work.
8. The Carthaginians had been unwilling to send reinforcements.
9. Those Gauls preferred to fight for the Romans than for the Carthaginians.
10. Your (s.) horse seems to be unwilling to drink.

EXERCISE 86.

'Do not repeal the Oppian Law. Today women wish to be equal to us, or even superior. Roman power has indeed[1] grown, not only in Sicily, but even in Greece and Asia; but luxury is wont to grow with power, and if this law is repealed, our power will soon be destroyed by excessive luxury. We Romans do not wish to be captured by the statues and spoils which our generals have transported to Rome from other countries. In prosperity we ought still to prefer our own gods. Besides, if we yield to the women, they will struggle with each other because of their love of purple and gold; husbands will become wretched, because their wives will beg them for those things which they will not be able to buy.'

[1] sānē.

Chapter 21
Eō and ferō

	Eō	īre	iī	itum	*I go*

Present	*Future*	*Imperfect*
eō	ībō	ībam
īs	ībis	ībās
it	ībit	ībat
īmus	ībimus	ībāmus
ītis	ībitis	ībātis
eunt	ībunt	ībant

Perfect	*Future Perfect*	*Perfect Infin.*
iī	ierō	isse
istī	ieris, etc.	
iit		
iimus	*Pluperfect*	*Imperative*
istis	ieram	ī, īte
iērunt	ierās, etc.	

This verb is more commonly found in its compounds:

abeō,[1] *I go away.*

adeō,[1] *I go towards, approach.*

exeō, *I go out.*

ineō, *I go into, enter.*

pereō,[1] *I perish*

redeō, *I return, come back.*

subeō,[1] *I go up to* or *under, undergo.*

transeō, *I go over, cross.*

[1] -iisse also found as well as -isse in Perf. Infin., e.g. abiisse.

Adeō is used Transitively or with ad and Acc.; ineō is most often used Transitively; subeō when meaning *I go under* or *undergo* is used Transitively; transeō, *I cross* (*river, bridge, etc.*) is used Transitively.

Compounds of eō which are used Transitively are conjugated also in the Passive Voice, e.g. inībātur, transīrī.

Eō and ferō

EXERCISE 87.

1. Multae feminae eo die ad forum ibant.
2. Hannibal Alpes multis cum copiis transierat.
3. Pater Pontii, ubi sententiam dedit, domum rediit.
4. Exercitus Romanus angustias sine exploratoribus init.
5. Pax erit vobis, si ab agro Samnitium abibitis.
6. Multi equites cum Marcello perierunt.
7. Perfugae Romani portam Salapiae adibant.
8. Mox campos Italiae transieritis.
9. Imperator Romanus omnibus cum copiis Syracusas iniit.
10. Hoc flumen facile transiri potest.

EXERCISE 88.

1. We will go by the shorter road.
2. Many of the Carthaginians wanted to return home.
3. Go (pl.) away home; do not stay in the market-place.
4. Hannibal's army had undergone many dangers.
5. The Carthaginians crossed the Rhone with many elephants and horses.
6. The Roman women dared to approach even the consuls.
7. Hannibal went up to the very walls of Rome.
8. The Romans went into the river up to their chests.
9. The wall could not be approached without danger.
10. Many out of both armies had perished on account of the pestilence.

Ferō	**ferre**	**tulī**	**lātum**	*I carry, bear, endure.*

Active

Present	*Future*	*Imperfect*
ferō	feram	ferēbam
fers	ferēs	ferēbās
fert	feret	ferēbat
ferimus	ferēmus	ferēbāmus
fertis	ferētis	ferēbātis
ferunt	ferent	ferēbant

Passive

feror	**ferar**	**ferēbar**
ferris	**ferēris**	**ferēbāris**
fertur	**ferētur**	**ferēbātur**
ferimur	**ferēmur**	**ferēbāmur**
feriminī	**ferēminī**	**ferēbāminī**
feruntur	**ferentur**	**ferēbantur**

Imperative Active, **fer, ferte**; Passive, **ferre, ferimini**.
Present Infinitive Active, **ferre**; Passive, **ferrī**.

Perfect Tenses and Infinitives follow the 3rd Conjugation:

Perfect Active, **tulī**, etc.; Infinitive, **tulisse**.

Perfect Passive, **lātus sum**, etc.; Infinitive, **lātus esse**.

There are many compounds of **ferō**; the following should be noticed:

auferō	**auferre**	**abstulī**	**ablātum**	*I carry away*
conferō	**conferre**	**contulī**	**collātum**	*I contribute*
	mē conferō, *I betake myself.*			

inferō	**inferre**	**intulī**	**illātum**	*I carry against*
	bellum inferō in (with Acc.), *I wage war against.*			
referō	**referre**	**rettulī**	**relātum**	*I carry back*
	pedem referō, *I retreat.*			

EXERCISE 89.
1. Perfugae arma Romana ferebant.
2. Nostri vim frigoris vix ferunt.
3. Socii nobis auxilium tulerant.
4. Difficile erat bellum tam longum ferre.
5. Naves ad portum tempestate relatae sunt.
6. Nolite bellum in Romanos inferre.
7. Frumentum Romanis a Britannis collatum erat.
8. Hannibal ab urbe Roma mox pedem rettulit.
9. Romulus e conspectu civium subito ablatus est.
10. Equites Romani in fugam se contulerunt.

EXERCISE 90.
1. The Carthaginians bear both heat and cold.
2. Shall we endure the folly of such leaders?

3. We are being carried from the shore by the wind.
4. The Romans carried away many statues from Syracuse.
5. Our men were not able to retreat across the river Trebia.
6. The Romans were waging war against their enemies in many places.
7. The reply of the general of the Samnites was brought back by the consuls.
8. Many tribes were compelled to contribute corn.
9. Carry (pl.) away booty, if you wish, but spare Archimedes.
10. You will not have endured all these dangers in vain.

EXERCISE 91.

ROMAN LADIES AND THEIR ADORNMENT (3)

Tum L. Valerius 'Non possum', inquit, 'tacitus suffragia vestra exspectare. M. Porcius, vir gravissimus, oratione longa matronas culpavit. Nunquam ante hoc tempus matronae in publico apparuerunt? Olim Capitolium a Sabinis captum erat et in medio foro nostri pugnabant; nonne matronae inter acies duas exierunt et proelium impediverunt?[1] Deinde urbs a Gallis capta est; nonne aurum matronae consensu omnium in publicum contulerunt?[2]

Adeo nunc ad rem. Eas leges, quae in bello latae sunt,[3] pax saepe abrogat. Ista lex est nova. Simpliciter vixerunt matronae Romanae permultos annos sine hac lege. Solum ob magnum reipublicae periculum ista lex lata est. Tum Hannibal in Italia erat, Cannis vicerat, non pecuniam in aerario habebamus; aurum et argentum omne in publicum conferebamus. Tali tempore nulla luxuria matronas corrumpebat. Lex Oppia lata

[1] This happened in the reign of Romulus, when Sabine women, married to Romans after their seizure at the games, interceded between their husbands and indignant fathers. See Part I, Ex. 141.

[2] The Gauls withdrew after capturing the whole of Rome except the Capitol in 390 B.C., in return for a large payment of gold. See Part I, Ex. 127.

[3] **lēgem ferre**, *to propose a law* to the people.

est, solum quia illo tempore aurum et argentum in usum
publicum omnes privati conferre debebant.'

EXERCISE 92.

Then Lucius Valerius made this speech against the Oppian
Law: 'I cannot endure in silence the bitter words of Marcus
Cato. For why does he thus blame the ladies of Rome? Not for
the first time have they now appeared in public: once they were
not afraid to go out and forbid our ancestors to enter a useless
battle; once by their help gold was contributed, because the
state was in great danger.

'Besides, laws, which we propose in war, are often repealed
in peace. This law of yours is not ancient. Women can again
live simply without it. Hannibal is not now in Italy, we have
money in the treasury. We did not propose this law because of
women's luxury, but because in a great crisis all gold and silver
should be contributed by private citizens for the public benefit.'

Chapter 22

Interrogative Pronoun, Adjectives, and Adverbs

Quis? *who?*   **Quī?** *what?*

Singular

	M.	F.	N.
Nom.	{quis quī	(quis) quae	quid quod
Acc.	{quem quem	quam quam	quid quod

The remaining Cases, sing. and plur., are declined like the Relative Pronoun (Ch. 15).

Quis clārior fuit in Graeciā Themistocle?
Who was more famous in Greece than Themistocles?

Quī homō clārior fuit?
What man was more famous?

Quis, quid, etc., are used as Interrogative **Pronouns; quī, quae, quod,** etc., as Interrogative **Adjectives.**

Many words which introduce Direct Questions have already been met, e.g. **ubi?** *where?* **cūr?** *why?* Others are:

quālis? (decl. like **omnis**) *of what kind?*   **quandō?** *when?*
quantus, -a, -um? *how big?*   **quotiēs?** *how often?*
quōmodo? *how (in what way)?*

Quālia arma sunt Gallīs?
What kind of arms have the Gauls?

Quantam villam vīs vendere?
How big a country-house do you want to sell?

Quandō redībunt consulēs?
When will the consuls come back?

EXERCISE 93.

1. Quid dulcius est quam amicitia?
2. Quis Romam defendet, si exercitus deletus erit?
3. Quomodo Hannibal tot elephantos trans flumen transmisit?
4. Quod bellum Graeci sine consilio deorum susceperunt?
5. Quanta castra prope flumen Hannibal posuit?
6. Quoties hunc librum legisti?
7. Quando iterum purpuram induemus?
8. Qualia animalia Britanniam incolunt?
9. Cui placet lex Oppia?
10. Cuius orationem mavultis audire?

EXERCISE 94.

ROMAN LADIES AND THEIR ADORNMENT (4)

'Hodie pax nobis reddita est et respublica nostra iterum floret. Quis coniugibus nostris fructum pacis negabit? Purpuram viri induunt; liberi nostri togas induunt purpura praetextas;[1] id ius vel infimo generi magistratuum permittimus. Quis vult vel equum pulchrius quam uxorem ornari? Praeterea, uxores sociorum nostrorum ornamenta aurea habent, insignes sunt auro et purpura; illae vehuntur per urbem, nostrae pedibus ambulant. Virorum animos hoc vulnerare potest, mulierum etiam magis. Mulieribus nunquam sunt honores, nec triumphi,[2] nec spolia belli. Ornatus et vestis, haec feminarum gaudia sunt. Quid aliud in rebus adversis, quam purpuram atque aurum, deponunt? Quid aliud in rebus secundis sumunt? Si legem Oppiam abrogaveritis, filiae, uxores, sorores non minus in manu erunt. Ipsae enim ornatum suum in manu maritorum potius quam in legis habere malunt; et vos appellari patres aut viri potius quam domini malle debetis.'

[1] *fringed* (from **praetexō**): this outer garment was worn by Roman free-born boys until they were sixteen, when they changed to a man's gown, **toga virīlis**.

[2] A triumph was a grand procession into Rome, decreed to a general after an important victory.

EXERCISE 95.

1. What did the Britons import from Gaul?
2. In which year was Rome captured by the Gauls?
3. How often have you (s.) approached the magistrate?
4. Whose advice did Pontius obey?
5. Who does not prefer to play rather than to be taught?
6. To whom shall we now entrust the command?
7. What woman does not wish to put on purple again?
8. How big is Sicily and what are the inhabitants like?
9. When shall we at last capture Syracuse?
10. Whom do you (pl.) wish to put in command of the army?

EXERCISE 96.

'We are not now fighting against the Carthaginians. Who therefore is unwilling to restore to women their adornment? We men put on purple and allow this right to our children and even to our very horses. Who wishes to deny to the wives of Romans those things which are allowed to the wives of our allies? Our wives can scarcely bear this wrong. What man is not delighted by the fruits of peace? Why do we not share these fruits with our wives, daughters, sisters? Besides, they do not wish to obey a law in this matter; they prefer not only to obey but also to delight you, their husbands, fathers, brothers.'

Chapter 23
Active Participles

A **Participle** is a Verbal Adjective, as was explained in Chapter 2: the Perfect Participle Passive is used, together with parts of **sum,** in the formation of the Perfect Passive Tenses, e.g. **oppugnātī sumus,** *we have been attacked.*

Latin has two more Participles, both in the **Active** Voice:

1. Present Participle

1st Conjug.	2nd Conjug.	3rd Conjug.	4th Conjug.
amans	**monens**	**regens**	**audiens**
loving	*advising*	*ruling*	*hearing*

| Stem | **amanti-** | **monenti-** | **regenti-** | **audienti-** |

Present Participles are declined like **ingens.**

Note.—**Sum, possum, mālo** have no Present Participles; **capiō** has **capiens,** and **eō** has **iens** (Gen. **euntis**).

The Present Participle is only used when the time of the action (or state) represented by the Participle is the same as the time of the action of the Verb with which it is used, e.g. in English, *I hear you calling,* where the *calling* and *hearing* happen at the same time.

Fēminae virōs dēscendentēs ad forum ōrābant.

The women were beseeching the men going down (or *while they were going down*) *to the forum.*

In this example, the *going down* (action of the Participle) takes place at the same time as the *beseeching* (action of the Main Verb). It should be noticed that in English we often put in *while* or *when* in translating a Present Participle. They are not expressed in Latin.

Because a Participle is partly an Adjective, **dēscendentēs** agrees with **virōs;** at the same time **dēscendentēs** has partly the nature of a Verb.

101

As the Present Participle is Active in Voice, it may itself govern an Object:

Perfugae, neglegenter arma gerentēs, oppidum intrāverant.
The deserters had entered the town, carrying their arms carelessly.

In this example **gerentēs** is Nom., agreeing with **perfugae**, and itself governs **arma** as its Direct Object.

2. Future Participle

The Future Participle is formed by adding **-ūrus** to the Supine Base, e.g. **amātūrus** (from **amāt-um**), **monitūrus, rectūrus, audītūrus,** and is declined like **bonus**. The Future Participle of **sum** is **futūrus**.

It may be translated in various ways according to the sense:

Speculātor nostrōs oppugnātūrōs cōnspexit.
The scout caught sight of our men, when they were about to (going to, ready to, intending to, etc.) attack.

The Future Participle is often used with parts of **sum**:

Nostrī oppugnātūrī erant.
Our men were about to attack (or *were on the point of attacking*).

EXERCISE 97.
1. Miles Archimedem formas spectantem interfecit.
2. Hannibal, omnia circumspectans, cum peditibus incedit.
3. Samnites Romanos per angustias pergentes exspectabant.
4. Romulus exercitum recensens e conspectu civium ablatus est.
5. Poeni Alpes ascensuri erant.
6. Perfugae, Latine exclamantes, vigiles excitare incipiunt.
7. Hannibal milites in Italiam descensuros confirmavit.
8. Vigiles, deditionem simulantes, circa portam trepidant.
9. Romani Marcellum ex equo cadentem viderunt.
10. Crispinus, dolum metuens, nuntios ad socios mittet.

Exercise 98.

THE RECALL OF HANNIBAL

After the death of Marcellus, Rome was suffering from lack of men and money. Hasdrubal, Hannibal's brother, evaded the Romans in Spain, crossed the Alps and hoped to join forces with him. Before this could happen, Nero and Līvius, the consuls, forced Hasdrubal to fight at the river Metaurus in Umbria and annihilated his army (207). Hannibal retired to Bruttium in south Italy, where he held out for four years. He was recalled in 203 to Africa, which Publius Cornēlius Scīpiō (son of the Scipio defeated at the Trebia) had now invaded, after driving the Carthaginians out of Spain. Scipio won the decisive battle of the war at Zama, south of Carthage, in 202.

Legati ad Hannibalem, in Africam eum revocantes, venerunt. Gemens et vix lacrimas cohibens dicitur legatorum verba audivisse. 'Vicit Hannibalem', inquit, 'non populus Romanus, quem toties superavi atque fugavi, sed senatus Carthaginiensis, qui ob invidiam novas copias mitti vetuerunt.' Iam hoc ipsum providens, naves antea paraverat: itaque robur exercitus in Africam transvexit. Pauci homines, patriam exsilii causa relinquentes, tristiores abierunt, quam Hannibal ex hostium terra decedens: respexit saepe Italiae litora, deos et homines et se ipsum accusans. 'Cur non milites', inquit, 'post Cannensem victoriam Romam duxi? Scipio Carthaginem ire audet, qui hostem in Italia Poenum non vidit; ego, qui centum milia armatorum in magnis proeliis cecidi, circa parva oppida Italiae consenui.' Ita se accusans, ex longa possessione Italiae detractus est.

Exercise 99.
1. Horatius saw the Etruscans running down towards the bridge.
2. Hannibal found the body of Marcellus lying on the hillock.
3. I saw a crowd of women besieging the roads.
4. The Carthaginians, while advancing through a pass, were attacked by Gauls.

5. The Sabine women besought their fathers and husbands, when on the point of fighting.
6. I hear many men praising the statues which have been brought away from Syracuse.
7. Retreating, the Romans fled to the river.
8. Marcellus began to weep, looking at that most beautiful city.
9. The Romans are about to climb the wall with ladders.
10. The Samnites were laughing, as they watched the unarmed Romans.

Exercise 100.

Hannibal was at length recalled to Carthage by ambassadors. Groaning and almost weeping, he listened to their words. 'Hannibal', said he, 'has not been overcome by the arms of the Romans, but by the jealousy of the Carthaginian senators, refusing to send reinforcements.' Because he feared this, he had already prepared a fleet; he disbanded a useless rabble of soldiers, and with the rest of his forces sailed to Africa. No one about to leave his own country has gone away more sadly than Hannibal, on the point of departing from the land of his enemies. Often looking back at the coast of Italy, he began to accuse even himself. 'Why did I not advance at once to Rome, when we had defeated the enemy at Cannae? Did not those enemies laugh, seeing Scipio daring to go to Carthage, and Hannibal growing old in Bruttium?'

Chapter 24

Passive Participle

Latin has only one Participle in the **Passive** Voice, namely the **Perfect Participle.** It is the most commonly used of all the Participles. Besides being used in the formation of the Perfect Passive Tenses, it is often used, in agreement with Nouns or Pronouns, to express an action that has already been completed:

Horātius, in ponte positus, impetum sustinēbat.
Horatius, stationed on the bridge, was resisting the attack.

Rōmānī alteram viam clausam inveniunt.
The Romans find the other road closed.

The Perfect Participles are used in these examples, because in the first, Horatius had been stationed on the bridge **before** he began to resist; in the second, the road had been closed **before** the Romans came upon it.

There are various ways of translating a Perfect Participle into English:

Herennius consultus nuntium remīsit.

Herennius, having been consulted,
Herennius, when consulted,
When H. was consulted, he
When H. had been consulted, he } *sent back a message.*
After being consulted, H.
On being consulted, H.

Having-been-consulted is a literal translation, but the other translations are more natural. Sometimes a Perfect Participle may be naturally translated by using a Relative Clause in English, e.g. **Horātius, in ponte positus,** *Horatius, who had been stationed on the bridge.* A good translation all depends upon the sense of the particular sentence.

105

EXERCISE 101.

1. Crispinus, morte Marcelli territus, in loco tuto castra posuit.
2. Sabini invitati spectaculo se dedunt.
3. Romani muros desertos ascenderunt.
4. Legati ad senatum introducti haec verba dixerunt.
5. Victi a vobis et ab imperatore vestro nos vobis dedimus.
6. Hannibal milites itinere fatigatos incitavit.
7. Nolite cedere genti toties a vobis victae.
8. Hannibal classem iam paratam habebat.
9. Ira commotus Camillus magistrum domum remisit.
10. Impediti flumine nostri ad oppidum effugerunt.

EXERCISE 102.

CAESAR'S INVASION OF BRITAIN:
(1) THE VOYAGE AND LANDING

Caesar had felt that if Britain remained independent, it would always threaten the peace of Gaul. Severe storms, insufficient troops, and the lateness of its start had brought little success to the first expedition in 55 B.C. A second expedition embarked on about July 6, in 54 B.C.

Caesar omnes naves, quas instructas habebat, ad portum Itium[1] convenire iussit; ipse cum legionibus ad eundem locum pervenit. Labienus, legatus eius, cum tribus legionibus in Gallia praesidii causa relictus est. Multos dies vento adverso impeditus, tandem cum quinque legionibus et equitum duobus milibus Caesar ad solis occasum naves solvit. Media tamen nocte noniam leni Africo provectus, sed longius delatus aestu, cursum non tenebat; prima luce Britanniam sub sinistra relictam[2] conspexit. Tum eam partem[3] insulae remis petere constituit, in qua optimum egressum superiore aestate invenerat. Omnes naves ad Britanniam meridiano fere tempore accesserunt, neque in eo loco hostis est visus; ut postea Caesar

[1] **Portus Itius,** probably Boulogne.
[2] This would be the South Foreland.
[3] Between Walmer and Sandwich.

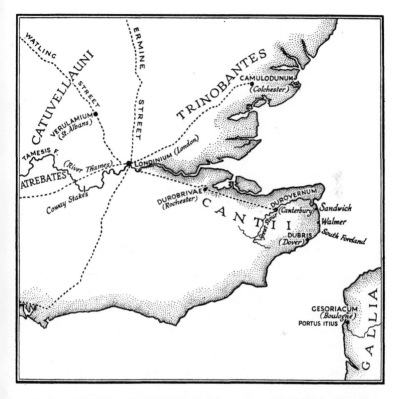

Map to illustrate Caesar's Second Invasion of Britain. His exact route is still disputed; suggestions in this book are based on the arguments of Dr. Rice Holmes. The dotted lines represent Roman roads.

ex captivis cognovit, permulti eo convenerant, sed multitudine navium perterriti (plus enim quam octingentae uno tempore visae erant), a litore discesserant et se in superiora loca abdiderant. Caesar igitur exercitum exposuit et locum castris idoneum cepit.

EXERCISE 103.

1. Having been deceived by the Samnites, the consuls struck camp.
2. The Romans attacked walls fortified by the skill of Archimedes.
3. Provoked by the enemy's cavalry, the Romans began to attack.
4. The deserters, who had been placed in the vanguard, reached the gate.
5. Look (pl.) at the statues transported from Syracuse.
6. On being recalled home, Hannibal blamed the Carthaginian senate.
7. The women again put on purple, for a long time laid aside.
8. After they had been surrounded, the Romans resisted in vain.
9. Marcellus gave the soldiers the promised booty.
10. Overcome by wine and sleep, the sentries could not resist.

EXERCISE 104.

After a long delay Caesar at last set sail. Because the loyalty of the Gauls was not certain, Labienus, left behind in Gaul, had been ordered to defend the harbours. Caesar himself, carried forward by a favourable wind until midnight, was then brought too far from his course by the tide; hindered only for a short time by this difficulty, he reached a good landing-place by means of rowing at about noon. He found no enemy drawn up on the shore, as he had expected; many had indeed assembled there,[1] as was found out afterwards from prisoners; but they had now retreated, terrified by the large number of ships, and, hidden on higher ground, were waiting for the Romans' attack.

[1] *thither.*

Participles of Deponent Verbs

(1) Deponent Verbs and Semi-Deponent Verbs have a Present and a Future Participle, Active in both form and meaning, e.g. **morans**, *delaying*, **morātūrus**, *about to delay;* **sequens**, *following*, **secūtūrus**, *about to follow* (N.B. **morior, orior**, have Future Participles **moritūrus, oritūrus**) :

Rōmānī Marcellum ex equō lābentem vidērunt.
The Romans saw Marcellus slipping from his horse.

Profectūrus in Britanniam Caesar ventō impediēbātur.
On the point of starting for Britain Caesar was delayed by the wind.

(2) The Perfect Participle of Deponent and Semi-Deponent Verbs is **Passive** in **form,** but **Active** in **meaning,** e.g. **morātus**, *after delaying* (*having delayed*), **secūtus**, *after following* (*having followed*):

Scīpiō prōgressus ad Trebiam ibi castra pōnit.
Scipio after advancing to the Trebia pitches his camp there.

EXERCISE 105.
1. Romani Poenos sequentes non effugerunt.
2. Saepe me querentem de feminarum sumptibus audivistis.
3. Dux, periculum veritus, obsides recepit.
4. Hannibal, suos hortatus, agmen procedere iussit.
5. Crispinus, nocte profectus, in loco tuto castra posuit.
6. Transgressus Anienem Hannibal omnes copias eduxit.
7. Milites Marcellum iam moriturum viderunt.
8. Perfugae ad portam venerunt, Latine loquentes.
9. Horatius, rem praeclaram ausus, salutem tandem petivit.
10. Barbari, undique ex insidiis exorti, agmen oppugnant.

EXERCISE 106.
1. Trying to escape, the Romans were hindered by the river.
2. The Gaul, about to fall, caught sight of Manlius.
3. After delaying for four days, the Gauls advanced towards Italy.
4. Hannibal encouraged his men, about to set out across the Alps.

5. The Gauls stood in the streets, wondering at the temples.
6. The Romans drove Hannibal back, after he had crossed the river.
7. Complaining about the disaster, the soldiers waited for the night.
8. Caesar set sail when he had obtained a suitable wind.
9. After saying wise words to his son, Herennius returned home.
10. The streets were full of men and women, rejoicing on account of the victory.

Chapter 25
Indirect Statement (1)

Rōmānī oppugnant.
The Romans are attacking.

Rōmānī oppugnant is a Main Clause and a Direct Statement of a fact, and the Verb is in the Indicative Mood.

Nuntius dīcit Rōmānōs oppugnāre.
The messenger says that the Romans are attacking.

The Main Clause in this sentence is **nuntius dīcit,** and our original Directly Stated fact has now become an **Indirect Statement,** expressed by **Rōmānōs oppugnāre.**

Rōmānōs oppugnāre is a Noun Clause and is the Object of **dīcit;** it is *what the messenger says.*

The Verb of the message (*are attacking*) is put into the Infinitive and the Subject of the Verb (*the Romans*) is put into the Accusative.

An Indirect Statement, then, is expressed in Latin by an **Infinitive with Subject Accusative.** It may be introduced by Verbs meaning *say, think, feel, believe, know, see, hear, perceive.*

N.B. Latin never uses **dīcō ... nōn (nunquam, nullus,** etc.); **negō,** *I deny* or *say ... not* (with **unquam, ullus,** etc.), is used instead:

Nuntius putat Rōmānōs nōn oppugnāre.
The messenger thinks that the Romans are not attacking.

But **Nuntius negat Rōmānōs oppugnāre.**
The messenger says that the Romans are not attacking.

EXERCISE 107.
1. Miles dicit murum esse humilem.
2. Romani audiunt Hannibalem bellum parare.
3. Milites nullam esse spem sentiunt.
4. Hannibal Alpes posse superari affirmat.

5. Romani putant legiones Samnitium esse in Apulia.
6. Syracusani Romanos murum ascendere non vident.
7. Omnes putamus amicitiam iucundissimam esse.
8. Caesar Britannos auxilium Gallis dare intellegit.
9. Salapitani agmen hostium appropinquare vident.
10. Dux negat pericula esse magna.

EXERCISE 108.
1. The commanders say that the ships are ready.
2. Caesar sees that the wind is favourable.
3. The consuls find out that the allies are fleeing.
4. The Roman ladies say that the law is not just.
5. Pontius thinks that his father's advice is foolish.
6. Hannibal sees that the soldiers fear the long journey.
7. Marcellus thinks that Syracuse is a very beautiful city.
8. Valerius says that beautiful adornment delights women.
9. We know that Hannibal wishes to deceive us.
10. Cato says that women ought to stay at home.

Tenses of the Infinitive in Indirect Statement

The following examples will make clear the use of the Infinitive in Indirect Statement:

(A) **Dīcit,** *he says*

    (1) **Rōmānōs oppugnāre,** *that the Romans are attacking*;
    (2) **Rōmānōs oppugnāvisse,** *that the Romans attacked* or
                     have attacked;
    (3) **Rōmānōs oppugnātūrōs esse,**[1] *that the Romans will attack.*

[1] The Future Infinitive Active is formed from the Future Participle and **esse,** e.g. **oppugnātūrus esse,** *to be about to attack.* The Participle must agree with the Subject of the Infinitive; here **oppugnātūrōs** agrees with **Rōmānōs.**
Note.—The Future Infinitive of **sum** is **futūrus esse** or **fore.**

In all the above examples, the Tense or time of the Infinitive is the same as the Tense used by the speaker in his Direct Statement, *the Romans are attacking, attacked, will attack.*

Indirect Statement (1) 113

(B) The tense of the Infinitive is chosen in exactly the same way after a Past Tense in the Main Verb; the Tense is the same as the Tense actually used by the speaker.

Dixit, *he said*
- (1) **Rōmānōs oppugnāre,** *that the Romans were attacking* (actual words *the R. are attacking*);
- (2) **Rōmānōs oppugnāvisse,** *that the Romans had attacked* (actual words *the R. have attacked*);
- (3) **Rōmānōs oppugnātūrōs esse,** *that the Romans would attack* (actual words *the R. will attack*).

EXERCISE 109.
1. Romani Hannibalem ad urbem appropinquare audiunt.
2. Non putamus novas copias adventuras esse.
3. Scisne Caesarem Androclum liberavisse?
4. Romani captivos vera dicere crediderunt.
5. Hannibal Romam mox in potestate Poenorum futuram esse dixit.
6. Marcellus sensit Romanos Syracusas frustra mari oppugnare.
7. Salapitani audiverunt Hannibalem anulum Marcelli invenisse.
8. Poeni iter difficillimum fore putabant.
9. Lentulus dixit milites per deditionem Romam ipsam conservaturos esse.
10. Romani Samnites locum praesidio occupavisse viderunt.

EXERCISE 110.
1. Hannibal says that the journey will now be easy.
2. The Romans learn that Archimedes has helped the Syracusans.
3. The scout reported that the enemy were in sight.
4. Marcellus thinks that the Romans will easily seize the hillock.
5. Horatius saw that the Etruscans had almost reached the bridge.
6. Caesar said that the weather would not be suitable.

7. The Britons saw that many ships were approaching the shore.
8. The Carthaginians knew that the Romans would make for the river.
9. The Greeks thought that Socrates was very wise.
10. The sentries saw that already a thousand Romans had entered the city.

EXERCISE 111.

1. Captivi dicunt Samnites Luceriam obsidere.
2. Credimus hostes urbem mox capturos esse.
3. Romani multos milites angustias occupavisse viderunt.
4. Herennius negavit tertium ullum consilium esse.
5. Hannibal dixit Poenos omnes gentes Hispanas superavisse.
6. Omnes scimus Hannibalem fuisse imperatorem fortissimum.
7. Lentulus putavit Romam non futuram esse tutam sine exercitu.
8. Romani Hasdrubalem Alpes transisse, et iam in Italiam procedere audiverunt.
9. Valerius negavit legem Oppiam esse necessariam.
10. Audivistine matronas Romanas purpuram rursus induere?

EXERCISE 112.

CAESAR'S INVASION OF BRITAIN: (2) FIRST SUCCESS FOLLOWED BY BAD NEWS

Caesar, quod naves defendere voluit, decem cohortes prope mare reliquit; Quintum Atrium praesidio praefecit. Minus anxius nunc erat, quod naves fore tutas credidit. Ipse noctu progressus circiter XII milia passuum hostium copias conspicatus est. Illi cum equitatu et essedis ad flumen[1] ex loco superiore progressi proelium commiserunt. Repulsi ab equitatu nostro se in silvas abdiderunt, nacti locum et natura et opere

[1] The Great Stour.

munitum, quem antea domestici belli causa paraverant: nam multis arboribus succisis omnes aditus erant obstructi. Modo pauci ex silvis exibant nostrosque intra munitiones ingredi prohibebant. At milites legionis septimae testudinem[1] fecerunt et aggerem iecerunt; locum ceperunt et hostes sine multo labore ex silvis expulerunt. Sed eos fugientes Caesar longius prosequi vetuit, et quod loci naturam ignorabat, et quod magna pars diei erat consumpta et tempus munitioni castrorum relinquere volebat.

Postridie mane milites equitesque in tres partes divisit et hostes persequi iussit. Ubi hi, multum progressi, iam extremos hostium conspexerunt, equites a Quinto Atrio ad Caesarem venerunt; nuntiaverunt nocte priore maximam tempestatem naves afflixisse, ancoras non satis validas fuisse, neque nautas et gubernatores vim tempestatis potuisse pati: itaque naves magnum incommodum accepisse.

[1] A body of men, closely packed together, with shields locked over their heads, and so looking like a *tortoise*.

EXERCISE 113.
1. The scout announces that the Romans are advancing.
2. Crispinus knew that Hannibal was preparing a trick.
3. The Romans heard that the Carthaginians had won a victory.
4. Hannibal said that the Carthaginians would soon conquer Italy.
5. Marcellus perceived that the walls of Syracuse were very long.
6. The Roman deserters said that the consul had arrived.
7. Cato said that the Romans ought not to repeal the law.
8. Valerius says that Roman women have often helped their country.
9. Do you (s.) think that Scipio will defeat Hannibal?
10. Caesar discovered that the Britons had all gone away from the shore.

EXERCISE 114.

Caesar thought that the ships would not be in danger, because he had left behind Quintus Atrius and a large garrison. After advancing for a few hours, our men caught sight of the enemy, who had retreated on the day before. The latter came down to lower ground and joined battle, but being driven back by our cavalry, betook themselves to the woods, in which they had prepared a strong position; they had blocked its entrances with trees. But our men quickly captured the place by means of a tortoise and a rampart. Caesar forbade them to pursue the retreating enemy, because only a few hours of the day were left.

On the next day our men were ordered to pursue the enemy. When at last they saw the enemy, messengers came to Caesar from Quintus Atrius. He heard that on the previous night, owing to a big storm, the anchors of the ships had given way and that many of the ships themselves, thrown[1] on to the shore, were now useless.

[1] ēiciō.

Chapter 26
Indirect Statement (2)

(1) **Caesar nostrōs ab hostibus premī vīdit.**
Caesar saw that our men were being hard pressed by the enemy.

(2) **Rōmānī audīvērunt Syrācūsās captās esse.**
The Romans heard that Syracuse had been captured.

(3) **Marcellus sensit urbem nōn facile captum īrī.**
Marcellus perceived that the city would not easily be captured.

The above examples illustrate the use of the Passive Infinitives in Indirect Statement.

In (1) what Caesar saw was *my men are being hard pressed*, and therefore the Present Infinitive is used.

In (2) it should be noticed carefully that the Participle part of the Perfect Infinitive, **captās,** agrees with **Syrācūsās,** the Subject of the Infinitive.

In (3) we have an example of the Future Infinitive Passive, made up of **īrī** (*it is being gone*) and **captum,** the Supine of **capiō,** *to capture.* Supines in **-um** are used to express Purpose after Verbs of Motion. The example literally means *there was a going to capture the city*, with **urbem** as the Direct Object of **captum.** It will be seen that no question of agreement arises in the use of the Fut. Infin. Passive.

Note.—Occasionally an Accusative and Infinitive Clause is found with the Passive of a Verb of *saying*, e.g. with **nuntiātum est,** *it was announced;* **trāditum est,** *it has been handed down* :

> **Nuntiātum est Saguntum captum esse,**
> **Poenōs Saguntum cēpisse.**
> *It was announced that Saguntum had been captured,*
> *that the Carthaginians had captured Saguntum.*

118 *Indirect Statement (2)*

1. Sempronius exercitum a Poenis repelli vidit.
2. Romani Syracusanos illa nocte somno et vino superatum iri crediderunt.
3. Caesar magnam partem diei consumptam esse sensit.
4. Valerius dixit equos pulchrius ornari quam mulieres.
5. Caesar vidit aditus loci obstructos esse.
6. Traditum est Romam a Romulo conditam esse.
7. Multi Romani Romulum in caelum ablatum esse putabant.
8. Hannibal non credere poterat milites talibus periculis territum iri.
9. Nonnulli scriptores elephantos in ratibus trans flumen transportatos esse narrant.
10. Caesar multas naves tempestate afflictas esse cognovit.

EXERCISE 116.

1. Marcellus heard that Archimedes had been killed.
2. Herennius said that hatred would be increased by severe conditions of peace.
3. Caesar saw that all the hills were being held by the enemy.
4. It was announced that one consul had been killed, the other wounded.
5. Hannibal saw that the column had been led into an ambush.
6. Do you (s.) think that the law will be repealed?
7. The commander knew that the soldiers were being hindered by cold and hunger.
8. The inhabitants know that the letter was composed by Hannibal.
9. The Syracusans realized that reinforcements would not be sent.
10. Cato said that Roman power was being destroyed by luxury.

Pronouns of 3rd Person in Indirect Statement

(1) **Horātius dixit sē impetum eōrum exceptūrum esse.**
Horatius said that he would receive their attack.

(2) **Hannibal cognōvit ducēs sē (suōs) fefellisse.**
Hannibal discovered that the guides had deceived him (his men).

He, she, it, they or *his, her, its, their* inside an Accusative and Infinitive Clause are expressed by the Reflexive Pronoun, when they refer to the **same** person as the Subject of the Verb of *saying, thinking, etc.* In (1) above, sē refers to **Horātius,** in (2) sē (suōs) refers to Hannibal.

Verbs of *Hoping, Promising,* etc.

Verbs of *hoping* (**spērō**), *promising* (**prōmittō**), *threatening* (**minor**), *swearing* (**iūrō**), are followed by an Accusative and Infinitive:

Britannī prōmisērunt sē obsidēs datūrōs esse.
The Britons promised to give (that they would give) hostages

These Verbs require a Future Infinitive, if they refer to the Future. But a *hope* or an *oath* may refer to the Present and require a Present Infinitive. In translating into Latin, the right Infinitive must be chosen according to the sense.

Spērō vōs valēre.
I hope you are well.

EXERCISE 117.
1. Cato dixit se deos patrios malle.
2. Hannibal speravit novas copias venturas esse.
3. Lentulus se paratum esse pro patria mori affirmavit.
4. Hannibal se suosque circumventos esse vidit.
5. Promittimus nos vobis viam facilem monstraturos esse.
6. Multi e Poenis se nunquam domum redituros esse putabant.
7. Galli dixerunt amicitiam Poenorum sibi gratiorem esse quam vim.
8. Hannibal se a Fortuna relictum esse sensit.
9. Syracusani se salutem sibi liberisque petere dixerunt.
10. Speramus Gallos vera dicere neque nos decepturos esse.

EXERCISE 118.

1. Porsenna promised to send back Cloelia to the Romans.
2. Hannibal learnt that many of his men had been killed by the Salapitani.
3. I hope that you have received my letter.
4. The ladies said that they wanted to drive through the streets.
5. Marcellus swore that he would spare the citizens.
6. The Britons announced to Boadicea that they were being injured by the Romans.
7. Caesar hoped to conquer the Britons in a short time.
8. Cato said that he would not give way to the Roman ladies.
9. Hannibal, when recalled home, said that he had been overcome by the jealousy of the Carthaginian senate.
10. The Romans heard that Hannibal was offering for sale their own shops.

Infinitives of Deponent Verbs

All the Infinitives of Deponent Verbs are Active in meaning; the Present and Perfect are Passive in form, e.g. **prōgredī, prōgressus esse**; the Future is Active in form, e.g. **prōgressūrus esse.** The same applies to Semi-Deponent Verbs, except that they have a Present Infinitive in the Active form, e.g. **audēre.**

Notes.—(*a*) In Indirect Statements, the word *that* is never expressed in Latin; it is often omitted in English, e.g. *he said it was raining.*

(*b*) An Accusative of the person, followed by **certiōrem faciō,** *I inform* (literally *I make someone more certain*), is found very frequently, e.g. **mē certiōrem fēcit,** *he informed me.* When this is turned Passively, the person informed becomes the Subject, e.g. **certior factus sum,** *I was informed.*

EXERCISE 119.

1. Crispinus Marcellum occisum esse nuntiavit.
2. Herennius audivit exercitus Romanos captos esse.
3. Captivi Luceriam mox expugnatum iri nuntiaverunt.

4. Galli dixerunt agros suos sine causa vastari.
5. Nuntiatum est magnam tempestatem ortam esse.
6. Caesar speraverat se celerius ad Britanniam perventurum esse.
7. Caesar certior factus est naves fractas esse.
8. Hannibal se semper hostem Romanis futurum esse iuravit.
9. Multi crediderant Hannibalem post hanc victoriam Romam statim progressurum esse.
10. Miles Marcellum certiorem fecit murum in uno loco ascendi posse.

EXERCISE 120.

CAESAR'S INVASION OF BRITAIN: (3) RALLY OF BRITONS DURING CAESAR'S ABSENCE

Caesar, ubi hoc audivit, legiones equitatumque revocari iubet, ipse ad naves regreditur; eadem fere quae ex nuntiis cognoverat ipse perspicit; invenit enim circiter quadraginta naves amissas esse, reliquas tamen magno labore refici posse. Itaque ex legionibus fabros deligit et ex continenti alios arcessi iubet; ad Labienum litteras scribit eumque iubet auxilio aliarum legionum quam plurimas naves aedificare. Ipse omnes naves subducere constituit et eas cum castris una munitione coniungere. In his rebus circiter dies decem consumit; ne noctu quidem milites opus intermittere patitur. Ubi opus est perfectum, easdem copias, quas ante, praesidii causa relinquit: ipse eodem unde redierat, proficiscitur. Eo progressus invenit maiores Britannorum copias in eum locum convenisse et omnium consensu imperium Cassivellauno mandatum esse. Huius fines a maritimis civitatibus flumen dividit, quod appellatur Tamesis, a mari circiter milia passuum octoginta. Hic superiore tempore bella continua cum reliquis civitatibus gesserat;[1] sed nostro adventu permoti, Britanni hunc toti bello praefecerant.

[1] In one of these wars he had defeated and killed the king of the Trinobantes. Cassivellaunus was prince of the Catuvellauni and his capital was near **Verulāmium** (St. Albans).

EXERCISE 121.

1. Messengers informed Caesar that the enemy's forces were being increased.
2. Hannibal thought that the Romans had been frightened by the death of the consul.
3. The famous general realized that he had been caught by his own trick.
4. Marcellus promised to give booty to the soldiers.
5. Hannibal said the city of Rome itself would soon be captured.
6. We swear that this is true and that we will be faithful allies.
7. The Romans perceived that they had been surrounded.
8. The citizens did not think that Hannibal would delay after the battle.
9. I hope to follow you, but I cannot promise to start before night.
10. The Romans rejoiced, when they had been informed that the army had defeated Hasdrubal.

EXERCISE 122.

Caesar at once returned to the coast and found that the message was true. He perceived that many ships had been lost through the storm and that the rest had been damaged. He resolved to repair the damaged ships as quickly as possible; by means of a despatch he ordered Labienus to build others. Because he realized that the ships had not been in a safe place, he ordered them to be beached and a fortification to be built round them. This work was completed within ten days. Then after returning to the place from which he had set out, he was informed that many troops had now been collected by Cassivellaunus, king of the Catuvellauni, and that the other tribes, joined with them, had put him in command of the whole army.

Additional Exercises on Indirect Statement will be found on p. 250.

Chapter 27
Present Subjunctive

There is one more Mood in Latin in addition to the Indicative and Imperative, namely the **Subjunctive**. The Tenses of the Subjunctive are fully conjugated in the Summary of Grammar, but for the sake of convenience the Present Subjunctive Tenses, Active and Passive, of the four Conjugations are set out below:

Present Subjunctive Active

amem	moneam	regam	audiam
amēs	moneās	regās	audiās
amet	moneat	regat	audiat
amēmus	moneāmus	regāmus	audiāmus
amētis	moneātis	regātis	audiātis
ament	moneant	regant	audiant

Present Subjunctive Passive

amer	monear	regar	audiar
amēris	moneāris	regāris	audiāris
amētur	moneātur	regātur	audiātur
amēmur	moneāmur	regāmur	audiāmur
amēminī	moneāminī	regāminī	audiāminī
amentur	moneantur	regantur	audiantur

Present Subjunctive of **Sum**

Sing.		*Plur.*	
	sim		sīmus
	sīs		sītis
	sit		sint

No meanings are here given for the Subjunctive, because they vary according to its use.

Here are some examples which will show some of its uses:

(1) **Occupēmus illum collem.** Exhortation
   Let us seize that hill.

123

(2) **Discēdat populus.** Exhortation, almost Command
Let the people depart.

(3) **Vincant nostrī exercitūs.** Wish
May our armies conquer!

The 1st and 3rd Persons of the Present Subjunctive are thus used to express *exhortation, command,* or *wish*; if these are negatived, **nē** is used:

Nē hostibus cēdāmus.
Let us not give way to the enemy.

(4) **Cum fessī sītis, requiescite.** Cause
Since you are tired, have a rest.

When a negative is used with a **cum,** *since,* clause, it is **nōn.** In some books the form **quum** is used instead of **cum.**

EXERCISE 123.
1. Naves statim paremus.
2. Lex Oppia abrogetur.
3. Ne desperemus.
4. Discedant pueri.
5. Cum nox appropinquet, domum abite.
6. Redeat tale tempus.
7. Ne hoc opere superemur.
8. Nos a Romanis liberemus.
9. Ne Poeni vos fallant.
10. Cedamus, cum nulla sit spes fugae.

EXERCISE 124.
1. Let us rejoice today.
2. May the better man win!
3. Stay (pl.) here, since you do not know the way.
4. May the gods be praised!
5. Let the soldiers be sent under the yoke.
6. Since the city is in danger, let us appoint a dictator.
7. May we hear better news!
8. Let us not be unworthy of our ancestors.
9. Let the prisoners depart.
10. Let not Archimedes be killed.

Imperfect, Perfect, and Pluperfect Subjunctive

(See Summary of Grammar for conjugation)

Cum, *since*, is regularly used with all Tenses of the Subjunctive.

(1) The Imperfect Subjunctive has the idea of incomplete action, just as the Imperfect Indicative has:

Cum ventus esset adversus, Caesar morātus est.
Since the wind was contrary, Caesar waited.

(2) The Perfect Subjunctive corresponds to the true Perfect (with *have*) in English:

Cum fēminās Rōmānās culpāveris, nōn possum tacēre.
Since you have blamed Roman women, I cannot keep silent.

(3) The Pluperfect Subjunctive corresponds to the English Pluperfect:

Cum Rōmam conservāvisset, Horātius laudātus est.
Since he had saved Rome, Horatius was praised.

EXERCISE 125.
1. Cum Alpes timerent, Poeni progredi nolebant.
2. Ne proelium in campo aperto committamus.
3. Cum iam superati sitis, cur vos dedere nonvultis?
4. Tuta perveniat classis exspectata.
5. Caesar ad litus rediit, cum tot naves fractae essent.
6. Caesar Britanniam invasit, cum incolae Gallos semper iuvarent.
7. Hac nocte murum scalis ascendamus.
8. Milites ante proelium prandeant et corpora somno curent.
9. Cum vigiles vino superati essent, facile erat murum ascendere.
10. Bona sit fortuna agricolis.

EXERCISE 126.
1. The Salapitani were ready, since they had been warned.
2. Caesar left Labienus behind, since he wanted the harbours to be defended.

3. Since the war has been finished, let us repeal this law.
4. Let us not forbid the women to ride through the streets.
5. Hannibal was defeated, since the Carthaginian senate was unwilling to send reinforcements.
6. Since night is approaching, do (pl.) not pursue the enemy.
7. May the women not be defeated by the words of Cato!
8. The deserters began to shout, since the gate had been shut.
9. Crispinus sent out messengers, since he feared a trick.
10. Caesar easily landed his troops, since the enemy had departed from the coast.

EXERCISE 127.

CAESAR'S INVASION OF BRITAIN: (4) SUPERIOR BRITISH TACTICS

Equites hostium essedariique acriter cum equitatu nostro in itinere pugnaverunt; nostri tamen, cum superiores essent, eos in silvas collesque reppulerunt, sed longius hostes secuti, nonnullos ex suis amiserunt. At illi post breve temporis intervallum, dum nostri in munitione castrorum occupati manent, subito se ex silvis eiecerunt et impetum fecerunt in eos qui in statione pro castris collocati erant. Quanquam Caesar statim duas cohortes[1] eis succurrere iussit, hostes per mediam aciem audacissime perruperunt, cum nostros novo genere pugnae perterruissent.

Nostri propter gravitatem armorum, cum neque persequi hostes fugientes possent neque ab signis[2] discedere auderent, minus apti erant ad hostem huius generis; equites magno cum periculo pugnabant, cum hostes saepe de industria[3] cederent, et ubi paulum ab legionibus nostros removerunt, ex essedis desilirent et comminus oppugnarent. Praeterea hostes nunquam universi acie conferta sed pauci[4] magnis intervallis dimicabant. Nihilominus, ubi Caesar plures cohortes submisit, repulsi sunt.

---

[1] A cohort was a tenth part of a legion.
[2] **signum,** here, *military standard* or *banner*.
[3] A Prepositional phrase, *on purpose*.
[4] *in small numbers.*

EXERCISE 128.

Our cavalry were attacked on the march by the enemy, but easily routed them. Since, however, they followed them too far towards the woods, some of our men were lost. Next the enemy made an attack against our outposts, since they had seen that the rest of the troops were busied in the fortification of the camp. At first our men resisted in vain, because the enemy were employing a novel kind of combat.

Since the battle had been joined under the eyes of all and in front of the camp, Caesar could understand the cause. Our infantry could not pursue the enemy, because their arms were too heavy and they did not dare to leave the standards without lighter weapons; besides, the enemy's cavalry kept retreating on purpose, and then leapt down from their chariots; then they easily attacked our cavalry, since the latter had now been removed a little from the legions. Nevertheless Caesar at length drove the enemy back with the help of more cohorts.

Chapter 28
Consecutive Clauses

Tanta erat tempestās, ut nulla nāvis cursum tenēret.
So great was the storm that no ship held its course.

The second part of this sentence is a **Consecutive Clause** (or an Adverbial Clause of Result), expressing the result of the size of the storm. In Latin a result is expressed by **ut,** *that,* with the Verb in the Subjunctive; a negative result is expressed by **ut nōn, ut nēmō, ut nullus,** etc.

The choice of the Tense of the Subjunctive depends entirely upon the sense. As a general rule, Latin uses the same Tense of the Subjunctive as would be used if the Verb were a Main Clause Verb in the Indicative.

In the above example, *no ship **was holding** its course* because of the storm, therefore the Imperfect Subjunctive is used, to express continuous action.

Tot mīlia passuum herī ambulāvī, ut hodiē fessus sim.
I walked so many miles yesterday that I am tired today.

Tanta erat tempestās, ut nāvis submersa sit.
So great was the storm that the ship was sunk.

The ship was sunk: the result was not continuous, therefore the Perfect is used, and not the Imperfect.

Note.—**Tam,** *so,* is used with Adjectives and Adverbs: **Tam fortis est,** *he is so brave.* **Tantus,** *so great,* is used instead of **tam magnus,** and **tot,** *so many,* instead of **tam multī.**

Adeō, *so (so much),* is used with Verbs: **Adeō terrēbantur,** *they were so frightened.*

EXERCISE 129.
1. Galli tanto silentio Capitolium ascenderunt, ut custodes fallerent.
2. Tantum erat frigus, ut Romani arma tenere non possent.

3. Tam bona est amicitia, ut omnes eam petant.
4. Roma erat in tanto periculo, ut Camillus dictator creatus sit.
5. Tam fortis erat Horatius, ut ab omnibus civibus laudaretur.
6. Adeo terrebantur Poeni propter Alpium altitudinem, ut Hannibal eos multis verbis hortaretur.
7. Tot milites in illo proelio occisi erant, ut Romanis nulla spes esset.
8. Manlius Gallum tanto ictu percussit, ut statim ceciderit.
9. Archimedes muros tam bene muniverat, ut Syracusani diu resisterent.
10. Vigiles somno et vino adeo superati erant, ut Romani Syracusas facile intrarent.

EXERCISE 130.

CAESAR'S INVASION OF BRITAIN:
(5) BRITISH RASHNESS LEADS TO DISASTER

Postero die procul a castris hostes in collibus constiterunt rarique[1] se ostendere et minus quam pridie nostros equites proelio lacessere inceperunt. Caesar, cum pabulum deesset, tres legiones et omnes equites emiserat. Sed meridie hostes tam repente ex omnibus partibus ad pabulatores advolaverunt, ut usque ad signa ipsa et legiones pervenirent. Nostri acriter in eos impetum fecerunt; equites, cum post se legiones viderent, hostes praecipites egerunt magnumque numerum eorum interfecerunt; tam celeriter reliquos reppulerunt, ut neque se colligere neque consistere neque ex essedis desilire possent. Post hanc fugam auxilia,[2] quae undique convenerant, statim discesserunt neque post id tempus unquam tot copiis nobiscum hostes contenderunt.

[1] *in small numbers*; compare previous use of **paucī.**
[2] **auxilium** (s.), *help* ; **auxilia** (pl.), *allied troops.*

EXERCISE 131.

1. So sad were the soldiers that for a long time they were silent.

2. The Romans were so weary that they did not defeat the enemy.
3. The Romans built roads so well that many survive today.
4. So great was the folly of the consuls that the army fell into the ambush.
5. Archimedes was so skilful that the Romans could not enter the city.
6. Valerius spoke so well that the law was repealed.
7. We are so delighted by the show that we want to see it again.
8. The soldier was so foolish that he killed Archimedes.
9. This law is so unjust that no one is willing to obey it.
10. I have said this so often that you ought to know it.

EXERCISE 132.

The enemy had retreated to the hills and were not now challenging our cavalry so often. Since there was a great scarcity of fodder, three legions had been sent out by Caesar in the morning together with all the cavalry. At midday, the enemy, who had been hiding themselves in the woods, flew out so suddenly that they attacked the foragers unawares and even broke away as far as the standards. Soon, however, our men attacked so fiercely that they killed many; they drove the rest back with so great a speed that they did not allow them to use their usual kind of combat. Having thus made trial of the strength of the Romans, many soldiers deserted from Cassivellaunus; never afterwards did our men fight against so big an army.

Additional Exercises on Consecutive Clauses will be found on p. 251.

Chapter 29
Further Use of Participles (1)

Latin is always economical in words (it is cheaper to send a telegram in Latin!), and this economy is especially seen in its use of the Participles. We have become familiar with their simple use in Chapters 23 and 24.

Here are examples of the use of Participles, with great economy of words:

(A) **The Perfect Participle of Deponent Verbs,** the only Verbs with a Perfect Participle with **Active** meaning.

> **Prōgressus ad flūmen, castra posuit.**
> *Having advanced to the river, he pitched his camp.*

or, better:

> *He advanced to the river **and** pitched his camp.*

Here we should notice that in English we often get rid of the Participle altogether and use two Main Verbs joined by *and*.

Note.—In English we often loosely use a Present Participle, e.g. *Advancing to the river, he pitched his camp.* In Latin a Present Participle is only used when the two actions happen at the same time (see Chapter 23, 1).

(B) **The Perfect Participle Passive agreeing with the Object of the Main Verb.**

> **Marcellus locum captum mūnīvit.**
> *Marcellus, having captured the position, fortified it.*

or, better:

> *Marcellus captured the position and fortified it.*

Two things should be noticed:

(1) The Active Voice has no Perfect Participle, and therefore the use of the Participle in example (A) cannot be the same in example (B): Latin cannot say *having captured* with **capiō.**

(2) Marcellus did two things to the Object, *the position*: he *captured* it and he *fortified* it; so Latin can bring in the Perfect Participle Passive and say *Marcellus fortified the* **having-been-captured** *position.*

(C) **The Perfect Participle Passive agreeing with the Subject of the Main Verb** (exactly like type (A), only Passive).

Exercitus circumventus sē dēdidit.

The army, having been surrounded, gave itself up.

or, better:

The army was surrounded and gave itself up.

The following exercises contain examples of these three uses of the Participle. Attempts should be made to translate the Participles in different ways, e.g. by turning them into main verbs followed by *and*. Example (C) might be translated: *After the army had been surrounded, it gave itself up.*

EXERCISE 133.
1. Caesar in Galliam regressus ad exercitum proficiscitur.
2. Naves undique profectae ad portum Itium conveniunt.
3. Caesar litteras acceptas legit.
4. Incolae perterriti ab ora discesserunt.
5. Romani Britannos subito conspectos oppugnaverunt.
6. Nonnulli longius progressi interfecti sunt.
7. Hannibal inventum Marcelli corpus sepelivit.
8. Milites circumventi sub iugum missi sunt.
9. Caesar omnes copias collectas in Britanniam transportavit.
10. Romani Syracusas captas vastabant.

EXERCISE 134.

CAESAR'S INVASION OF BRITAIN:
(6) UNDER-WATER DEFENCES NO OBSTACLE

Caesar, ubi consilium Britannorum cognovit, ad flumen Tamesim in fines Cassivellauni exercitum duxit; hoc flumen solum in uno loco[1] pedibus, atque hoc aegre, transiri potest. Eo progressus vidit in altera fluminis ripa magnas copias

[1] Possibly at Coway Stakes, near Walton Bridge.

hostium esse instructas. Ripa autem acutis sudibus praefixis munita erat, eiusdemque generis sub aqua defixae sudes flumine tegebantur. Certior factus de his rebus a captivis perfugisque Caesar equites praemittit, legiones celeriter sequi iubet. Sed tanta celeritate et tanto impetu milites ierunt, quanquam capite solo ex aqua exstabant, ut hostes impetum legionum atque equitum sustinere non possent ripasque relinquerent et se fugae mandarent.

EXERCISE 135.

1. The Romans advanced to the river and were attacked by the Carthaginians.
2. Manlius saw the Gaul and hurled him headlong.
3. The Sabines overwhelmed Tarpeia with their shields and killed her.
4. Hannibal was recalled and sadly obeyed the senate.
5. The Carthaginians rose up from an ambush and attacked the cavalry.
6. Archimedes invented artillery and placed it on the walls.
7. Caesar delayed for twenty-five days and then set sail.
8. The Romans prepared ladders and carried them to the wall.
9. Archimedes had drawn some figures and was looking at them.
10. Herennius was sent for by his son and came to the camp.

EXERCISE 136.

The river Thames divides the lands of Cassivellaunus from Kent; only in one place is it easy to cross this river on foot. Here the Britons had been drawn up and were waiting for our troops; they had not only fortified the bank with pointed stakes, but had also fixed stakes under the water. Caesar had captured some Britons and questioned them; from them he found out that the enemy were defending themselves in this way. He was not, however, frightened by the danger and ordered first his cavalry, then his infantry, to advance across the river. The soldiers crossed the river and attacked so fiercely, that they drove the enemy back and routed them.

Chapter 30
Further Use of Participles (2): Ablative Absolute

(D) **A Participle, agreeing with a Noun or Pronoun, in the Ablative Case, when this Noun or Pronoun is *not* the Subject or the Object of the Main Verb.** This use is called the **Ablative Absolute.**

> **Caesar, exercitū expositō, locum castrīs cēpit.**
> *Caesar, his army having been landed, seized a place for his camp.*

or   *Caesar landed his army and seized a place for his camp.*

Here Latin cannot use a Deponent Participle (type (A) in previous chapter), because there is no Deponent Verb for *to land*. Nor can it use type (B) construction, because the Main Verb, **cēpit,** only governs **locum** and not *army*. Latin, therefore, shuts aside *landed his army* in a little construction of its own in the Ablative. For this use of the Ablative, compare in English: *With my work finished, I can now play.*

N.B. An Ablative Absolute can only be used when the Noun or Pronoun in the Ablative Absolute cannot be made the Subject or the Object of the Main Verb. This test should always be applied in translating English into Latin. *Absolute* comes from **absolvō** (perfect participle **absolūtus**), *I unloose*: the Noun and Participle are *unloosed* from the Subject or Object of the Main Verb of the sentence.

The Ablative Absolute is also very common with the Perfect Participle of a Deponent or with the Present Participle of any Verb.

N.B. When the Present Participle is used as a Verb rather than as an Adjective, the Abl. sing. ends in **-e**:

Lēgātīs locūtīs, mīlitēs diū tacēbant.
*When the ambassadors had spoken, the soldiers were silent
for a long time.*

Prōcēdente diē, vīrēs dēficiēbant.
As the day advanced, their strength began to fail.

Nostrīs mīlitibus cunctantibus, aquilifer in aquam dēsiluit.
*As our men were dallying, a standard-bearer leaped down
into the water.*

Note.—As explained before, the Present Participle may only
be used when the event in the Participle Clause occurs at the
same time as the action of the Main Verb.

(E) **No Participle possible. The use of *cum* [1].**

(*a*) **Cum eō vēnisset, vīdit hostēs instructōs esse.**
*When he had come there, he saw that the enemy had been
drawn up.*

or   *Having come there, etc.*

In translating English into Latin, no Perfect Participle with
Active meaning is possible, unless the Verb is Deponent;
another kind of clause must be used, e.g. **cum** and the Subjunctive in the above example.

(*b*) **Cum diū hostibus restitissent, tandem sē recēpērunt.**
*After resisting the enemy for a long time, they at last
retreated.*

Here, no Ablative Absolute is possible, because **resistō** does
not take a Direct Object in the Accusative, i.e. is Intransitive,
and cannot be used **personally** in the Passive Voice.

[1] **Cum,** *when.*

Cum (sometimes written **quum**) with a past Tense of the
Subjunctive can mean *when* as well as *since;* the sense of a
sentence will show the right translation.

EXERCISE 137.

1. Remo interfecto, Romulus Romae regnavit.
2. Bobus captis, Hercules domum redibat.
3. Romulo mortuo, Numa rex creatus est.
4. Civibus revocantibus, Horatius comites se recipere coegit.
5. Hannibal, obsidibus acceptis, equites praemisit.
6. Romani, consulibus hortantibus, impetum Poenorum sustinebant.
7. Caesar, cognito Britannorum consilio, ad flumen exercitum duxit.
8. Nocte appropinquante, Caesar suos vetuit hostes persequi.
9. Labieno in Gallia relicto, Caesar in Britanniam discessit.
10. Hannibal, cum Italiam petere constituisset, animos suorum confirmavit.

EXERCISE 138.

CAESAR'S INVASION OF BRITAIN: (7) GUERRILLA TACTICS AND GRADUAL SURRENDER

Cassivellaunus, omni spe victoriae deposita, magnam partem copiarum dimisit; quattuor milibus essedariorum relictis itinera nostra servabat[1]; paulum ex via excedebat et in locis silvestribus se abdebat; in eis regionibus, per quas nos iter facturos esse cognoverat, pecora atque homines ex agris in silvas compellebat; deinde, nostris equitibus praedae causa in agros egressis, essedarios ex silvis emittebat et equites latius vagari prohibebat. Caesar igitur non iam nostros longe ab agmine legionum discedere patiebatur.

Interim Trinobantes, legatis ad Caesarem missis, promittunt se ei sese dedituros esse; Mandubracium, filium regis, ab eo petunt; is, patre a Cassivellauno interfecto, ad Caesarem in Galliam confugerat. Caesar ab his obsides quadraginta et frumentum exercitui poscit, et ad eos Mandubracium mittit. Tum ab aliis gentibus, quae se dediderant, cognovit non longe ex eo loco oppidum[2] Cassivellauni abesse, silvis paludibusque

---

[1] *kept under observation.*
[2] *stronghold* rather than *town*, in this passage.

munitum. Eo cum legionibus profectus, locum duabus ex partibus oppugnare properavit. Hostes paulisper morati, cum militum nostrorum impetum sustinere non possent, sese ex alia parte oppidi eiecerunt. Magnus ibi numerus pecoris repertus est; multi in fuga comprehensi interfecti sunt.

EXERCISE 139.
1. The city having been captured, the soldiers were seeking booty.
2. After preparing an ambush, the Gauls awaited the Carthaginians.
3. When Marcellus had been killed, and Crispinus had been wounded, the Romans retreated.
4. As the soldiers were despairing, Hannibal made a speech.
5. The Romans prepared ladders and waited for an opportunity.
6. The soldier approached the wall and counted the stones.
7. While the enemy approached, the Salapitani were guarding the gate.
8. The Gauls attacked the column and blocked the way.
9. When Valerius had spoken, the law was repealed.
10. While Hannibal was hesitating, the Gauls made an attack.

EXERCISE 140.
No hope of victory being left, Cassivellaunus tried to hinder our troops by another plan. He sent back home most of his soldiers and kept with him four thousand charioteers. He withdrew the latter a little from the route and hid them in the woods; thither also he drove all the herds and inhabitants, and waited for our cavalry. Then, when our cavalry were wandering through the fields in search of plunder, he suddenly sent out the charioteers and drove them back. When this had been done repeatedly, Caesar was compelled to keep the cavalry near the line of march.

Meanwhile Caesar restored Mandubracius, son of the former king, to the Trinobantes, in return for hostages and corn, and received other tribes into surrender. Being informed that the stronghold of Cassivellaunus was not far away, he determined to attack it. While our men were attacking on two sides, the enemy escaped from another. Many, however, were killed while fleeing.

Additional Exercises on the use of the Participles:

EXERCISE 141.
1. Marcelli anulo invento, Hannibal litteras composuit.
2. Exercitus, ad alterum saltum progressus, subito constitit.
3. Romani multas statuas captas Romam transportaverunt.
4. Oratione Catonis audita, Valerius diu locutus est.
5. Litora Italiae respiciens, Hannibal deos accusabat.
6. Proelio commisso, nostri hostes statim reppulerunt.
7. Luxuria crescente, imperia deleri solent.
8. Britanni, cum ex essedis desiluissent, comminus pugnabant.
9. Hieme appropinquante, legiones in castra redire solebant.
10. Hannibal suos convocatos multis verbis confirmavit.

EXERCISE 142.
1. Hearing this, Caesar ordered the legions to be called back.
2. Crispinus, who had been wounded in the battle, was lamenting the death of Marcellus.
3. As the sentries had now been overcome by wine, the Romans climbed the wall.
4. Marcellus was killed while fighting.
5. Speaking in Latin, the deserters ordered the sentries to open the gate.
6. Caesar beached the ships and protected them with a fortification.
7. Hannibal almost wept, on the point of leaving Italy.
8. Our men pursued the Britons and drove them into the woods.
9. After reaching the top of the Alps, the Carthaginians could see the plains of Italy.
10. As the supply of fodder was failing, Caesar sent out three legions.

Chapter 31
Final Clauses

Hannibal equitēs mittit, ut hostēs oppugnent.
Hannibal sends cavalry (in order) that they may attack the enemy or to attack, etc.

Marcellus profectus est, ut tumulum caperet.
Marcellus set out to capture the hillock.

These are examples of a **Final Clause** (or Adverbial Clause, expressing Purpose), expressed by **ut** followed by the Subjunctive. The Latin Infinitive is never to be used to express a Final Clause.

Nē (*lest*) is used to introduce a negative Purpose, *in order that . . . not,* and **nēve** for a second negative clause, instead of **neque**:

Nē dēspērārent nēve prōgredī nollent, Hannibal mīlitibus quiētem dedit.

In order that they should not despair nor be unwilling to advance, Hannibal gave the soldiers a rest.

The following should be noticed, for use in Final Clauses:

nē quis,[1] *that no one.*	**nē ullus,** *that no* (Adj.).
nē quid,[1] *that nothing.*	**nē unquam,** *that never.*

[1] See Indefinite Pronouns in Summary of Grammar.

Noctū appropinquāvērunt, ne quis vidēret.
They approached by night, so that no one might see.

Sequence of Tenses

The Tense of the Verb in a Final Clause depends upon the Tense of the Main Verb.

Tenses are divided into **Primary** and **Historic**:

Indicative Primary	*Subjunctive Primary*
Present	Present
Future	Perfect
True Perfect	
(e.g. **mīsī,** *I have sent*)	

The Imperative is also Primary.

Indicative Historic	*Subjunctive Historic*
Imperfect	Imperfect
Indefinite (Aorist) Perfect	Pluperfect
(e.g. **mīsī,** *I sent*)	
Pluperfect	

In most types of Dependent Clause in Latin, including Final, **Primary** Tenses are followed by **Primary,** and **Historic** by **Historic.**

The rule for Final Clauses is simple:

If the Main Verb is Primary, the Verb in the Final Clause will be in the Present Subjunctive (*may*).

If the Main Verb is Historic, the Verb in the Final Clause will be in the Imperfect Subjunctive (*might*).

*The above scheme of the **Sequence of Tenses** will be needed in other constructions and will be referred to again. The Perfect and Pluperfect Tenses of the Subjunctive are given in the scheme, but they will not be required in Final Clauses.*

EXERCISE 143.
1. Caesar Labienum reliquit, ut portus defenderet.
2. Equites ad Caesarem venerunt, ut nuntiarent multas naves fractas esse.
3. Consules progrediuntur, ut locum capiant.
4. Nemo praemissus erat, ut saltum exploraret.
5. Fabius cunctatur, ne proelium committere cogatur.
6. Salapitani portam clauserant, ne quis oppidum iniret.
7. Feminae Romanae vias obsidebant, ut viros orarent.
8. Perfugae Latine loquuntur, ut Salapitanos fallant.

9. Ne Gallos sperneret neve falleretur, Hannibal benigne respondit et obsides accepit.
10. Essedarii e silvis emissi erant, ut nostros a praeda prohiberent.

EXERCISE 144.

CAESAR'S INVASION OF BRITAIN:
(8) EXPEDITION ENDS AFTER SURRENDER
OF CASSIVELLAUNUS

Interim Cassivellaunus ad quattuor reges, qui Cantio praeerant, nuntios misit; eos iussit omnes copias colligere ut castra navalia subito oppugnarent. Cum ei ad castra venissent, nostri, eruptione facta, multis eorum interfectis, suos incolumes reduxerunt. Cassivellaunus, hoc proelio nuntiato, tot detrimentis acceptis, vastatis finibus, maxime permotus defectione civitatium, legatos ad Caesarem misit, ut se dederet. Caesar, cum constituisset in Gallia hiemare propter repentinos Gallorum motus, neque multum aestatis superesset, obsides et vectigal a Britannia poscit; Cassivellaunum Mandubracio et Trinobantibus nocere vetat.

Obsidibus acceptis exercitum reducit ad mare, naves invenit refectas. His ad mare deductis, quod et captivorum magnum numerum habebat, et nonnullae tempestate amissae erant naves, sensit non omnes simul posse transportari. Perpaucae tamen ex eis navibus quae inanes post primam navigationem remittebantur et quas Labienus Caesari fecerat, in Britanniam advenerunt. Caesar igitur, ne anni tempore a navigatione prohiberetur, angustius milites in navibus collocavit; tempestatem nactus idoneam, cum secunda vigilia solvisset, prima luce terram attigit omnesque incolumes naves perduxit.

EXERCISE 145.
1. Hannibal sends out a scout to give the signal.
2. Archimedes had invented artillery, in order that the citizens might defend Syracuse.
3. The Samnites blocked the pass, in order to surround the Romans.

4. Hannibal has used the ring of Marcellus to deceive the Salapitani.
5. Ambassadors went to Italy to recall Hannibal.
6. Repeal (pl.) the law, so that the women may enjoy the fruits of peace.
7. The Sabine women went out of the city in order that their husbands and fathers should not fight.
8. The famous Fabius refused to join battle, lest he should be defeated.
9. We will shut the gate so that no one may escape.
10. The Syracusans had come to Marcellus to seek safety for their children.

EXERCISE 146.

The four kings, by order of Cassivellaunus, advanced with all their forces towards the sea, to storm Caesar's camp. Our men, however, sallied out to attack them, and drove them back. Cassivellaunus had now suffered so many losses that he surrendered to Caesar. The latter decided to return to Gaul to defend the Roman legions, and after demanding hostages, led his troops back to the coast. He had so many prisoners that everybody could not be taken across in[1] one voyage. He therefore sent over part of his men and then awaited the return of the ships, in order to take over the remainder. Since only a few came back, he adopted another plan, so that he might avoid bad[2] weather: he packed[3] the soldiers more tightly and set sail as soon as possible. Leaving Britain at the second watch, he reached harbour at dawn.

[1] No Preposition.   [2] Use **adversus**.   [3] **collocō**.

Further uses of the Relative Pronoun

(1) As a Conjunction, connecting sentences:

Horātius Rōmam conservāvit. Quī positus forte in ponte hostēs conspexit.

Horatius saved Rome. He, by chance stationed on the bridge, caught sight of the enemy.

Quī refers to **Horātius** in the preceding sentence. The beginning of a Latin sentence is often linked up by a Relative Pronoun with what came before. In English we use a Personal Pronoun, or a Demonstrative Pronoun, or, as in the next example, a Demonstrative Adjective:

> **Caesar exercitum ad Tamesim duxit; quod flūmen sōlum ūnō locō pedibus transīrī potest.**
> *Caesar led his army to the Thames; this river can only be crossed at one place on foot.*

(2) To express Purpose, (*a*) when the Antecedent is in the Accusative Case, or (*b*) when the Verb of which the Antecedent is the Subject is in the Passive Voice:

(*a*)   **Lēgātōs mīsit, quī pācem ōrārent.**
> *He sent ambassadors to ask* (literally *who might ask*) *for peace.*

(*b*)   **Lēgātī missī sunt, quī pācem ōrārent.**
> *Ambassadors were sent to ask for peace.*

EXERCISE 147.

Make up 10 sentences in Latin, correctly using the Relative Pronoun with the Subjunctive, to express a Final Clause.

Additional Exercises on Final Clauses will be found on p. 252, and some mixed Exercises on Final and Consecutive Clauses on p. 253.

Chapter 32
Indirect Commands and Petitions

---

(1) **Senātus Carthāginiensis Hannibalī imperat ut redeat.**
The Carthaginian senate orders Hannibal to return.

(2) **Hannibal ōrāverat ut novās cōpiās mitterent.**
Hannibal had asked them to send reinforcements.

Ut redeat and **ut novās cōpiās mitterent** are Noun Clauses in the form of (1) an **Indirect Command,** and (2) an **Indirect Petition;** these clauses state *what they order, what he had asked.*

Nearly all Verbs in Latin of *commanding, asking, advising, persuading, someone to do something,* are followed by **ut,** or if it is *not to do something,* by **nē,** and the Subjunctive. **Nēve** (or **neu**) is used for *and not,* and **nē quis, nē ullus,** etc. are used as in Final Clauses for *that no one,* etc.

The **Sequence of Tenses** is exactly the same for Indirect Commands as for Final Clauses (see Chapter 31).

Among Verbs which are used in this way are:

ōrō, *I ask, beg, entreat.*	**hortor,** *I exhort, encourage.*
petō (ā tē), *I beseech (you).*	**suādeō** (Dat.), *I urge.*
rogō, *I ask.*	**persuādeō** (Dat.), *I persuade.*
precor, *I pray.*	**imperō** (Dat.), *I order, command.*
moneō, *I advise, warn.*	**postulō,** *I demand.*

Note.—**Iubeō,** *I order,* and **vetō,** *I forbid,* are always followed by an Infinitive.

Quīdam, *a certain person, a certain*

Sing.	M.	F.	N.
Nom.	**quīdam**	**quaedam**	**quiddam (quoddam)**
Acc.	**quendam**	**quandam**	**quiddam (quoddam)**

The remaining Cases are declined like the Relative Pronoun with **-dam** added throughout, except that the Gen. pl. is written **quōrundam, quārundam, quōrundam.**

144

Quīdam is used as an Indefinite Pronoun or as an Indefinite Adjective; in the neuter **quiddam** is used as a Pronoun, **quoddam** as an Adjective:

Quīdam ē mīlitibus Marcellō consilium prōposuit.
One of the soldiers proposed a plan to Marcellus.

Mīles quīdam, etc.
A certain soldier or simply, *a soldier*, etc.

Coepī, *I began* or *have begun*

This Verb has no Present-Stem Tenses. Its Perfect Tenses, both in the Indicative and in the Subjunctive, follow the regular 3rd Conjug. The Infinitive is **coepisse;** Fut. Participle, **coeptūrus.**

EXERCISE 148.

1. Herennius Pontium monuit ut Romanos inviolatos dimitteret.
2. Uxores viros rogabunt ut sibi dent pecuniam.
3. Multae orabant ut Romani legem iniustam abrogarent.
4. Hannibal praeconem tabernas quasdam Romanas venditare iussit.
5. Marcellus Crispino persuaserat ut secum proficisceretur.
6. Consules hortabantur equites ut acrius hostibus resisterent.
7. Caesar equitibus imperavit ne longius ab agmine vagarentur.
8. Cives deos precari coeperant ut suos conservarent.
9. Caesar militibus imperaverat ut castra munirent, neve opus intermitterent.
10. Te moneo ut hoc opus diligentissime perlegas.

EXERCISE 149.

A MESSAGE THAT FLEW

The Nervii, a tribe in N.E. Gaul, suddenly in 54 B.C., after Caesar's return from Britain, attacked the winter-quarters of one of the Roman legions. The commander of the legion was Quintus Cicero, brother of the famous orator.

Nervii vallo novem pedum et fossa quindecim pedum hiberna cingunt. Septimo die oppugnationis ferventia iacula in casas, quae Gallico more stramentis erant tectae, iacere coeperunt; ventus ignem in omnem partem castrorum distulit. Hostes maximo clamore turres agere et scalis vallum ascendere coeperunt. Hic dies nostris longe gravissimus erat, sed tanta erat militum virtus, ut nemo hostium intrare auderet.

Caesar ex captivis cognovit Ciceronem esse in magno periculo. Tum cuidam ex equitibus Gallis magnis praemiis persuadet ut ad Ciceronem epistolam deferat. Quam Graecis scriptam litteris mittit, ne epistola intercepta nostra consilia ab hostibus cognoscantur. Salutis causa Gallum monet ut hastam cum epistola ad amentum deligata intra munitionem castrorum abiciat. In litteris scribit se cum legionibus profectum celeriter adfore; Ciceronem hortatur ut pristinam virtutem retineat. Gallus periculum veritus, ita ut Caesar imperaverat, hastam mittit. Quae casu ad turrim adhaesit neque ab nostris duobus diebus animadversa tertio die a quodam milite conspicitur et ad Ciceronem defertur. Cum ille perlectam apud milites recitavisset, omnes maxime gaudebant. Tum fumus incendiorum procul videbatur; quae res omnem dubitationem adventus legionum expulit.

EXERCISE 150.
1. Caesar ordered the legions to follow the cavalry quickly.
2. We beseech you (s.) to spare the women and children.
3. Afterwards Herennius advised his son to kill all the Romans.
4. Hannibal encouraged his soldiers not to be afraid of the Alps.
5. Why are you (pl.) demanding that the law should be repealed?
6. The Sabines began to urge a certain maiden, by name Tarpeia, to open the gate.
7. The consuls ought to have been warned not to advance without scouts.
8. Cassivellaunus has persuaded the four kings to attack Caesar's camp.

9. Marcellus had ordered that no one should harm Archimedes.

10. Pontius asked his father to give him advice.

EXERCISE 151.

The Nervii suddenly attacked Cicero's winter-quarters and tried by every means to take it by storm; they even threw red-hot javelins on to the thatch-covered huts. Thinking[1] that the Romans, frightened by the conflagration, would quickly surrender, they began to climb the rampart with ladders. In one place the Romans were even begging the Nervii by signs and words to enter; no one, however, dared to advance.

Caesar was informed about these matters by prisoners, and asked a Gallic cavalryman to convey a message to Cicero; the latter was at first unwilling because of the danger; finally Caesar persuaded him to do this, after offering a large reward. In order that the Gauls should not discover his plan, he wrote the letter in Greek characters; he advised the Gaul to fasten the letter to a spear and hurl the spear inside the fortification. The Gaul reached the walls and threw the spear; after two days a soldier found it sticking to a tower and carried it to Cicero. Caesar announced in the letter that he would soon bring help to the legion; he urged all to retain their former[2] courage and not to lose hope.

[1] Use **reor** and see Chapter 29 (A), note.
[2] **pristinus.**

Cautionary Note on Verbs of *persuading, telling, etc.*

In translating English into Latin, it should be carefully noticed whether after **moneō, suādeō, persuādeō** the sense requires an Indirect Command or an Indirect Statement. Compare *He warned the boy not to go on the ice* (Indirect Command) with *He warned the boy that the ice was thin* (Indirect Statement).

Great care, too, should be taken with the English Verb *tell*: it may be that (1) **narrō** is wanted, *I tell a story;* or (2) **certiōrem faciō**, *I inform* (or **nuntiō**); or (3) **imperō** or **iubeō**, *I command.*

EXERCISE 152.

1. Cicero was told that Caesar would soon arrive.
2. Caesar told the infantry to follow as quickly as possible.
3. Caesar had been warned that the banks of the river had been fortified with stakes.
4. Lentulus urged the Romans to surrender without a struggle.
5. It is one thing to tell a story, another to tell it well.
6. The prisoners persuaded the consuls that Luceria was being besieged.
7. Hannibal continued to urge the senate to send reinforcements.
8. After two days the Romans were told that Hasdrubal's army had been defeated.
9. Fabius warned the commanders not to join battle with Hannibal.
10. A soldier persuaded Marcellus to send soldiers over the wall.

Additional Exercises on Indirect Commands and Petitions will be found on p. 254.

Chapter 33
Indirect Questions (1)

(1) **Quid cōpiae parant?**
What are the troops preparing?

This is a Direct Question, expressed by an Interrogative word and the Indicative.

(2) **Hannibal rogat quid cōpiae parent.**
Hannibal asks what the troops are preparing.

Quid cōpiae parent is a Noun Clause in the form of an **Indirect Question** (the Noun Clause is *what Hannibal asks*).

An Indirect Question is introduced by an Interrogative word, but the Verb is always in the Subjunctive; apart from this it is like a Direct Question.

Sequence of Tenses is observed in Indirect Questions (see Chapter 31), with Primary Tenses of the Subjunctive following Primary Tenses of the Indicative, and Historic following Historic.

In Indirect Questions a Future Subjunctive is supplied by the Future Participle and **sim** (Primary), **essem** (Historic).

The following examples should be carefully studied:

Primary Indicative

Hannibal rogat	**rogābit**	**rogāvit**	**rogāverit**
Hannibal asks	*will ask*	*has asked*	*will have asked*

followed by Primary Subjunctive

quid cōpiae parent	**parātūrae sint**	**parāverint**
what the troops are preparing	*are going to prepare*	*(have) prepared*

Historic Indicative

Hannibal rogābat	**rogāvit**	**rogāverat**
Hannibal was asking	*asked*	*had asked*

followed by Historic Subjunctive

quid cōpiae parārent	**parātūrae essent**	**parāvissent**
what the troops were preparing	*were going to pre-prepare*	*had prepared*

Note.—The Imperative has Primary Sequence.

In translating English into Latin, we must do two things, (1) look at the Main Verb and see whether a Primary or a Historic Tense of the Subjunctive is wanted; (2) choose one of the Primary Tenses or one of the Historic Tenses according to the sense.

Interrogative words that are used in Direct Questions are also used in Indirect Questions, **cūr, quot, quantus,** etc.

N.B. **Quandō** (never **cum** or **ubi**) is used for *when* in these clauses:

Hannibal rogāvit quandō novae cōpiae ventūrae essent.
Hannibal asked when reinforcements would come.

Very important.—The Verb which introduces an Indirect Question in Latin is very often not a Verb of *asking* at all. Verbs of *saying, warning, seeing, hearing, finding out, knowing,* etc., can all introduce Indirect Questions:

Caesar certior factus est, monitus est, vīdit, audīvit, cognōvit, scīvit, quantum esset perīculum.
Caesar was informed, was warned, saw, heard, found out, knew, how great the danger was.

Like an Indirect Statement, an Indirect Question can be the Subject of the Main Verb:

Quot nāvēs fractae sint, incertum est.
How many ships have been broken is uncertain.

Exercise 153.
1. Hannibal milites rogat cur desperent.
2. Exploratores nuntiant quantus sit hostium exercitus.
3. Nostri cognoverant ubi hostes se abderent.
4. Caesar intellexit cur tot naves amissae essent.
5. Caesar certior factus erat in quanto periculo esset legio.
6. Titus Livius narrat qualia tormenta Archimedes invenerit.
7. Romani viderunt quid Hannibal facturus esset.
8. Caesar sensit quanta fuisset vis tempestatis.
9. Scisne quantas copias Caesar transportaturus sit?
10. Salapitani non ignorabant quis litteras composuisset.

Exercise 154.
1. The Britons knew why Caesar was building ships.
2. The Romans find out who is helping the Syracusans.
3. Caesar realized why so few ships had arrived.
4. Hannibal tells his men where he is going to lead them.
5. The consuls perceived how big was the disaster.
6. Have you (s.) heard who have been made consuls?
7. Fabius was asked when he was going to attack the Carthaginians.
8. Hannibal asked what was hindering the column.
9. Caesar understood why our men had been defeated on that day.
10. We all know which law displeases the Roman ladies.

Exercise 155.
1. Hannibal scire voluit quantae copiae hostium essent.
2. Caesar ex captivis cognovit quo hostes discessissent.
3. Non certiores facti sumus quando equites profecturi sint.
4. Caesar nondum audiverat quales essent portus Britanniae.
5. Caesar militibus ostendit quid fieri velit.
6. Galli non ignorabant ubi legio hiematura esset.
7. Scisne cur plebs hanc legem non abrogaverit?
8. Fabius sensit qualem hostem vincere conaretur.
9. Nescimus quomodo Hannibal elephantos trans flumen transmiserit.
10. Britanni viderunt quantas copias Caesar paravisset.

Exercise 156.

THE BEST GENERAL

According to one account, Publius Scīpiō Āfricānus (so called from his victory over Hannibal at Zama in Africa in 202 B.C.) was a member of an embassy that went in 193 B.C. to Ephesus, to protest against the aggression of Antiochus of Syria. By this time Hannibal was also at Ephesus; he had fled into exile from Carthage and was hoping to invade Italy once more with the help of Antiochus.

Publius Africanus et Hannibal Ephesi colloquebantur. Africanus Hannibalem rogavit, quem fuisse maximum imperatorem crederet; respondit Hannibal 'Alexandrum, regem Macedonum, maximum fuisse credo; paucis enim copiis innumerabiles exercitus fudit et ad oras, quas visere supra spem humanam est, pervenit'. Roganti deinde, quem secundum poneret, Hannibal 'Pyrrhum', inquit, 'secundum pono; nemo enim castris elegantius loca cepit, praesidia disposuit; praeterea ita homines sibi conciliavit, ut Italicae gentes regis externi quam populi Romani, tam diu principis in ea terra, imperium ferre mallent.' Rogatus, quem tertium poneret, respondit haud dubie se ipsum. Tum Scipio ridens affirmavit Hannibalem non se vicisse. 'Quid, si me viceris?' Respondit Hannibal: 'Tum vero me et ante Alexandrum et ante Pyrrhum et ante alios omnes imperatores ponam.'

EXERCISE 157.

1. Cato asks why the women are going down to the forum.
2. Caesar told the soldiers what he had found out from the scout.
3. Caesar found out from prisoners how the Britons had fortified the banks of the Thames.
4. The soldier perceived how many stones there were in the wall.
5. The Romans never knew when the Britons were going to fly out from the woods.
6. Caesar learns how many ships of war[1] the soldiers have built.
7. It is uncertain how big an army Hannibal led into Italy.
8. Valerius asked why the Romans did not allow the women to put on purple.
9. We want to know when Caesar is going to bring help to the legion.
10. Herennius told his son what he thought to be best.

[1] *ship of war*, **nāvis longa.**

EXERCISE 158.

Publius Africanus had gone to Ephesus to ask Antiochus not to injure the allies of the Romans. By chance Hannibal was also there, and the two generals began to converse. Asked by Africanus who had been the greatest general, Hannibal said that he thought that Alexander had been the greatest. 'Although', said he, 'he only had a few troops, he always conquered his enemies, and no general ever marched further than he.' When Africanus asked whom he wished to put second, he said that he put Pyrrhus second. 'I do not think that any general has ever chosen sites for camps more fitly. Besides, even the tribes of Italy preferred to be ruled by him than by the Roman people.' Africanus then asked whom he placed next. 'Without doubt', said he, 'I place myself next.' Scipio could not check his laughter and asked in what order he placed the conqueror of Scipio. 'The man[1] who shall conquer Scipio, I place before all.'

[1] is.

Indirect Questions (2)

Num in a single Indirect Question means *whether* or *if* (**sī** is never used in this way):

Caesar speculātōrem rogāvit num hostēs vīdisset.
Caesar asked the scout whether (or *if*) *he had seen the enemy.*

Double Questions

(1) Direct. **-ne** or **utrum** (introducing the question) . . . **an,** *or* (**annōn,** *or not*).

Vīdistīne hostēs an audīvistī?
or   **Utrum vīdistī,** etc.
Have you seen the enemy or heard them?

Vīdistīne hostēs annōn?
Have you seen the enemy or not?

(2) Indirect. **Utrum,** *whether* or *if,* . . . **an,** *or* (**necne,** *or not*).

Caesar speculātōrem rogāvit utrum hostēs vīdisset an audīvisset.
Caesar asked the scout whether he had seen the enemy or heard them.

Necne after **vīdisset** would mean *or not*.

Uter? Which of two?

Uter, utra, utrum? Which of two? is declined like **neuter,** and can be used either as a Pronoun or as an Adjective, in Direct or Indirect Questions:

> **Uter consul vulnerātus est?**
> *Which of the two consuls was wounded?*

Utrum, *whether,* thus literally means *which thing of the two.*

Note. Indirect Questions in Latin, introduced by **cūr, quālis, quantus,** etc., are often translated into English with the help of an abstract noun:

> **Hannibal rogāvit quantae et ubi essent cōpiae.**
> *Hannibal asked the size and whereabouts of the forces.*

So : **cūr,** *reason.*   **quōmodo,** *method.*
       quālis, *nature, sort.*   **quot,** *number.*
       quō, *destination.*   **unde,** *source, origin.*

N.B. **Quōmodo** is *how, in what way;* **quam** is *how,* when used with Adjectives and Adverbs.

EXERCISE 159.

1. Vultisne vos dedere annon?
2. Hannibal non cognoverat num Hasdrubal Alpes transisset.
3. Nescimus utrum falsa an vera captivi nuntiaverint.
4. Utra via exercitus profectus est?
5. Caesar reperire voluit qualis esset ora Britanniae.
6. Caesar nondum certior factus erat quomodo essedarii pugnare solerent.
7. Cicero ignorabat utrum Caesar mox venturus esset necne.
8. Nescio utro oculo Hannibal fuerit caecus.
9. Romani mirabantur cur tot milites sine exploratoribus essent profecti; senserunt quam stulti fuissent consules.
10. Conati sumus cognoscere utrum hostes a dextra an a sinistra oppugnaturi essent.

EXERCISE 160.
1. Did you (s.) hear this from our men or from the enemy?
2. Marcellus soon saw the size and nature of the fortifications.
3. Caesar doubted whether all the ships would arrive from Gaul.
4. Pontius did not know the reason for this advice of his father.
5. The Syracusans were asking whether a new fleet had started from Carthage or not.
6. Which of the two generals advised the Romans to attack?
7. The destination of the troops was not uncertain for long.
8. The Salapitani could see the nature of the soldiers' arms.
9. Many women wanted to know if the law had been repealed.
10. The Syracusan soldier did not know the identity of Archimedes.

Additional Exercises on Indirect Questions will be found on p. 255.

Chapter 34
Notes on Various Uses and Constructions

Intransitive Verbs in Passive Voice

Intransitive Verbs which take the Dative Case do not have a full Passive Voice. They are, however, used **impersonally** in the 3rd person sing. in the Passive:

Magistrīs pārētur, *the masters are obeyed (obedience is done to the masters).*

Caesarī persuāsum est, *Caesar has been persuaded (persuasion has been brought about to Caesar).*

Quisque, uterque, quisquam

(1) **Quisque, quaeque, quidque** or **quicque (quodque,** when used as an Adjective), declined like **quis,** means *each one (each)* and is used of more than two persons or things:

Reliquī suam quisque domum rediērunt.
The rest returned each to his own home.

Quisque is often used idiomatically after a Superlative, e.g **fortissimus quisque,** *all the bravest men.*

(2) **Uterque, utraque, utrumque** (a compound of **uter)** means *each of two:*

Ab utrōque cornū oppugnāvērunt.
They attacked on each wing.

(3) **Quisquam, quidquam** or **quicquam,** declined like **quis** in the masc. and neut. sing., means *anyone* when preceded by a word with negative meaning (Latin does not use **et nēmō**):

Hannibal suōs in silvā abdiderat, nec quisquam ā locō movēbātur.
Hannibal had hidden his men in the wood, and no one moved from his place.

156

Partitive Genitive, Genitive of Value, Ablative of Price

(1) **Partitive Genitive.** Some uses of this have been met before, e.g. **māior pars cōpiārum,** *most of the troops.* It is commonly found after the neuter sing. (Nom. and Acc. only) of Adjectives and after certain words expressing amount or degree:

multum, *much.*	**paulum,** *little.*	**parum,** *too little.*
plūs, *more.*	**minus,** *less.*	**nimium** ⎫
plūrimum, *very much.*	**minimum,** *very little.*	**nimis** ⎬ *too much*
tantum, *so much.*	**satis,** *enough.*	

> **Nōn erat Caesarī satis nāvium.**
> *Caesar had not enough ships.*

(2) **Genitive of Value.** The following Genitives of Adjectives (**pretiī,** *price,* being understood) are used for indefinite value or price after Verbs of *buying, selling, valuing* (**aestimō**): **magnī,** *at a high price*; **plūris,** *at a higher price*; **maximī,** *at a very high price*; **parvī,** *at a low price*; **minōris,** *at a lower price*; **minimī,** *at a very low price*; **tantī,** *at so high a price.*

> **Amīcitiam bonōrum maximī aestimāmus.**
> *We value the friendship of good men very highly.*

(3) **Ablative of Price.** The Ablative is used when a definite price is stated:

> **Librum sex dēnāriīs ēmī.**
> *I bought a book for six denarii* (about 5s.).

Two uses of the Consecutive Clause

(1) **Is quī** with the Subjunctive, *the kind of man to* ...:

> **Caesar nōn erat is quī tālī rē superārētur.**
> *Caesar was not the kind of man to be overcome by a thing like that.*

(2) **Accidit ut** with the Subjunctive, *it happens that*:

> **Accidit ut Hannibal Ephesī adesset.**
> *It happened that Hannibal was present at Ephesus.*

EXERCISE 161.

1. Hannibalī nunquam ut se dedat persuadebitur.
2. Gallus, ut ei imperatum erat, hastam intra urbem mittit.

3. Parum frumenti in castris Romanorum erat.
4. Uterque consul suos hortabatur, ut hostibus resisterent.
5. Vix cuiquam persuasum erat illam legem esse utilem.
6. Marcellus imperaverat ut civibus parceretur.
7. Fabius Hannibalis ingenium maximi aestimavit.
8. Optimus quisque in eo proelio interfectus esse videbatur.
9. Accidit ut Syracusani festum diem Dianae celebrarent.
10. Uxoribus sociorum invidebatur a matronis Romanis, quia illis erat satis purpurae atque auri.

EXERCISE 162.
1. All the wisest men value highly the words of Socrates.
2. Cato said that the Romans had transported too much booty to the city.
3. Pontius was not the kind of man to obey good advice.
4. The Romans fled from the battle, each seeking a way for himself.
5. Caesar left Labienus behind, so that the Romans would not be injured by the Gauls.
6. In this crisis the soldiers looked at each other and no one spoke.
7. From each of the two sides the Gauls rose from their ambush.
8. No one had been ordered to reconnoitre the route.
9. That writer sold six books for thirty denarii.
10. The Carthaginians were now weary, after suffering so much toil.

EXERCISE 163.
1. Dux promisit feminis atque liberis parsum iri.
2. Nihil pluris quam libertatem aestimamus.
3. Romani non putaverant quemquam cum tot militibus Alpes posse transire.
4. Post hanc cladem parum militum Romanis supererat.
5. Ne Archimedi noceatur.
6. Matronae Romanae non erant eae quae tantam iniuriam sine certamine ferrent.

7. Quot talentis villam istam emisti?
8. Accidit ut Hannibal anulum Marcelli invenisset.
9. Cum hostes adessent, Romani pro se quisque in urbem ex agris migrabant.
10. Caesar redire constituit, cum paulum aestatis superesset.

EXERCISE 164.

1. It happened that on that day Horatius had been stationed on the bridge.
2. The Gaul was at last persuaded to carry the letter to Cicero's camp.
3. Not for long were the enemy resisted.
4. Hannibal did not believe that anyone had been a better general than Alexander.
5. Since not much of the day was left, Caesar ordered his men not to pursue the enemy.
6. All the best men believe that it is sometimes good to be silent.
7. Some books we value very highly, others at very little.
8. Each of the two Scipios was brave; the son was more fortunate than the father.
9. Sometimes even the poor are envied by the rich.
10. It happens that you (s.) have read the last words of this book.

Additional Exercises of miscellaneous sentences will be found on p. 256.

Summary of Grammar

Nouns

1st Declension

Sing.		*Plur.*
Nom.	**mensa** (f.), *table*	**mensae**
Voc.	**mensa**	**mensae**
Acc.	**mensam**	**mensās**
Gen.	**mensae**	**mensārum**
Dat.	**mensae**	**mensīs**
Abl.	**mensā**	**mensīs**

Note. **Fīlia,** *daughter,* and **dea,** *goddess,* have Dat. and Abl. plur. **fīliābus, deābus.**

2nd Declension

Sing.

Nom.	**dominus** (m.), *master*	**magister** (m.), *master*	**puer** (m.),
Voc.	**domine** (*of household*)	**magister** (*of school*)	**puer** [*boy*
Acc.	**dominum**	**magistrum**	**puerum**
Gen.	**dominī**	**magistrī**	**puerī**
Dat.	**dominō**	**magistrō**	**puerō**
Abl.	**dominō**	**magistrō**	**puerō**

Plur.

Nom.	**dominī**	**magistrī**	**puerī**
Voc.	**dominī**	**magistrī**	**puerī**
Acc.	**dominōs**	**magistrōs**	**puerōs**
Gen.	**dominōrum**	**magistrōrum**	**puerōrum**
Dat.	**dominīs**	**magistrīs**	**puerīs**
Abl.	**dominīs**	**magistrīs**	**puerīs**

Note. **Fīlius,** *son,* has Voc. sing. **fīlī,** and Gen. sing. **fīlī** or **fīliī; deus,** *god,* has Voc. sing. **deus; vir,** *man,* keeps **vir-** throughout.

Sing.		Plur.
Nom.	bellum (n.), *war*	bella
Voc.	bellum	bella
Acc.	bellum	bella
Gen.	bellī	bellōrum
Dat.	bellō	bellīs
Abl.	bellō	bellīs

Note. Neuter Nouns in -ium, e.g. auxilium, *help*, form Gen. sing. in -ī or -iī.

3rd Declension

(1) Nouns with Consonant Stems

Sing.

Nom.	rex (m.), *king*	mīles (c.), *soldier*	consul (m.), *consul*
Voc.	rex	mīles	consul
Acc.	rēgem	mīlitem	consulem
Gen.	rēgis	mīlitis	consulis
Dat.	rēgī	mīlitī	consulī
Abl.	rēge	mīlite	consule

Plur.

Nom.	rēgēs	mīlitēs	consulēs
Voc.	rēgēs	mīlitēs	consulēs
Acc.	rēgēs	mīlitēs	consulēs
Gen.	rēgum	mīlitum	consulum
Dat.	rēgibus	mīlitibus	consulibus
Abl.	rēgibus	mīlitibus	consulibus

Sing.		Plur.
Nom.	leō (m.), *lion*	leōnēs
Voc.	leō	leōnēs
Acc.	leōnem	leōnēs
Gen.	leōnis	leōnum
Dat.	leōnī	leōnibus
Abl.	leōne	leōnibus

Sing.

Nom.	caput (n.), *head*	opus (n.), *work*	carmen (n.) *song*
Voc.	caput	opus	carmen
Acc.	caput	opus	carmen
Gen.	capitis	operis	carminis
Dat.	capitī	operī	carminī
Abl.	capite	opere	carmine

Plur.

Nom.	capita	opera	carmina
Voc.	capita	opera	carmina
Acc.	capita	opera	carmina
Gen.	capitum	operum	carminum
Dat.	capitibus	operibus	carminibus
Abl.	capitibus	operibus	carminibus

(2) Nouns with **I**- Stems

(*a*) Nom. sing. in **-is, -er,** or **-ēs**

Sing.

Nom.	hostis (c.), *enemy*	imber (m.), *shower*	nūbēs (f.), *cloud*
Voc.	hostis	imber	nūbēs
Acc.	hostem	imbrem	nūbem
Gen.	hostis	imbris	nūbis
Dat.	hostī	imbrī	nūbī
Abl.	hoste	imbre	nūbe

Plur.

Nom.	hostēs	imbrēs	nūbēs
Voc.	hostēs	imbrēs	nūbēs
Acc.	hostēs (or -īs)	imbrēs (or -īs)	nūbēs (or -īs)
Gen.	hostium	imbrium	nūbium
Dat.	hostibus	imbribus	nūbibus
Abl.	hostibus	imbribus	nūbibus

Note. **Pater, patris,** *father*; **māter, mātris,** *mother*; **frāter, frātris,** *brother*, have Gen. pl. in **-um**; so also **iuvenis** (c.), *young person*, and **canis** (c.), *dog*. Abl. of **ignis** (m.), *fire*, is usually **ignī**.

(*b*) Neuter

Sing.

Nom.	cubīle (n.), *couch*	animal (n.), *animal*	calcar (n.), *spur*
Voc.	cubīle	animal	calcar
Acc.	cubīle	animal	calcar
Gen.	cubīlis	animālis	calcāris
Dat.	cubīlī	animālī	calcārī
Abl.	cubīlī	animālī	calcārī

Plur.

Nom.	cubīlia	animālia	calcāria
Voc.	cubīlia	animālia	calcāria
Acc.	cubīlia	animālia	calcāria
Gen.	cubīlium	animālium	calcārium
Dat.	cubīlibus	animālibus	calcāribus
Abl.	cubīlibus	animālibus	calcāribus

(*c*) Nom. sing. of one syllable, ending in two consonants; also Nom. ending in -tās

Sing.

Nom.	urbs (f.), *city*	pons (m.), *bridge*	cīvitās (f.), *state*
Voc.	urbs	pons	cīvitās
Acc.	urbem	pontem	cīvitātem
Gen.	urbis	pontis	cīvitātis
Dat.	urbī	pontī	cīvitātī
Abl.	urbe	ponte	cīvitāte

Plur.

Nom.	urbēs	pontēs	cīvitātēs
Voc.	urbēs	pontēs	cīvitātēs
Acc.	urbēs (or -īs)	pontēs (or -īs)	cīvitātēs (or -īs)
Gen.	urbium	pontium	cīvitātium
Dat.	urbibus	pontibus	cīvitātibus
Abl.	urbibus	pontibus	cīvitātibus

Note. Nox, noctis (f.), *night*, is declined in the same way.

(3) Irregular Nouns

Sing.

Nom.	**senex**(m.), *old*	**bōs**(c.), *ox*	**sūs** (c.), *pig*	**Iuppiter** (m.),
Voc.	**senex** [*man*	**bōs**	**sūs**	**Iuppiter** [*Jupiter*
Acc.	**senem**	**bovem**	**suem**	**Iovem**
Gen.	**senis**	**bovis**	**suis**	**Iovis**
Dat.	**senī**	**bovī**	**suī**	**Iovī**
Abl.	**sene**	**bove**	**sue**	**Iove**

Plur.

Nom.	**senēs**	**bovēs**	**suēs**	
Voc.	**senēs**	**bovēs**	**suēs**	no plur.
Acc.	**senēs**	**bovēs**	**suēs**	
Gen.	**senum**	**boum**	**suum**	
Dat.	**senibus**	⎰**bōbus** or	⎰**suibus** or	
Abl.	**senibus**	⎱**būbus**	⎱**subus**	

Sing.   *Plur.*

Nom.	**vīs** (f.), *force*	**vīrēs** (*strength*)
Voc.	—	**vīrēs**
Acc.	**vim**	**vīrēs**
Gen.	—	**vīrium**
Dat.	—	**vīribus**
Abl.	**vī**	**vīribus**

Sing.   *Plur.*

N.V.A.	**iter** (n.), *journey*	**itinera**
Gen.	**itineris**	**itinerum**
Dat.	**itinerī**	**itineribus**
Abl.	**itinere**	**itineribus**

4th Declension

Sing.   *Plur.*

Nom.	**gradus** (m.), *step*	**gradūs**
Voc.	**gradus**	**gradūs**
Acc.	**gradum**	**gradūs**
Gen.	**gradūs**	**graduum**
Dat.	**graduī**	**gradibus**
Abl.	**gradū**	**gradibus**

Sing.		Plur.
N.V.A.	**cornū** (n.), *horn*	**cornua**
Gen.	**cornūs**	**cornuum**
Dat.	**cornū**	**cornibus**
Abl.	**cornū**	**cornibus**

Note. **Domus** (f.), *house*, can be declined like **gradus** in all Cases except in the Abl. where it takes the form **domō.**

5th Declension

Sing.		Plur.		Sing.		Plur.
Nom.	**diēs** (m.), *day*	**diēs**		**rēs** (f.), *thing*		**rēs**
Voc.	**diēs**	**diēs**		**rēs**		**rēs**
Acc.	**diem**	**diēs**		**rem**		**rēs**
Gen.	**diēī**	**diērum**		**reī**		**rērum**
Dat.	**diēī**	**diēbus**		**reī**		**rēbus**
Abl.	**diē**	**diēbus**		**rē**		**rēbus**

Adjectives

(1) 1st and 2nd Declensions

(a) in -us, -a, -um: bonus, *good*

Sing.	M.	F.	N.
Nom.	**bonus**	**bona**	**bonum**
Voc.	**bone**	**bona**	**bonum**
Acc.	**bonum**	**bonam**	**bonum**
Gen.	**bonī**	**bonae**	**bonī**
Dat.	**bonō**	**bonae**	**bonō**
Abl.	**bonō**	**bonā**	**bonō**

Plur.			
Nom.	**bonī**	**bonae**	**bona**
Voc.	**bonī**	**bonae**	**bona**
Acc.	**bonōs**	**bonās**	**bona**
Gen.	**bonōrum**	**bonārum**	**bonōrum**
Dat.	**bonīs**	**bonīs**	**bonīs**
Abl.	**bonīs**	**bonīs**	**bonīs**

Note. **meus,** *my,* has Voc. sing. masc. **mī.**

(b) in **-er, -ra, -rum: niger,** *black*

Sing.	M.	F.	N.
Nom.	niger	nigra	nigrum
Voc.	niger	nigra	nigrum
Acc.	nigrum	nigram	nigrum
Gen.	nigrī	nigrae	nigrī
Dat.	nigrō	nigrae	nigrō
Abl.	nigrō	nigrā	nigrō

Plur.			
Nom.	nigrī	nigrae	nigra
Voc.	nigrī	nigrae	nigra
Acc.	nigrōs	nigrās	nigra
Gen.	nigrōrum	nigrārum	nigrōrum
Dat.	nigrīs	nigrīs	nigrīs
Abl.	nigrīs	nigrīs	nigrīs

(c) in **-er, -era, -erum: tener,** *tender*

Sing.	M.	F.	N.
Nom.	tener	tenera	tenerum
Voc.	tener	tenera	tenerum
Acc.	tenerum	teneram	tenerum
Gen.	tenerī	tenerae	tenerī
Dat.	tenerō	tenerae	tenerō
Abl.	tenerō	tenerā	tenerō

Plur.			
Nom.	tenerī	tenerae	tenera
Voc.	tenerī	tenerae	tenera
Acc.	tenerōs	tenerās	tenera
Gen.	tenerōrum	tenerārum	tenerōrum
Dat.	tenerīs	tenerīs	tenerīs
Abl.	tenerīs	tenerīs	tenerīs

Adjectives

(2) 3rd Declension

(i) I-Stems

(a) with three endings in Nom. sing.: ācer, *keen*

Sing.	M.	F.	N.
Nom.	ācer	ācris	ācre
Voc.	ācer	ācris	ācre
Acc.	ācrem	ācrem	ācre
Gen.	ācris	ācris	ācris
Dat.	ācrī	ācrī	ācrī
Abl.	ācrī	ācrī	ācrī

Plur.			
Nom.	ācrēs	ācrēs	ācria
Voc.	ācrēs	ācrēs	ācria
Acc.	ācrēs (or -īs)	ācrēs (or -īs)	ācria
Gen.	ācrium	ācrium	ācrium
Dat.	ācribus	ācribus	ācribus
Abl.	ācribus	ācribus	ācribus

Note. **Celer, celeris, celere,** *swift,* keeps **-er** throughout, and has Gen. plur. **celerum.**

(b) with two endings in Nom. sing.: omnis, *all*

Sing.	M. and F.	N.	Plur. M. and F.	N.
Nom.	omnis	omne	omnēs	omnia
Voc.	omnis	omne	omnēs	omnia
Acc.	omnem	omne	omnēs (or -īs)	omnia
Gen.	omnis	omnis	omnium	omnium
Dat.	omnī	omnī	omnibus	omnibus
Abl.	omnī	omnī	omnibus	omnibus

(c) with one ending in Nom. sing.: ingens, *huge*

Sing.	M. and F.	N.	Plur. M. and F.	N.
Nom.	ingens	ingens	ingentēs	ingentia
Voc.	ingens	ingens	ingentēs	ingentia
Acc.	ingentem	ingens	ingentēs (or -īs)	ingentia
Gen.	ingentis	ingentis	ingentium	ingentium
Dat.	ingentī	ingentī	ingentibus	ingentibus
Abl.	ingentī	ingentī	ingentibus	ingentibus

fēlix, *fortunate*

Sing.	M. and F.	N.	*Plur.* M. and F.	N.
Nom.	fēlix	fēlix	fēlicēs	fēlicia
Voc.	fēlix	fēlix	fēlicēs	fēlicia
Acc.	fēlicem	fēlix	fēlicēs (or -īs)	fēlicia
Gen.	fēlicis	fēlicis	fēlicium	fēlicium
Dat.	fēlicī	fēlicī	fēlicibus	fēlicibus
Abl.	fēlicī	fēlicī	fēlicibus	fēlicibus

(ii) Consonant Stems
   With one ending in Nom. sing.: **vetus,** *old*

Sing.	M. and F.	N.	*Plur.* M. and F.	N.
Nom.	vetus	vetus	veterēs	vetera
Voc.	vetus	vetus	veterēs	vetera
Acc.	veterem	vetus	veterēs	vetera
Gen.	veteris		veterum	
Dat.	veterī		veteribus	
Abl.	vetere		veteribus	

Note. **Inops, inopis,** *poor*; **memor, memoris,** *mindful*; **immemor, immemoris,** *forgetful*, have Abl. sing. in **-ī.**

Comparison of Adjectives

(1) (*a*) Regular

densus, *thick*	densior	densissimus
fortis, *brave*	fortior	fortissimus
ingens, *huge*	ingentior	ingentissimus
audax, *bold*	audācior	audācissimus
pulcher, *beautiful*	pulchrior	pulcherrimus
miser, *wretched*	miserior	miserrimus
ācer, *keen*	ācrior	ācerrimus

(*b*) With Superlative Irregular

facilis, *easy*	facilior	facillimus

So: **difficilis,** *difficult*; **similis,** *like*; **dissimilis,** *unlike*; **gracilis,** *slender*; **humilis,** *low*.

Declension of Comparatives (**except plūs**)

Stem			**altiōr-,** *higher, deeper*	
Sing.	M. and F.	N.	*Plur.* M. and F.	N.
N.V.	**altior**	**altius**	**altiōrēs**	**altiōra**
Acc.	**altiōrem**	**altius**	**altiōrēs**	**altiōra**
Gen.	**altiōris**		**altiōrum**	
Dat.	**altiōrī**		**altiōribus**	
Abl.	**altiōre**		**altiōribus**	

(2) Irregular

  (*a*) With different Stems

bonus, *good*	**melior**	**optimus**
malus, *bad*	**pēior**	**pessimus**
magnus, *great*	**māior**	**maximus**
parvus, *small*	**minor**	**minimus**
multus, *much*	**plūs** (n.)	**plūrimus**

Declension of **plūs**

Sing.	N.	*Plur.* M. and F.	N.
N.V.A.	**plūs**	**plūrēs**	**plūra**
Gen.	**plūris**	**plūrium**	
Dat.	—	**plūribus**	
Abl.	**plūre**	**plūribus**	

Note **Plūs** in sing. is a neut. Noun, followed by Gen. It is an Adj. in plur.

  (*b*) Compounds in **-dicus, -ficus, -volus,** etc.

maledicus, *evil-speaking*	**maledīcentior**	**maledīcentissimus**
magnificus, *splendid*	**magnificentior**	**magnificentissimus**
benevolus, *kind*	**benevolentior**	**benevolentissimus**
egēnus, *needy*	**egentior**	**egentissimus**
prōvidus, *provident*	**prōvidentior**	**prōvidentissimus**

  (*c*) Adjectives ending in **-us** preceded by a vowel, except those ending in **-quus**

dubius, *doubtful*	**magis dubius**	**maximē dubius**
But **antīquus,** *ancient*	**antīquior**	**antīquissimus**

(*d*) With no normal Positive

infrā, *below*	**inferior,** *lower*	**infimus, īmus,** *lowest*
prae, *before*	**prior,** *earlier, former*	**prīmus,** *first*
suprā, *above*	**superior,** *higher, earlier*	**suprēmus, summus, highest*
prope, *near*	**propior,** *nearer*	**proximus,** *nearest, next*
ultrā, *beyond*	**ulterior,** *further*	**ultimus,** *last*

Adverbs and their Comparison

(1) Regular

dignus	**dignē,** *worthily*	**dignius**	**dignissimē**
miser	**miserē,** *wretchedly*	**miserius**	**miserrimē**
pulcher	**pulchrē,** *beautifully*	**pulchrius**	**pulcherrimē**
ācer	**ācriter,** *keenly*	**ācrius**	**ācerrimē**
celer	**celeriter,** *swiftly*	**celerius**	**celerrimē**
fortis	**fortiter,** *bravely*	**fortius**	**fortissimē**
constans	**constanter,** *firmly*	**constantius**	**constantissimē**
But **audax**	**audacter,** *boldly*	**audācius**	**audācissimē**
facilis	**facile,** *easily*	**facilius**	**facillimē**

(2) Irregular

bonus	**bene,** *well*	**melius**	**optimē**
malus	**male,** *badly*	**pēius**	**pessimē**
magnus	**magnopere,** *greatly*	**magis**	**maximē**
parvus	**paulum,** *little*	**minus**	**minimē**
multus	**multum,** *much*	**plūs**	**plūrimum**

Note. **Magis** is *more*, of degree; **plūs** is *more*, of quantity.

diū, *for a long time*	**diūtius**	**diūtissimē**
nūper, *lately*	—	**nūperrimē**
—	**potius,** *rather*	**potissimum,** *especially*
saepe, *often*	**saepius**	**saepissimē**

Numerals

	Roman Numerals	Cardinals	Ordinals	Numeral Adverbs
1	I	ūnus, -a, -um	prīmus, -a, -um, *first*	semel, *once*
2	II	duo, duae, duo	secundus	bis, *twice*
3	III	trēs, tria	tertius	ter, *three times*
4	IV, IIII	quattuor	quartus	quater
5	V	quīnque	quīntus	quīnquiēs
6	VI	sex	sextus	sexiēs
7	VII	septem	septimus	septiēs
8	VIII	octō	octāvus	octiēs
9	IX	novem	nōnus	noviēs
10	X	decem	decimus	deciēs
11	XI	ūndecim	ūndecimus	ūndeciēs
12	XII	duodecim	duodecimus	duodeciēs
13	XIII	tredecim	tertius decimus	terdeciēs
14	XIV	quattuordecim	quartus decimus	quattuordeciēs
15	XV	quīndecim	quīntus decimus	quīndeciēs
16	XVI	sēdecim	sextus decimus	sēdeciēs
17	XVII	septendecim	septimus decimus	septiēsdeciēs
18	XVIII	duodēvīgintī or octōdecim	duodēvīcēsimus	duodēvīciēs
19	XIX	ūndēvīgintī or novendecim	ūndēvīcēsimus	ūndēvīciēs
20	XX	vīgintī	vīcēsimus	vīciēs
21	XXI	ūnus et vīgintī	ūnus et vīcēsimus	semel et vīciēs
22	XXII	duo et vīgintī	alter et vīcēsimus	bis et vīciēs
30	XXX	trīgintā	trīcēsimus	trīciēs
40	XL	quadrāgintā	quadrāgēsimus	quadrāgiēs
50	L	quīnquāgintā	quīnquāgēsimus	quīnquāgiēs
60	LX	sexāgintā	sexāgēsimus	sexāgiēs
70	LXX	septuāgintā	septuāgēsimus	septuāgiēs
80	LXXX	octōgintā	octōgēsimus	octōgiēs
90	XC	nōnāgintā	nōnāgēsimus	nōnāgiēs
100	C	centum	centēsimus	centiēs
200	CC	ducentī, -ae, -a	ducentēsimus	ducentiēs
300	CCC	trecentī	trecentēsimus	trecentiēs
400	CCCC	quadringentī	quadringentēsimus	quadringentiēs
500	D	quīngentī	quīngentēsimus	quīngentiēs
600	DC	sescentī	sescentēsimus	sescentiēs
700	DCC	septingentī	septingentēsimus	septingentiēs
800	DCCC	octingentī	octingentēsimus	octingentiēs
900	DCCCC	nōngentī	nōngentēsimus	nōngentiēs
1,000	M	mīlle	mīllēsimus	mīliēs
2,000	MM	duo mīlia	bis mīllēsimus	bis mīliēs

Sing.	M.	F.	N.
Nom.	ūnus	ūna	ūnum
Voc.	ūne	ūna	ūnum
Acc.	ūnum	ūnam	ūnum
Gen.	ūnĭus	ūnĭus	ūnĭus
Dat.	ūnī	ūnī	ūnī
Abl.	ūnō	ūnā	ūnō

Notes. Plural like **bonus**. Like **ūnus** are declined: **sōlus**, *only*; **tōtus**, *whole*; **nullus**, *no, none*; **ullus**, *any*.

	M.	F.	N.
Nom.	duo	duae	duo
Voc.	duo	duae	duo
Acc.	duōs or duo	duās	duo
Gen.	duōrum	duārum	duōrum
Dat.	duōbus	duābus	duōbus
Abl.	duōbus	duābus	duōbus

Note. Like **duo** is declined **ambō**, *both*.

	M. and F.	N.
Nom.	trēs	tria
Voc.	trēs	tria
Acc.	trēs or trīs	tria
Gen.	trium	trium
Dat.	tribus	tribus
Abl.	tribus	tribus

Notes (i). In Compound Numbers from 20 to 99, either the English order is followed, or the smaller comes first with **et**, e.g. **vīgintī trēs** or **trēs et vīgintī**, but **ūnus** generally comes first. After 100, the larger number comes first, with or without **et**, e.g. **ducentī et quinque** or **ducentī quinque**.

(ii) The only Cardinals from 1 to 100 that are declined are **ūnus, duo, trēs**; the hundreds from **ducentī** to **nongentī** are declined like the plur. of **bonus**, but with Gen. pl. in **-um**.

(iii) **Mille** is an indeclinable Adjective; **mille passūs**, *a mile*. The plur., **mīlia** (-ium, -ibus), is a Noun, always followed by the Gen., e.g. **duo mīlia passuum**, *two miles*.

Pronouns

(1) 1st and 2nd Persons

(*a*) Personal Pronouns

Sing.		*Plur.*
Nom.	**ego,** *I*	**nōs**
Acc.	**mē**	**nōs**
Gen.	**meī**	**nostrī, nostrum**
Dat.	**mihi**	**nōbīs**
Abl.	**mē**	**nōbīs**

Nom.	**tū,** *you* (also Voc.)	**vōs** (also Voc.)
Acc.	**tē**	**vōs**
Gen.	**tuī**	**vestrī, vestrum**
Dat.	**tibi**	**vōbīs**
Abl.	**tē**	**vōbīs**

(*b*) Reflexive Pronouns

As above, omitting the Nom. and Voc.

(*c*) Possessive Pronouns

1st Person, **meus** (Voc. **mī**), **mea, meum,** *my*; **noster, nostra, nostrum,** *our*.

2nd Person, **tuus, tua, tuum,** *your* (*of you*, sing.); **vester vestra, vestrum,** *your* (*of you*, plur.).

(2) 3rd Person

(*a*) Pronoun

There is no Personal Pronoun for the 3rd Person. Instead Latin uses the Demonstrative Pronoun, **is, ea, id.**

When used as a Personal Pronoun, **is, ea, id,** means *he, she, it.*

When used as a Demonstrative Pronoun or Adjective, **is, ea, id,** means *this* or *that* (without emphasis).

Sing.	M.	F.	N.	*Plur.*	M.	F.	N.
Nom.	**is**	**ea**	**id**		**eī**	**eae**	**ea**
Acc.	**eum**	**eam**	**id**		**eōs**	**eās**	**ea**
Gen.	**ēius**	**ēius**	**ēius**		**eōrum**	**eārum**	**eōrum**
Dat.	**eī**	**eī**	**eī**		**eīs**	**eīs**	**eīs**
Abl.	**eō**	**eā**	**eō**		**eīs**	**eīs**	**eīs**

(*b*) Reflexive Pronoun
Sing. and Plur., all genders

Acc.	**sē** or **sēsē**, *himself, herself, itself, themselves*
Gen.	**suī**
Dat.	**sibi**
Abl.	**sē** or **sēsē**

(*c*) Possessive Pronouns

(i) **ēius** (Gen. sing. of **is, ea, id**), *his, her, its*;
   eōrum, eārum, eōrum (Gen. plur. of **is, ea, id**), *their*, when
   these persons are **not** the same as the Subject of the
   sentence in which they occur.

(ii) **suus, sua, suum**, *his own, her own, its own, their own*, when
   these persons **are** the same as the Subject of the sentence in which they occur.

Demonstrative Pronouns
   (*a*) **hīc**, *this (near me)*

Sing.	M.	F.	N.	*Plur.*	M.	F.	N.
Nom.	**hīc**	**haec**	**hōc**		**hī**	**hae**	**haec**
Acc.	**hunc**	**hanc**	**hōc**		**hōs**	**hās**	**haec**
Gen.	**hūius**	**hūius**	**hūius**		**hōrum**	**hārum**	**hōrum**
Dat.	**hūīc**	**hūīc**	**hūīc**		**his**	**his**	**his**
Abl.	**hōc**	**hāc**	**hōc**		**his**	**his**	**his**

   (*b*) **ille**, *that (over there)*

Sing.	M.	F.	N.	*Plur.*	M.	F.	N.
Nom.	**ille**	**illa**	**illud**		**illī**	**illae**	**illa**
Acc.	**illum**	**illam**	**illud**		**illōs**	**illās**	**illa**
Gen.	**illĭus**	**illĭus**	**illĭus**		**illōrum**	**illārum**	**illōrum**
Dat.	**illī**	**illī**	**illī**		**illīs**	**illīs**	**illīs**
Abl.	**illō**	**illā**	**illō**		**illīs**	**illīs**	**illīs**

Note. Like **ille** is declined **iste, ista, istud**, *that (near you)*.

(c) **īdem,** *the same*

Sing.	M.	F.	N.	Plur. M.	F.	N.
Nom.	īdem	eadem	idem	eīdem or īdem	eaedem	eadem
Acc.	eundem	eandem	idem	eōsdem	eāsdem	eadem
Gen.	ēiusdem	ēiusdem	ēiusdem	eōrundem	eārundem	eōrundem
Dat.	eīdem	eīdem	eīdem	eīsdem or īsdem		
Abl.	eōdem	eādem	eōdem	eīsdem or īsdem		

Emphatic Pronoun, **ipse,** *self*

Sing.	M.	F.	N.	Plur. M.	F.	N.
Nom.	ipse	ipsa	ipsum	ipsī	ipsae	ipsa
Acc.	ipsum	ipsam	ipsum	ipsōs	ipsās	ipsa
Gen.	ipsĭus	ipsĭus	ipsĭus	ipsōrum	ipsārum	ipsōrum
Dat.	ipsī	ipsī	ipsī	ipsīs	ipsīs	ipsīs
Abl.	ipsō	ipsā	ipsō	ipsīs	ipsīs	ipsīs

Pronominal Adjectives

(a) **alius,** *other, another (of any number)*

Sing.	M.	F.	N.	Plur. M.	F.	N.
Nom.	alius	alia	aliud	aliī	aliae	alia
Acc.	alium	aliam	aliud	aliōs	aliās	alia
Gen.	alīus	alīus	alīus	aliōrum	aliārum	aliōrum
Dat.	aliī	aliī	aliī	aliīs	aliīs	aliīs
Abl.	aliō	aliā	aliō	aliīs	aliīs	aliīs

(b) **alter,** *the one* or *the other of two*

Sing.	M.	F.	N.	Plur. M.	F.	N.
N.	alter	altera	alterum	alterī	alterae	altera
A.	alterum	alteram	alterum	alterōs	alterās	altera
G.	alterĭus	alterĭus	alterĭus	alterōrum	alterārum	alterōrum
D.	alterī	alterī	alterī	alterīs	alterīs	alterīs
Ab.	alterō	alterā	alterō	alterīs	alterīs	alterīs

Note. Like **alter** are declined **neuter,** *neither;* **uter?** *which of two?* **uterque,** *each of two,* except that e is dropped before **r,** after the Nom. sing. masc.

6666666666

Relative Pronoun, quĭ, *who, which*

Sing.	M.	F.	N.	Plur.	M.	F.	N.
Nom.	quĭ	quae	quod		quĭ	quae	quae
Acc.	quem	quam	quod		quōs	quās	quae
Gen.	cūius	cūius	cūius		quōrum	quārum	quōrum
Dat.	cūī	cūī	cūī		quibus or quīs		
Abl.	quō	quā	quō		quibus or quīs		

Interrogative Pronoun, quis? *who?* **quī?** *what?*

Sing.	M.	F.	N.	
Nom.	quis	(quis)	quid	used as Pronouns
	quī	quae	quod	used as Adjectives
Acc.	quem	quam	quid	*Note.* The remaining Cases
	quem	quam	quod	are declined like the Relative Pronoun.

Indefinite Pronoun

(a) **quis,** *anyone;* **quĭ,** *any* (used after **sī, nisi, num, nē**)

Sing.	M.	F.	N.	
Nom.	⎰quis	qua	quid	used as Pronouns
	⎱quĭ	quae	quod	used as Adjectives
		or qua		
Acc.	⎰quem	quam	quid	*Note.* The remaining Cases
	⎱quem	quam	quod	are declined like the Relative Pronoun.

(b) Compounds of **quis,** *any*

	Sing.	M.	F.	N.	
(i)	Nom.	quīdam	quaedam	quiddam (quoddam)	*a certain person, a certain*
	Acc.	quendam	quandam	quiddam (quoddam)	
	G. pl.	quōrundam	quārundam	quōrundam	
(ii)	Nom.	quisque	quaeque	quidque or quicque (quodque)	*each one, each*
(iii)	Nom.	quisquam	—	quidquam or quicquam	*anyone,* after negative

Verbs

Verbs

The Verb **sum**

Indicative	Subjunctive	Imperative
Present		
sum	**sim**	**es, estō** (s.)
es	**sīs**	**este** (pl.)
est	**sit**	
sumus	**sīmus**	
estis	**sītis**	
sunt	**sint**	

Future

erō
eris
erit
erimus
eritis
erunt

Imperfect

		Infinitives
eram	**essem**	
erās	**essēs**	Pres. **esse**
erat	**esset**	Perf. **fuisse**
erāmus	**essēmus**	Fut. **futūrus esse**
erātis	**essētis**	or **fore**
erant	**essent**	

Perfect

fui	**fuerim**
fuisti	**fueris**
fuit	**fuerit**
fuimus	**fuerīmus**
fuistis	**fuerītis**
fuērunt	**fuerint**

Future Perfect

	Participle
fuerō	
fueris	Fut. **futūrus**
fuerit	
fuerimus	
fueritis	
fuerint	

Pluperfect

fueram	**fuissem**
fuerās	**fuissēs**
fuerat	**fuisset**
fuerāmus	**fuissēmus**
fuerātis	**fuissētis**
fuerant	**fuissent**

Verbs

1st Conjugation, Active

Indicative	Subjunctive	Imperative

Present

amō	amem	amā (s.)
amās	amēs	amāte (pl.)
amat	amet	
amāmus	amēmus	
amātis	amētis	
amant	ament	

Future

amābō
amābis
amābit
amābimus
amābitis
amābunt

Imperfect

amābam	amārem		**Infinitives**
amābās	amārēs	Pres.	amāre
amābat	amāret	Perf.	amāvisse
amābāmus	amārēmus	Fut.	amātūrus esse
amābātis	amārētis		
amābant	amārent		

Perfect

amāvī	amāverim
amāvistī	amāverīs
amāvit	amāverit
amāvimus	amāverīmus
amāvistis	amāverītis
amāvērunt	amāverint

Future Perfect

amāverō		**Participles**
amāveris	Pres.	amans
amāverit	Fut.	amātūrus
amāverimus		
amāveritis		
amāverint		

Pluperfect

amāveram	amāvissem	**Supine**
amāverās	amāvissēs	amātum
amāverat	amāvisset	
amāverāmus	amāvissēmus	
amāverātis	amāvissētis	
amāverant	amāvissent	

Verbs 179

1st Conjugation, Passive

	Indicative	Subjunctive	Imperative
Present	amor	amer	amāre (s.)
	amāris	amēris	amāminī (pl.)
	amātur	amētur	
	amāmur	amēmur	
	amāminī	amēminī	
	amantur	amentur	

Future

amābor
amāberis
amābitur
amābimur
amābiminī
amābuntur

Imperfect / Infinitives

Indicative	Subjunctive	
amābar	amārer	
amābāris	amārēris	Pres. amārī
amābātur	amārētur	Perf. amātus esse
amābāmur	amārēmur	Fut. amātum īrī
amābāminī	amārēminī	
amābantur	amārentur	

Perfect

amātus sum	amātus sim
amātus es	amātus sīs
amātus est	amātus sit
amātī sumus	amātī sīmus
amātī estis	amātī sītis
amātī sunt	amātī sint

Future Perfect / Participle

amātus erō
amātus eris — Perf. amātus
amātus erit
amātī erimus
amātī eritis
amātī erunt

Pluperfect

amātus eram	amātus essem
amātus erās	amātus essēs
amātus erat	amātus esset
amātī erāmus	amātī essēmus
amātī erātis	amātī essētis
amātī erant	amātī essent

Verbs

2nd Conjugation, Active

Indicative	Subjunctive	Imperative
Present		
moneō	moneam	monē (s.)
monēs	moneās	monēte (pl.)
monet	moneat	
monēmus	moneāmus	
monētis	moneātis	
monent	moneant	

Future

monēbō
monēbis
monēbit
monēbimus
monēbitis
monēbunt

Imperfect

		Infinitives
monēbam	monērem	
monēbās	monērēs	Pres. monēre
monēbat	monēret	Perf. monuisse
monēbāmus	monērēmus	Fut. monitūrus esse
monēbātis	monērētis	
monēbant	monērent	

Perfect

monuī	monuerim
monuistī	monueris
monuit	monuerit
monuimus	monuerīmus
monuistis	monuerītis
monuērunt	monuerint

Future Perfect

		Participles
monuerō		
monueris		Pres. monens
monuerit		Fut. monitūrus
monuerimus		
monueritis		
monuerint		

Pluperfect

		Supine
monueram	monuissem	
monuerās	monuissēs	monitum
monuerat	monuisset	
monuerāmus	monuissēmus	
monuerātis	monuissētis	
monuerant	monuissent	

2nd Conjugation, Passive

Indicative	Subjunctive	Imperative
Present		
moneor	monear	monēre (s.)
monēris	moneāris	monēminī (pl.)
monētur	moneātur	
monēmur	moneāmur	
monēminī	moneāminī	
monentur	moneantur	

Future

monēbor
monēberis
monēbitur
monēbimur
monēbiminī
monēbuntur

Imperfect

Indicative	Subjunctive	Infinitives
monēbar	monērer	
monēbāris	monērēris	Pres. monērī
monēbātur	monērētur	Perf. monitus esse
monēbāmur	monērēmur	Fut. monitum īrī
monēbāminī	monērēminī	
monēbantur	monērentur	

Perfect

monitus sum	monitus sim
monitus es	monitus sīs
monitus est	monitus sit
monitī sumus	monitī sīmus
monitī estis	monitī sītis
monitī sunt	monitī sint

Future Perfect

	Participle
monitus erō	
monitus eris	Perf. monitus
monitus erit	
monitī erimus	
monitī eritis	
monitī erunt	

Pluperfect

monitus eram	monitus essem
monitus erās	monitus essēs
monitus erat	monitus esset
monitī erāmus	monitī essēmus
monitī erātis	monitī essētis
monitī erant	monitī essent

Verbs

3rd Conjugation Active

Indicative	Subjunctive	Imperative
Present		
regō	regam	rege (s.)
regis	regās	regite (pl.)
regit	regat	
regimus	regāmus	(But dīc, dūc, fac, fer)
regitis	regātis	
regunt	regant	

Future

regam
regēs
reget
regēmus
regētis
regent

Imperfect

		Infinitives
regēbam	regerem	
regēbās	regerēs	Pres. regere
regēbat	regeret	Perf. rexisse
regēbāmus	regerēmus	Fut. rectūrus esse
regēbātis	regerētis	
regēbant	regerent	

Perfect

rexī	rexerim
rexistī	rexeris
rexit	rexerit
reximus	rexerīmus
rexistis	rexerītis
rexērunt	rexerint

Future Perfect

	Participles
rexerō	
rexeris	Pres. regens
rexerit	Fut. rectūrus
rexerimus	
rexeritis	
rexerint	

Pluperfect

		Supine
rexeram	rexissem	
rexerās	rexissēs	rectum
rexerat	rexisset	
rexerāmus	rexissēmus	
rexerātis	rexissētis	
rexerant	rexissent	

3rd Conjugation, Passive

Indicative	Subjunctive	Imperative

Present

regor	regar	regere (s.)
regeris	regāris	regiminī (pl.)
regitur	regātur	
regimur	regāmur	
regiminī	regāminī	
reguntur	regantur	

Future

regar
regēris
regētur
regēmur
regēminī
regentur

Imperfect

Infinitives

regēbar	regerer		
regēbāris	regerēris	Pres.	regī
regēbātur	regerētur	Perf.	rectus esse
regēbāmur	regerēmur	Fut.	rectum īrī
regēbāminī	regerēminī		
regēbantur	regerentur		

Perfect

rectus sum	rectus sim
rectus es	rectus sīs
rectus est	rectus sit
rectī sumus	rectī sīmus
rectī estis	rectī sītis
rectī sunt	rectī sint

Future Perfect

Participle

rectus erō	
rectus eris	Perf. rectus
rectus erit	
rectī erimus	
rectī eritis	
rectī erunt	

Pluperfect

rectus eram	rectus essem
rectus erās	rectus essēs
rectus erat	rectus esset
rectī erāmus	rectī essēmus
rectī erātis	rectī essētis
rectī erant	rectī essent

4th Conjugation, Active

Indicative	Subjunctive	Imperative
Present		
audiō	audiam	audī (s.)
audīs	audiās	audīte (pl.)
audit	audiat	
audīmus	audiāmus	
audītis	audiātis	
audiunt	audiant	
Future		
audiam		
audiēs		
audiet		
audiēmus		
audiētis		
audient		

Imperfect		Infinitives	
audiēbam	audīrem		
audiēbās	audīrēs	Pres.	audīre
audiēbat	audīret	Perf.	audīvisse
audiēbāmus	audīrēmus	Fut.	audītūrus esse
audiēbātis	audīrētis		
audiēbant	audīrent		

Perfect

audivī	audīverim
audīvistī	audīveris
audīvit	audīverit
audīvimus	audīverimus
audīvistis	audīverītis
audīvērunt	audīverint

Future Perfect		Participles	
audīverō			
audīveris		Pres.	audiens
audīverit		Fut.	audītūrus
audīverimus			
audīveritis			
audīverint			

Pluperfect		Supine
audīveram	audīvissem	
audīverās	audīvissēs	auditum
audīverat	audīvisset	
audīverāmus	audīvissēmus	
audīverātis	audīvissētis	
audīverant	audīvissent	

Verbs

185

4th Conjugation, Passive

Indicative	Subjunctive	Imperative
Present		
audior	audiar	audīre (s.)
audīris	audiāris	audīminī (pl.)
audītur	audiātur	
audīmur	audiāmur	
audīminī	audiāminī	
audiuntur	audiantur	

Future
audiar
audiēris
audiētur
audiēmur
audiēminī
audientur

Imperfect		Infinitives
audiēbar	audīrer	
audiēbāris	audīrēris	Pres. audīrī
audiēbātur	audīrētur	Perf. audītus esse
audiēbāmur	audīrēmur	Fut. audītum īrī
audiēbāminī	audīrēminī	
audiēbantur	audīrentur	

Perfect

audītus sum	audītus sim
audītus es	audītus sīs
audītus est	audītus sit
audītī sumus	audītī sīmus
audītī estis	audītī sītis
audītī sunt	audītī sint

Future Perfect   Participle

audītus erō
audītus eris   Perf. audītus
audītus erit
audītī erimus
audītī eritis
audītī erunt

Pluperfect

audītus eram	audītus essem
audītus erās	audītus essēs
audītus erat	audītus esset
audītī erāmus	audītī essēmus
audītī erātis	audītī essētis
audītī erant	audītī essent

Deponent Verbs

1st Conjugation

	Indicative	Subjunctive	Imperative
Pres.	moror, *I delay*	morer	morāre (s.), morāminī (pl.)
Fut.	morābor		
Imperf.	morābar	morārer	Infinitives
Perf.	morātus sum	morātus sim	Pres. morārī
Fut. Perf.	morātus erō		Perf. morātus esse
Pluperf.	morātus eram	morātus essem	Fut. morātūrus esse

Participles—Present, morans; Future, morātūrus; Perfect, morātus.
Supine—morātum.

2nd Conjugation

	Indicative	Subjunctive	Imperative
Pres.	vereor, *I fear*	verear	verēre (s.), verēminī (pl.)
Fut.	verēbor		
Imperf.	verēbar	verērer	Infinitives
Perf.	veritus sum	veritus sim	Pres. verērī
Fut. Perf.	veritus erō		Perf. veritus esse
Pluperf.	veritus eram	veritus essem	Fut. veritūrus esse

Participles—Present, verens; Future, veritūrus; Perfect, veritus.
Supine—veritum.

3rd Conjugation

	Indicative	Subjunctive	Imperative
Pres.	ūtor, *I use*	ūtar	ūtere (s.), ūtiminī (pl.)
Fut.	ūtar		
Imperf.	ūtēbar	ūterer	Infinitives
Perf.	ūsus sum	ūsus sim	Pres. ūtī
Fut. Perf.	ūsus erō		Perf. ūsus esse
Pluperf.	ūsus eram	ūsus essem	Fut. ūsūrus esse

Participles—Present, ūtens; Future, ūsūrus; Perfect, ūsus.
Supine—ūsum.

4th Conjugation

	Indicative	Subjunctive	Imperative
Pres.	mentior, *I tell a lie*	mentiar	mentīre (s.), mentīminī (pl.
Fut.	mentiar		
Imperf.	mentiēbar	mentīrer	Infinitives
Perf.	mentītus sum	mentītus sim	Pres. mentīrī
Fut. Perf.	mentītus erō		Perf. mentītus esse
Pluperf.	mentītus eram	mentītus essem	Fut. mentītūrus esse

Participles—Present, mentiens; Future, mentītūrus; Perfect, mentītus.
Supine—mentītum.

Verbs of 3rd Conjugation in -iō

	Active		Passive	
	Indicative	Subjunctive	Indicative	Subjunctive

Present

Indicative	Subjunctive	Indicative	Subjunctive
capiō, *I take*	capiam	capior	capiar
capis	capiās	caperis	capiāris
capit	capiat	capitur	capiātur
capimus	capiāmus	capimur	capiāmur
capitis	capiātis	capiminī	capiāminī
capiunt	capiant	capiuntur	capiantur

Future

Indicative	Indicative
capiam	capiar
capiēs	capiēris
capiet	capiētur
capiēmus	capiēmur
capiētis	capiēminī
capient	capientur

Imperfect

Indicative	Subjunctive	Indicative	Subjunctive
capiēbam	caperem	capiēbar	caperer
capiēbās	caperēs	capiēbāris	caperēris
capiēbat	caperet	capiēbātur	caperētur
capiēbāmus	caperēmus	capiēbāmur	caperēmur
capiēbātis	caperētis	capiēbāminī	caperēminī
capiēbant	caperent	capiēbantur	caperentur

Imperative

cape, capite (but **fac**)   capere, capiminī

Infinitives

Pres.	capere		Pres.	capī
Perf.	cēpisse		Perf.	captus esse
Fut.	captūrus esse		Fut.	captum īrī

Perfect Tenses follow the 3rd Conjugation, Active, **cēpī**, etc.; Passive, **captus sum**, etc.

Participles—Present, **capiens**; Future, **captūrus**; Perfect, **captus**.
Supine—**captum**.

The following Verbs and their compounds are conjugated in Present Stem Tenses like the above: **capiō, cupiō, faciō, fodiō, fugiō, iaciō, rapiō**; **-spiciō** (Compounds only); Deponent—**gradior** and Compounds, **patior, morior**. **Orior** follows 4th Conjugation except for **oreris, oritur**, in Pres. Indic., and **orerer, orerētur, orerentur**, in Imperf. Subj.

For Passive of **faciō** and its Compounds, see next page.

Fīō, *I become* or *am made*

Present Stem Tenses and forms for the Passive of **faciō** are supplied by **fīō**, but the Compounds **cōnficiō, interficiō, praeficiō, reficiō** all have a regular Passive, e.g. **cōnficior**, Infin., **cōnficī**.

	Indicative	Subjunctive	Imperative

Present

	fīō	**fīam**	**fī** (s.)
	fīs	**fīās**	**fīte** (pl.)
	fit	**fīat**	
	(**fīmus**)	**fīāmus**	
	(**fītis**)	**fīātis**	
	fīunt	**fīant**	

Future   Pres. Infinitive

fīam	
fīēs	**fierī**
fīet	
fīēmus	
fīētis	
fīent	

Imperfect

fīēbam	**fierem**	
fīēbās	**fierēs**	
fīēbat	**fieret**	
fīēbāmus	**fierēmus**	
fīēbātis	**fierētis**	
fīēbant	**fierent**	

Perfect Tenses are formed regularly from the Supine, **factus sum**, etc.

Perfect Infinitive, **factus esse**; Future Infinitive, **factum īrī**.

Verbs

Possum, posse, potuī, *I am able*

Indicative	Subjunctive

Present

possum	possim
potes	possīs
potest	possit
possumus	possīmus
potestis	possītis
possunt	possint

Future

poterō
poteris
poterit
poterimus
poteritis
poterunt

Imperfect

Indicative	Subjunctive	Infinitives	
poteram	possem		
poterās	possēs	Pres.	posse
poterat	posset	Perf.	potuisse
poterāmus	possēmus		
poterātis	possētis		
poterant	possent		

Perfect

potuī	potuerim
potuistī	potuerīs
potuit	potuerit
potuimus	potuerīmus
potuistis	potuerītis
potuērunt	potuerint

Future Perfect

potuerō
potueris
potuerit
potuerimus
potueritis
potuerint

Pluperfect

potueram	potuissem
potuerās	potuissēs
potuerat	potuisset
potuerāmus	potuissēmus
potuerātis	potuissētis
potuerant	potuissent

190 *Verbs*

Volō, nōlō, mālō

Indicative	Subjunctive	Indicative	Subjunctive
Present			
volō, *I wish*	velim	nōlō, *I do not wish* nōlim	
vīs	velīs	nōnvīs	nōlīs
vult	velit	nōnvult	nōlit
volumus	velīmus	nōlumus	nōlīmus
vultis	velītis	nōnvultis	nōlītis
volunt	velint	nōlunt	nōlint

Future

volam
volēs, etc.

nōlam
nōlēs, etc.

Imperfect

volēbam	vellem	nōlēbam	nollem
volēbās	vellēs	nōlēbās	nollēs
volēbat	vellet	nōlēbat	nollet
volēbāmus	vellēmus	nōlēbāmus	nollēmus
volēbātis	vellētis	nōlēbātis	nollētis
volēbant	vellent	nōlēbant	nollent

Present — Imperative

mālō, *I prefer*	mālim
māvīs	mālis
māvult	mālit
mālumus	mālīmus
māvultis	mālītis
mālunt	mālint

nōlī (s.)
nōlīte (pl.)
(volō and mālō have none)

Future — Infinitive

mālam
mālēs, etc.

Pres. velle
nolle
malle

Imperfect

mālēbam	mallem
mālēbās	mallēs
mālēbat	mallet
mālēbāmus	mallēmus
mālēbātis	mallētis
mālēbant	mallent

Participle

Pres. volens
nōlens
—

Tenses formed from the Perfect Bases are regular: voluī, nōluī, māluī; Perfect Infinitives, voluisse, nōluisse, māluisse.

Eō, īre, iī, itum, *I go*

Indicative	Subjunctive	Imperative
Present		
eō	eam	ī (s.)
īs	eās	īte (pl.)
it	eat	
īmus	eāmus	
ītis	eātis	
eunt	eant	

Future

ībō
ībis
ībit
ībimus
ībitis
ībunt

Imperfect

		Infinitives
ībam	īrem	
ībās	īrēs	Pres. īre
ībat	īret	Perf. isse
ībāmus	īrēmus	Fut. itūrus esse
ībātis	īrētis	
ībant	īrent	

Perfect

iī	ierim
istī	ierīs
iit	ierit
iimus	ierīmus
istis	ierītis
iērunt	ierint

Future Perfect

		Participles
ierō		Pres. iens (Stem eunt-)
ieris, etc.		Fut. itūrus

Pluperfect

		Supine
ieram	issem	
ierās, etc.	issēs, etc.	itum

-iisse is found as well as -isse in Perfect Infin. of abeō, adeō, pereō, subeō.

Compounds of eō which are Transitive are conjugated in the Passive Voice, e.g. transīrī.

Ferō, ferre, tulī, lātum, *I bear*

Active		Passive	
Indicative	Subjunctive	Indicative	Subjunctive

Present

ferō	feram	feror	ferar
fers	ferās	ferris	ferāris
fert	ferat	fertur	ferātur
ferimus	ferāmus	ferimur	ferāmur
fertis	ferātis	feriminī	ferāminī
ferunt	ferant	feruntur	ferantur

Future

feram		ferar	
ferēs		ferēris	
feret		ferētur	
ferēmus		ferēmur	
ferētis		ferēminī	
ferent		ferentur	

Imperfect

ferēbam	ferrem	ferēbar	ferrer
ferēbās	ferrēs	ferēbāris	ferrēris
ferēbat	ferret	ferēbātur	ferrētur
ferēbāmus	ferrēmus	ferēbāmur	ferrēmur
ferēbātis	ferrētis	ferēbāminī	ferrēminī
ferēbant	ferrent	ferēbantur	ferrentur

Imperative

fer, ferte	ferre, feriminī

Infinitives

Pres.	ferre		Pres.	ferrī
Perf.	tulisse		Perf.	lātus esse
Fut.	lātūrus esse		Fut.	lātum īrī

Perfect Tenses follow the 3rd Conjugation, Active, **tulī**, etc.; Passive, **lātus sum**, etc.

Participles—Present, **ferens**; Future, **lātūrus**; Perfect, **lātus**.

Supine—**lātum**.

Coepī, *I began* or *have begun*

This Verb in Perfect-Stem Tenses is conjugated like **rexī**, etc. Infinitive, **coepisse**. Future Participle, **coeptūrus**.

Verbs

Principal parts of Verbs

(The Future Participle is given instead of a Supine where no other form from the Supine-Base is in common use.)

First Conjugation

Present	Infinitive	Perfect	Supine	
secō	-āre	secuī	sectum	*I cut*
sonō	-āre	sonuī	sonitum	*I sound*
vetō	-āre	vetuī	vetitum	*I forbid*
iuvō	-āre	iūvī	iūtum	*I help*
dō	-are	dedī	datum	*I give*
stō	-āre	stetī	statum	*I stand*
praestō	-āre	praestitī	praestitum	*I show*

Second Conjugation

Present	Infinitive	Perfect	Supine	
doceō	-ēre	docuī	doctum	*I teach*
ferveō	-ēre	ferbuī	—	*I glow*
teneō	-ēre	tenuī	-tentum	*I hold*
retineō	-ēre	retinuī	retentum	*I hold back, keep*
recenseō	-ēre	recensuī	recensum	*I review*
dēleō	-ēre	dēlēvī	dēlētum	*I destroy*
fleō	-ēre	flēvī	flētum	*I weep*
impleō	-ēre	implēvī	implētum	*I fill*
ardeō	-ēre	arsī	(arsūrus)	*I am on fire*
augeō	-ēre	auxī	auctum	*I increase* (tr.)
fulgeō	-ēre	fulsī	—	*I shine*
haereō	-ēre	haesī	(haesūrus)	*I stick* (intr.)
iubeō	-ēre	iussī	iussum	*I order*
maneō	-ēre	mansī	(mansūrus)	*I remain*
rideō	-ēre	rīsī	rīsum	*I laugh*
suādeō	-ēre	suāsī	suāsum	*I urge, advise*
prandeō	-ēre	prandī	pransum	*I breakfast*
respondeō	-ēre	respondī	responsum	*I reply*
caveō	-ēre	cāvī	cautum	*I am on my guard (against)*
faveō	-ēre	fāvī	fautum	*I favour*
moveō	-ēre	mōvī	mōtum	*I move* (tr.)
sedeō	-ēre	sēdī	sessum	*I sit*
obsideō	-ēre	obsēdī	obsessum	*I besiege*
videō	-ēre	vīdī	vīsum	*I see*
voveō	-ēre	vōvī	vōtum	*I vow, dedicate*
pendeō	-ēre	pependī	—	*I hang* (intr.)

Third Conjugation

Present	Infinitive	Perfect	Supine	
intellegō	-ere	intellexī	intellectum	*I understand*
neglegō	-ere	neglexī	neglectum	*I neglect*
pergō	-ere	perrexī	perrectum	*I proceed*
porrigō	-ere	porrexī	porrectum	*I stretch* (tr.)
surgō	-ere	surrexī	surrectum	*I rise*
tegō	-ere	texī	tectum	*I cover*
afflīgō	-ere	afflīxī	afflictum	*I dash* (tr.)
cingō	-ere	cinxī	cinctum	*I surround*
contemnō	-ere	contempsī	contemptum	*I despise*
dīcō	-ere	dīxī	dictum	*I say*
dūcō	-ere	duxī	ductum	*I lead*
fingō	-ere	finxī	fictum	*I imagine, feign*
gerō	-ere	gessī	gestum	*I carry*
instruō	-ere	instruxī	instructum	*I draw up, equip*
iungō	-ere	iunxī	iunctum	*I join*
scrībō	-ere	scripsī	scriptum	*I write*
sūmō	-ere	sumpsī	sumptum	*I take*
trahō	-ere	traxī	tractum	*I drag*
vehō	-ere	vexī	vectum	*I carry*
vīvō	-ere	vixī	victum	*I live*
cēdō	-ere	cessī	cessum	*I go away, yield*
claudō	-ere	clausī	clausum	*I shut*
dīvidō	-ere	dīvīsī	dīvīsum	*I divide*
fīgō	-ere	fixī	fixum	*I fix*
laedō	-ere	laesī	laesum	*I hurt, damage*
lūdō	-ere	lūsī	lūsum	*I play*
mergō	-ere	mersī	mersum	*I sink* (tr.)
mittō	-ere	misī	missum	*I send*
premō	-ere	pressī	pressum	*I press*
opprimō	-ere	oppressī	oppressum	*I overwhelm*
vādō	-ere	-vāsī	-vāsum	*I go, stride*
cognoscō	-ere	cognōvī	cognitum	*I find out*
crescō	-ere	crēvī	crētum	*I grow*
pascō	-ere	pāvī	pastum	*I feed* (tr.)
quiescō	-ere	quiēvī	quiētum	*I rest*
sinō	-ere	sīvī	situm	*I allow*
sternō	-ere	strāvī	strātum	*I strew*
consenescō	-ere	consenuī	—	*I grow old*
consulō	-ere	consuluī	consultum	*I consult*
dēserō	-ere	dēseruī	dēsertum	*I desert*
gemō	-ere	gemuī	gemitum	*I groan*
incolō	-ere	incoluī	—	*I inhabit*
occumbō	-ere	occubuī	occubitum	*I die*
pōnō	-ere	posuī	positum	*I place*
arcessō	-ere	arcessivī	arcessitum	*I send for*
lacessō	-ere	lacessivī	lacessitum	*I provoke*
petō	-ere	petivī	petitum	*I seek*
quaerō	-ere	quaesivī	quaesitum	*seek, ask*

Present	Infinitive	Perfect	Supine	
acuō	-ere	acuī	acūtum	*I sharpen*
constituō	-ere	constituī	constitūtum	*I determine*
induō	-ere	induī	indūtum	*I put on*
metuō	-ere	metuī	—	*I fear*
minuō	-ere	minuī	minūtum	*I lessen*
ruō	-ere	ruī	(ruitūrus)	*I rush*
ascendō	-ere	ascendī	ascensum	*I climb*
bibō	-ere	bibī	—	*I drink*
comprehendō	-ere	comprehendī	comprehensum	*I seize*
contendō	-ere	contendī	contentum	*I march, fight*
dēfendō	-ere	dēfendī	dēfensum	*I defend*
incendō	-ere	incendī	incensum	*I set on fire*
ostendō	-ere	ostendī	ostensum⎫ ostentum⎭	*I show*
revellō	-ere	revellī	revulsum	*I pull away*
solvō	-ere	solvī	solūtum	*I loose, pay*
suspendō	-ere	suspendī	suspensum	*I hang* (tr.)
vertō	-ere	vertī	versum	*I turn* (tr.)
vīsō	-ere	vīsī	vīsum	*I visit*
volvō	-ere	volvī	volūtum	*I roll* (tr.)
agō	-ere	ēgī	actum	*I do, drive, spend (time)*
cōgō	-ere	coēgī	coactum	*I compel*
redigō	-ere	redēgī	redactum	*I reduce*
emō	-ere	ēmī	emptum	*I buy*
frangō	-ere	frēgī	fractum	*I break* (tr.)
fundō	-ere	fūdī	fūsum	*I pour, rout*
legō	-ere	lēgī	lectum	*I choose, read*
colligō	-ere	collēgī	collectum	*I collect*
dēligō	-ere	dēlēgī	dēlectum	*I choose*
relinquō	-ere	relīquī	relictum	*I leave behind*
rumpō	-ere	rūpī	ruptum	*I break* (tr.)
vincō	-ere	vīcī	victum	*I conquer*
abdō	-ere	abdidī	abditum	*I hide*

So also: most compounds of dō—addō, *I add*; condō, *I found, hide*; crēdō, *I believe*; dēdō, *I give up*; prōdō, *I betray*; reddō, *I give back*; trādō, *I hand over* or *down*; vendō, *I sell*; but circumdō, -dare, -dedī, -datum, *I surround*.

cadō	-ere	cecidī	cāsum	*I fall*
excidō	-ere	excidī	—	*I fall out*
incidō	-ere	incidī	—	*I fall into*
caedō	-ere	cecīdī	caesum	*I cut, beat, kill*
occīdō	-ere	occīdī	occīsum	*I kill*
succīdō	-ere	succīdī	succīsum	*I cut through, fell*
canō	-ere	cecinī	—	*I sing*
currō	-ere	cucurrī	cursum	*I run*

concurrō, perf. concurri; dēcurrō, perfect usually dēcucurrī; prōcurrō, perf. prōcurrī or prōcucurrī; succurrō, perf. succurrī.

Verbs

Present	Infinitive	Perfect	Supine	
dēsistō	-ere	dēstitī	dēstitum	*I cease*
discō	-ere	didicī	—	*I learn*
fallō	-ere	fefellī	falsum	*I deceive*
parcō	-ere	pepercī	parsum	*I spare*
pellō	-ere	pepulī	pulsum	*I drive*

compound perfects—compulī, expulī, reppulī

poscō	-ere	poposcī	—	*I demand*
resistō	-ere	restitī	—	*I resist*
tangō	-ere	tetigī	tactum	*I touch*
attingō	-ere	attigī	attactum	*I reach*

-iō Verbs of mixed Conjugation

conspiciō	-ere	conspexī	conspectum	*I catch sight of*
percutiō	-ere	percussī	percussum	*I strike*
cupiō	-ere	cupīvī	cupītum	*I desire*
rapiō	-ere	rapuī	raptum	*I seize*
capiō	-ere	cēpī	captum	*I take*
faciō	-ere	fēcī	factum	*I make*
fodiō	-ere	fōdī	fossum	*I dig*
fugiō	-ere	fūgī	(fugitūrus)	*I flee*
iaciō	-ere	iēcī	iactum	*I throw*

(For list of compounds, see Chapter 17)

Fourth Conjugation

sepeliō	-īre	sepelīvī	sepultum	*I bury*
aperiō	-īre	aperuī	apertum	*I open*
saliō	-īre	saluī	—	*I leap, dance*
dēsiliō	-īre	dēsiluī	dēsultum	*I leap down*
transiliō	-īre	transiluī	—	*I leap over*
saepiō	-īre	saepsī	saeptum	*I enclose*
sentiō	-īre	sensī	sensum	*I feel, perceive*
vinciō	-īre	vinxī	vinctum	*I bind*
reperiō	-īre	repperī	repertum	*I discover*
veniō	-īre	vēnī	ventum	*I come*

Deponent and Semi-Deponent Verbs

Second Conjugation

confiteor	-ērī	confessus sum	*I confess*
reor	-ērī	ratus sum	*I think*
tueor	-ērī	—	*I defend, protect*

Semi-Deponent

soleō	-ēre	solitus sum	*I am accustomed*
audeō	-ēre	ausus sum	*I dare*
gaudeō	-ēre	gāvīsus sum	*I rejoice*

Third Conjugation

fruor	-ī	**fructus sum**	*I enjoy*
īrascor	-ī	**īrātus sum**	*I am angry*
lābor	-ī	**lapsus sum**	*I slip, fall*
loquor	-ī	**locūtus sum**	*I speak*
nanciscor	-ī	**nactus sum**	*I obtain*
nascor	-ī	**nātus sum**	*I am born*
oblīviscor	-ī	**oblītus sum**	*I forget*
proficiscor	-ī	**profectus sum**	*I set out, start*
queror	-ī	**questus sum**	*I complain*
sequor	-ī	**secūtus sum**	*I follow*
ūtor	-ī	**ūsus sum**	*I use*

Mixed Conjugation

gradior	-ī	**gressus sum**	*I step, walk*
morior	-ī	**mortuus sum**	*I die*
patior	-ī	**passus sum**	*I suffer, allow*

Semi-Deponent

fīdō	-ere	**fīsus sum**	*I trust*

Fourth Conjugation

experior	-īrī	**expertus sum**	*I try, make trial of*
orior	-īrī	**ortus sum**	*I rise*

Note. Future Participles—**fruitūrus, moritūrus, oritūrus.**

Prepositions

(1) With Accusative

ad, *to, towards, for* (*the purpose of*)

adversus, *against*

ante, *before, in front of*

apud, *near, among, at the house of*

circā, circum, *round*

contrā, *against, opposite*

extrā, *outside*

in, *into, on to, against*

infrā, *under, beneath*

inter, *between, among*

intrā, *within*

ob, *on account of, because of*

per, *through, throughout, by means of*

pōne, *behind*

post, *after, behind*

praeter, *along, except*

prope, *near*

propter, *on account of, because of*

secundum, *according to*

sub, *under* (after Verb of motion)

suprā, *above, beyond*

trans, *across, over*

ultrā, *beyond*

(2) With Ablative

ā, ab, *from, by* (Agent)

cum, (*in company*) *with*

dē, *down from, concerning, about*

ex, ē, *out of, from, of* (after a number)

in, *in, on, over, among*

prō, *on behalf of, for, in return for, instead of*

sine, *without*

sub, *under* (of situation)

tenus (following Noun, sometimes in Gen.), *as far as, up to*

Memorandum of some of the usages and constructions covered by Latin Course for Schools, Part I

Accusatives, two, are often used after Verbs of *hiding, asking, teaching* (**cēlō,** *I hide*; **flāgitō,** *I demand*; **ōrō,** *I beg*; **rogō,** *I ask,* when followed by **sententiam**; **doceō,** *I teach*). **Aquam incolās ōrāmus,** *we are begging the natives for water*.

Adjectives: Agreement. An Adjective must agree with its Noun in Gender, Number, and Case.

Order. Adjectives are more often placed *after* their Nouns than *before*, but Adjectives expressing quantity, such as **multus,** are placed *before,* as in English. **Populus Rōmānus multa bella movēbat,** *the Roman people started many wars.*

> **Used as Nouns. Nostrī,** *our men*; **pauca,** *few things.*
> **Two Adjectives with one Noun** follow the Noun and are joined by **et. Templum pulchrum et antīquum intrāmus,** *we are entering a beautiful old temple.*

Apposition. When a Noun is followed by another Noun in such a way that the second explains or describes the first, the second Noun agrees in Case with the first, and is said to be in Apposition to it. **Agricola, vir bonus, prōvinciam administrat,** *Agricola, a good man, is governing the province. N.B.* **Urbs Rōma,** *the city of Rome.*

Commands: Positive—Imperative, **Scrībe epistolam hodiē,** *write the letter today.*

> **Negative—Nōlī** (s.), **nōlīte** (pl.), with Infinitive. **Nōlī amīcōs neglegere,** *do not neglect your friends.*

Conjunctions, with Negative. *N.B.* **Nec, neque,** *and not*; **nōn tamen** or **nec tamen,** *but not.*

Future Perfect Tense in an *if* or *when* clause. In English we often use a Present Tense after *if* and *when,* but in Latin a Future Perfect is used, if that is the Tense which precisely represents the time of the action. **Sī bellum parāveris, pācem servābis,** *if you prepare war, you will preserve peace.*

Infinitive: as a Noun. Vidēre est crēdere, *seeing is believing.*

> **Neuter in gender. Falsa dīcere est turpe,** *telling lies is disgraceful.*
> **Prolative Infinitive.** Many Verbs require another Verb in the Infinitive to complete their sense, e.g. **properō,** *I hasten*; **constituō,** *I resolve, determine.*

Locative Case is used with Proper Nouns, giving the actual names of towns or small islands, to express *at* or *in,* e.g. 1st Decl., **Rōmae,** *at Rome*; **Athēnīs,** *in Athens*; 2nd Decl., **Londīniī,** *in London*; **Vēiīs,** *in Veii*; 3rd Decl., **Carthāginī** or **-e,**

at Carthage; **Gādibus**, *at Cadiz*. *N.B.* **Humī**, *on the ground*; **rūrī** or **-e**, *in the country*; **domī**, *at home*.

Place *to* and *from*, with Proper names. When a Proper Noun is used, giving the actual name of a town or small island, and also with **domus** and **rūs**, the Accusative without a Preposition is used to express motion *to*, and the Ablative without a Preposition to express *from*, e.g. **Rōmam**, *to Rome*; **Athēnīs**, *from Athens*; **rūs**, *into the country*.

Possessor, Dative of, is often used with the Verb **sum**, with the thing possessed in the Nom. Case. **Erat Alexandrō equus,** *Alexander had a horse*.

Pronouns: Composite Subject of different Persons. The Verb is Plural and agrees with the 1st Person rather than the 2nd, and the 2nd rather than the 3rd. **Ego et leō antrum intrāverāmus,** *the lion and I had entered the cave*.

Reflexive Pronouns, sē, suus, are only to be used when the person they refer to is the **same** person as the Subject of their sentence. **Mīlitēs ad proelium sē parābant,** *the soldiers were getting themselves ready for battle*. **Caesar suōs confirmāvit,** *Caesar encouraged his men*.

That of, those of. No Pronoun is used in Latin to express *that* or *those* before a Genitive. **Cūrā librōs tuōs et amīcī,** *look after your own books and your friend's*.

Questions, Direct: (*a*) **-ne** is attached to the important word in a simple question which asks for information. **Fīliamne exspectās?** *Are you waiting for your daughter?* (*b*) **nonne** is used to introduce a question which contains the negative and of which the expected answer is *yes*. **Nonne epistolam exspectās?** *You are expecting a letter, aren't you?* (*c*) **num** is used to introduce a question, when an answer is not expected and is already felt to be *no*. **Num amīcitiam vītās?** *Surely you don't avoid friendship?*

Time: (*a*) **Length of Time,** Accusative. **Septem annōs,** *for seven years*. (*b*) **Point of Time,** Ablative. **Septimō annō,** *in the seventh year*; **septimō diē,** *on the seventh day*. (*c*) **Limit of Time,** Ablative. **Septem diēbus,** *within seven days*.

Latin-English Vocabulary

Verbs which are followed by 1 *or* 2 *or* 4, *to show the number of their Conjugation, are conjugated regularly.*

Proper Nouns are usually not given, if they are the same in English as in Latin.

The long quantity of the final -o *of Verbs has been omitted.*

Ā, ab (Abl.), *from; by* (agent).

abdo, -ere, -didī, -ditum, *I remove, hide.*

abdūco, -ere, -duxī, -ductum, *I lead away.*

abeo, -īre, -iī, -itum, *I go away.*

abicio, -icere, -iēcī, -iectum, *I throw away, cast.*

abrogo, 1, *I repeal.*

abrumpo, -ere, -rūpī, -ruptum, *I break off.*

absum, -esse, -fuī, *I am away, distant.*

absūmo, -ere, -sumpsī, -sumptum, *I destroy.*

ac, *and.*

accēdo, -ere, -cessī, -cessum, ad, *I reach.*

accidit (impers.), *it happens, happened.*

accipio, -cipere, -cēpī, -ceptum, *I receive; I suffer (loss).*

accūso, 1, *I accuse.*

ācer, ācris, ācre, *keen, fierce.*

acētum, -ī (n.), *vinegar.*

aciēs, aciēī (f.), *line of battle.*

ācriter, *fiercely.*

acūtus, -a, -um, *sharpened, pointed.*

ad (Acc.), *to, towards, at.*

addo, -ere, -didī, -ditum, *I add.*

adeo, -īre, -iī, -itum, *I approach.*

adeō (Advb.), *so much, to such an extent.*

adhaereo, -ēre, -haesī, -haesum (intrans.), *I stick.*

adhūc, *still.*

aditus, -ūs (m.), *entrance.*

adiuvo, -āre, -iūvī, -iūtum, *I help.*

administro, 1, *I govern.*

admitto, -ere, -mīsī, -missum, *I let in.*

admoveo, -ēre, -mōvī, -mōtum (trans.), *I move towards.*

adsum, -esse, -fuī, *I am present or near.*

advenio, -īre, -vēnī, -ventum, ad, *I arrive at, reach.*

adventus, -ūs (m.), *arrival.*

adversus, -a, -um, *contrary, unfavourable; rēs adversae (f. pl.), misfortune.*

adversus (Prep. with Acc.), *against.*

advoco, 1, *I summon.*

advolo, 1, *I fly towards.*

aedificium, -ī (n.), *building, house.*

aedifico, 1, *I build.*

aergē, *scarcely, with difficulty.*

Aenēās, Aenēae (m.), *Aeneas.*

aequus, -a, -um, *level, fair, just.*

aerārium, -ī (n.), *treasury.*

aestās, -tātis (f.), *summer.*

aestimo, 1, *I reckon, value.*

aestus, -ūs (m.), *heat, tide.*

affirmo, 1, *I declare.*

afflīgo, -ere, -flixī, -flictum, *I dash together.*

Āfricus, -ī (m.), *South West wind.*

ager, agrī (m.), *field, estate, territory.*

agger, -eris (m.), *rampart.*

aggredior, -gredī, -gressus sum, *I attack.*

agmen, agminis (n.), *column.*

ago, -ere, ēgī, actum, *I drive, push forward, do, spend (time).*

agricola, -ae (m.), *farmer.*

alacer, alacris, alacre, *eager, energetic.*

Albānus, -ī (m.), *an Alban.*

Alexander, Alexandrī (m.), *Alexander.*

aliēnus, -a, -um, *belonging to another.*

aliquamdiū, *for some time.*

aliquot, *some.*

alius, -a, -ud, *other, another.* For uses, see Ch. 12.

Alpēs, -ium (f. pl.), *the Alps.*

alter, altera, alterum, *the one* or *the other (of two).*

altitūdō, -dinis (f.), *height.*

altus, -a, -um, *high, deep.*

ambō, ambae, ambō, *both.*

ambulo, 1, *I walk.*

āmentum, -ī (n.), *strap.*

amīcitia, -ae (f.), *friendship.*

amīcus, -ī (m.), *friend.*

āmitto, -ere, -mīsī, -missum, *I lose.*

amo, 1, *I love.*

an (in indir. question), *or.*

ancora, -ae (f.), *anchor.*

angustiae, -ārum (f. pl.), *pass.*

angustus, -a, -um, *narrow.*

angustē, *closely.*

animadverto, -ere, -vertī, -versum, *I notice.*

animal, animālis (n.), *animal.*

animus, -ī (m.), *mind, heart.*

Aniō, -iēnis (m.), *the river Anio.*

annōn (in dir. question), *or not.*

annus, -ī (m.), *year.*

anser, anseris (m.), *goose.*

ante (Prep. with Acc.), *before;* (Advb.), *before.*

anteā (Advb.), *before.*

antīquus, -a, -um, *ancient.*

ānulus, -ī (m.), *signet-ring.*

anxius, -a, -um, *anxious.*

aperio, -īre, aperuī, apertum, *I open.*

apertus, -a, -um, *open.*

appāreo, 2, *I appear, am evident.*

appello, 1, *I call (by name).*

appropinquo, 1 (intrans.), *I approach.*

aptus, -a, -um, *suitable, suited.*

apud (Acc.), *among.*

aqua, -ae (f.), *water.*

arbor, arboris (f.), *tree.*

arcesso, -ere, arcessīvī, arcessītum, *I send for.*

Archimēdēs, Archimēdis (m.), *Archimedes.*

argentārius, -a, -um, *of money.*

argentum, -ī (n.), *silver.*

arma, -ōrum (n. pl.), *arms.*

armātus, -a, -um, *armed.*

ars, artis (f.), *skill, trick.*

arx, arcis (f.), *citadel.*

ascendo, -ere, -scendī, -scensum (trans. and intrans.), *I climb.*

asper, aspera, asperum, *rough, troublesome.*

at, *but.*

Athēniensēs, -ium (m. pl.), *the Athenians.*

atque, *and.*

attingo, -ere, -tigī, -tactum, *I reach.*

auctōritās, -tātis (f.), *authority.*

audācia, -ae (f.), *daring, boldness.*

audax, Gen. **audācis,** *daring, bold.*

audeo, -ēre, ausus sum, *I dare.*

audio, 4, *I hear.*

aufero, -ferre, abstulī, ablātum, *I take away.*

augeo, -ēre, auxī, auctum (trans.), *I increase.*

aureus, -a, -um, *golden.*

aurum, -ī (n.), *gold.*

aut, *or;* **aut . . . aut,** *either . . . or.*

autem, *but, moreover.*

auxilium, -ī (n.), *help;* **auxilia, -ōrum** (n. pl.), *allied troops.*

avāritia, -ae (f.), *greed.*

Barbarus, -ī (m.), *barbarian, foreigner.*

beātus, -a, -um, *happy.*

Belgae, -ārum (m. pl.), *the Belgians.*

bellicus, -a, -um, *of war.*

bellum, -ī (n.), *war.*

bene, *well.*

benignē, *kindly.*

blandus, -a, -um, *coaxing.*

bonus, -a, -um, *good.*

bōs, bovis (c.), *ox, cow.*

brevis, -e, *short.*

Britannī, -ōrum (m. pl.), *the Britons.*

Britannia, -ae (f.), *Britain.*

Cado, -ere, cecidī, cāsum, *I fall.*

caecus, -a, -um, *blind.*

caedo, -ere, cecīdī, caesum, *I cut, kill.*

caelum, -ī (n.), *sky.*

Caesar, Caesaris (m.), *Caesar.*

calidus, -a, -um, *hot.*

campus, -ī (m.), *plain.*

canis, canis (c.), *dog.*

Cannae, -ārum (f. pl.), *Cannae.*

Cannensis, -e, *of* or *at Cannae.*

capio, capere, cēpī, captum, *I take, capture, captivate, choose.*

Capitōlium, -ī (n.), *the Capitol.*

captīvus, -ī (m.), *prisoner.*

caput, capitis (n.), *head, capital.*

Carthāginiensis, -e, *Carthaginian.*

Carthāgō, -ginis (f.), *Carthage.*

cārus, -a, -um, *dear, popular.*

casa, -ae (f.), *hut.*

castra, -ōrum (n. pl.), *camp.*

cāsus, -ūs (m.), *fall;* **cāsū,** *by chance.*

204 *Latin-English Vocabulary*

cataracta, -ae (f.), *portcullis.*

Catō, -ōnis (m.), *Cato.*

causa, -ae (f.), *reason, cause;* **causā** (after Gen.), *for the sake of, for, because of.*

cautus, -a, -um, *cautious, careful.*

caverna, -ae (f.), *hole.*

cedo, -ere, cessī, cessum, *I yield, give in.*

celebro, 1, *I celebrate.*

celer, celeris, celere, *quick.*

celeritās, -tātis (f.), *speed.*

celeriter, *quickly.*

centum, *a hundred.*

centuriō, -ōnis (m.), *centurion.*

certāmen, -minis (n.), *struggle, fight.*

certo, 1, *I struggle, strive.*

certus, -a, -um, *certain;* **certiōrem facio,** *I inform.*

cēterī, -ae, -a, *the rest.*

cibus, -ī (m.), *food.*

Cicerō, -ōnis (m.), *Cicero.*

cingo, -ere, cinxī, cinctum, *I surround.*

circā (Acc.), *round.*

circiter (Advb.), *about (of number).*

circumdo, -dare, -dedī, -datum, *I surround.*

circumspecto, 1, *I look around at.*

circumsto, -stāre, -stetī, *I stand around.*

circumvenio, -īre, -vēnī, -ventum, *I surround.*

Circus, -ī (m.), *the Circus,* for chariot races, etc.

cīvis, -is (c.), *citizen.*

cīvitās, -tātis (f.), *state.*

clādēs, clādis (f.), *disaster.*

clam, *secretly.*

clāmor, clāmōris (m.), *shout.*

classis, classis (f.), *fleet.*

claudo, -ere, clausī, clausum, *I shut.*

cloāca, -ae (f.), *drain, sewer.*

coepī, coepisse, *I began.*

cognosco, -ere, -nōvī, -nitum, *I find out, learn, recognize.*

cōgo, -ere, coēgī, coactum, *I compel.*

cohibeo, 2, *I check, halt.*

cohors, cohortis (f.), *cohort.*

collēga, -ae (m.), *colleague.*

colligo, -ere, collēgī, collectum, *I collect, rally.*

collis, collis (m.), *hill.*

colloco, 1, *I place, station.*

colloquor, -ī, collocūtus sum, *I converse.*

colōnia, -ae (f.), *colony, settlement.*

comes, comitis (c.), *companion.*

commeātus, -ūs (m.), *provisions.*

comminus (Advb.), *at close quarters.*

committo, -ere, -mīsī, -missum, *I join.*

commoveo, -ēre, -mōvī, -mōtum (trans.), *I move, stir.*

comparo, 1, *I obtain.*

compello, -ere, -pulī, -pulsum, *I drive.*

compleo, -ēre, -plēvī, -plētum, *I fill.*

compōno, -ere, -posuī, -positum, *I compose, write.*

comprehendo, -ere, -prehendī, -prehensum, *I seize.*

concēdo, -ere, -cessī, -cessum, *I grant, allow.*

concilio, 1, *I win over.*

condiciō, -ōnis (f.), *term, condition.*

condo, -ere, -didī, -ditum, *I found.*

confero, -ferre, -tulī, collātum, *I contribute;* mē confero, *I betake myself.*

confertus, -a, -um, *pressed close;* aciēs conferta, *close order.*

conficio, -ficere, -fēcī, -fectum, *I finish, end.*

confīgo, -ere, -fixī, -fixum, *I pierce.*

confirmo, 1, *I strengthen, confirm, prove, encourage.*

confugio, -ere, -fūgī, *I flee for refuge.*

congero, -ere, -gessī, -gestum, *I pile together.*

congrego, 1, *I herd together.*

cōnicio, -icere, -iēcī, -iectum, *I throw.*

coniectus, -ūs (m.), *hurling, range.*

coniungo, -ere, -iunxī, -iunctum, *I join.*

coniux, coniugis (c.), *wife, husband.*

cōnor, -ārī, cōnātus sum, *I try.*

consenesco, -ere, -senuī, *I grow old.*

consensus, -ūs (m.), *agreement.*

conservo, 1, *I save, keep safe.*

consilium, -ī (n.), *plan, advice.*

consisto, -ere, -stitī, -stitum, *I halt, take up a position.*

conspectus, -ūs (m.), *sight.*

conspicio, -spicere, -spexī, -spectum, *I catch sight of.*

conspicor, -ārī, conspicātus sum, *I catch sight of, see.*

constans, Gen. constantis, *firm.*

constanter, *firmly.*

consterno, -ere, -strāvī, -strātum, *I strew.*

constituo, -ere, -stituī, -stitūtum, *I determine, resolve, decide.*

consul, consulis (m.), *consul.*

consulo, -ere, -suluī, -sultum, *I consult.*

consūmo, -ere, -sumpsī, -sumptum, *I take up, spend.*

consurgo, -ere, -surrexī, -surrectum, *I rise up.*

contemno, -ere, -tempsī, -temptum, *I despise.*

contendo, -ere, -tendī, -tentum, *I march, fight.*

continens, -entis (f.), *mainland.*

contineo, -ēre, -tinuī, -tentum, *I keep, hold back.*

continuus, -a, -um, *continuous.*

contiō, -ōnis (f.), *meeting, speech;* c. habēre, *to make a speech.*

contrā (Acc.), *against.*

convenio, -īre, -vēnī, -ventum, *I come together, meet.*

convoco, 1, *I call together.*

cōpiae, -ārum (f. pl.), *forces, troops;* novae c., *reinforcements.*

cōpulo, 1, *I join.*

corpus, corporis (n.), *body.*

corrumpo, -ere, -rūpī, -ruptum, *I corrupt, ruin.*

crās, *tomorrow.*

crēdo, -ere, crēdidī, crēditum (Dat.), *I believe, trust.*

creo, 1, *I appoint, elect.*

cresco, -ere, crēvī, crētum, *I grow.*

crucio, 1, *I torture.*

culpo, 1, *I blame.*

cum (Prep. with Abl.), *(in company) with.*

cum (Conjunction, with primary tenses of indic. and historic tenses of subj.), *when;* (with any tense of subj.), *since.*

cumulus, -ī (m.), *heap.*

cunctor, -ārī, cunctātus sum, *I delay.*

cupio, cupere, cupīvī, cupītum, *I desire.*

cūr? *why?*

cūro, 1, *I look after, see to, refresh.*

cursus, -ūs (m.), *course.*

custōdio, 4, *I guard.*

custōs, custōdis (c.), *guard.*

Dē (Abl.), *down from, about, concerning.*

dēbeo, 2, *I ought.*

dēcēdo, -ere, -cessī, -cessum, *depart.*

decem, *ten.*

dēcipio, -cipere, -cēpī, -ceptum, *I deceive.*

dēditiō, -ōnis (f.), *surrender.*

dēdo, -ere, -didī, -ditum (trans.), *I surrender.*

dēdūco, -ere, -duxī, -ductum, *I lead down, bring down.*

dēfectiō, -ōnis (f.), *desertion.*

dēfendo, -ere, -fendī, -fensum, *I defend.*

dēfero, -ferre, -tulī, -lātum, *I carry down, convey.*

dēfessus, -a, -um, *tired, exhausted.*

dēfīgo, -ere, -fixī, -fixum, *I fasten down.*

dēicio, -icere, -iēcī, -iectum, *I throw down, let down.*

dēinde, *then, next.*

dēlecto, 1, *I delight, please.*

dēleo, -ēre, dēlēvī, dēlētum, *I destroy.*

dēlībero, 1, *I deliberate, consider.*

dēligo, 1, *I bind.*

dēligo, -ere, -lēgī, -lectum, *I choose.*

dēmitto, -ere, -mīsī, -missum, *I send down, let down.*

densus, -a, -um, *thick.*

dēpello, -ere, -pulī, -pulsum, *I drive down.*

dēplōro, 1, *I lament.*

dēpōno, -ere, -posuī, -positum, *I lay aside.*

dēscendo, -ere, -scendī, -scensum (intrans.), *I go down, descend.*

dēscrībo, -ere, -scripsī, -scriptum, *I draw.*

dēsero, -ere, -seruī, -sertum, *I desert, abandon.*

dēsilio, -īre, -siluī, -sultum, *I leap down.*

dēspēro, 1, *I despair.*

dēsum, -esse, -fuī, *I am wanting.*

dētraho, -ere, -traxī, -tractum, *I drag away.*

dētrīmentum, -ī (n.), *loss.*

deus, -ī (m.), *god.*

dēvolvo, -ere, -volvī, -volūtum, *I roll down.*

dēvoveo, -ēre, -vōvī, -vōtum, *I dedicate.*

dexter, dextra, dextrum, *right;* ā dextrā, *on the right.*

dico, -ere, dixī, dictum, *I say.*

dictātor, -tōris (m.), *dictator.*

diēs, diēī (m.), *day.*

differo, differre, distulī, dīlātum, *I spread, scatter.*

difficilis, -e, *difficult.*

dīligenter (Advb. of dīligens), *carefully.*

dīmico, -āre, -āvī, *I fight.*

dīmitto, -ere, -mīsī, -missum, *I let go, disband.*

dīripio, -ripere, -ripuī, -reptum, *I plunder.*

discēdo, -ere, -cessī, -cessum, *I depart.*

disco, -ere, didicī, *I learn.*

displiceō, 2 (Dat.), *I displease.*

dispōno, -ere, -posuī, -positum, *I arrange.*

dissimilis, -e, *unlike.*

diū, *for a long time.*

dīves, Gen. dīvitis, *rich.*

dīvido, -ere, dīvīsī, dīvīsum, *I divide.*

do, dare, dedī, datum, *I give.*

doceo, -ēre, docuī, doctum, *I teach.*

dolus, -ī (m.), *trick.*

domesticus, -a, -um, *at home;* bellum d., *civil war.*

domicilium, -ī (n.), *home.*

dominus, -ī (m.), *master (of household).*

Domitiānus, -ī (m.), *Domitian.*

domus, -ūs or -ī (f.), *home, house;* domum, *homewards;* domī, *at home.*

dormio, 4, *I sleep.*

Druidae, -ārum (m. pl.), *Druids.*

dubiē, *doubtfully;* haud dubiē, *certainly.*

dubitātiō, -ōnis (f.), *doubt.*

dubito, 1, *I hesitate.*

ducentī, -ae, -a, *two hundred.*

dūco, -ere, duxī, ductum, *I lead.*

dulcis, -e, *sweet, pleasant.*

dum, *while.*

duo, duae, duo, *two.*

duodecim, *twelve.*

dux, ducis (c.), *leader, general, guide.*

Ē, ex (Abl.), *out of, from, of* (after a number).

ēdūco, -ere, -duxī, -ductum, *I lead out.*

effugio, -fugere, -fūgī (trans. and intrans.), *I escape (from).*

ego, *I.*

ēgredior, -gredī, -gressus sum, *I go out.*

ēgressus, -ūs (m.), *landing-place.*

ēicio, -icere, -iēcī, -iectum, *I hurl forth;* mē ēicio, *I rush out.*

ēleganter, *fitly.*

elephantus, -ī (m.), *elephant.*

ēmitto, -ere, -mīsī, -missum, *I send out, discharge.*

emo, -ere, ēmī, emptum, *I buy.*

emptor, -ōris (m.), *buyer.*

enim, *for.*

eo, īre, iī, itum, *I go.*

eō (Advb.), *thither.*

eōdem (Advb.), *to the same place.*

Ephesus, -ī (f.), *Ephesus.*

epistola, -ae (f.), *letter.*

epulae, -ārum (f. pl.), *feast, banquet.*

eques, equitis (m.), *cavalry-man;* equitēs, *cavalry.*

equester, equestris, equestre, *of cavalry, cavalry.*

equitātus (Collective Noun), -ūs (m.), *cavalry.*

equus, -ī (m.), *horse.*

ērigo, -ere, -rexī, -rectum, *I raise.*

ēruptiō, -ōnis (f.), *sally.*

esseda, -ae (f.), *war-chariot.*

essedārius, -ī (m.), *fighter in a war-chariot, charioteer.*

et, *and, even, also;* et . . . et, *both . . . and.*

etiam, *also, even.*

Etruscī, -ōrum (m. pl.), *the Etruscans.*

ēvādo, -ere, -vāsī, -vāsum, *I go out, escape.*

excēdo, -ere, -cessī, -cessum, *I go from.*

excido, -ere, -cidī, *I fall out.*

excito, 1, *I rouse, awake.*

exclāmo, 1, *I shout out.*

exemplum, -ī (n.), *example.*

exeo, -īre, -iī, -itum, *I go out.*

exerceo, 2, *I train.*

exercitus, -ūs (m.), *army.*

exitus, -ūs (m.), *way out.*

exorior, -orīrī, -ortus sum, *I spring up, rise.*

expello, -ere, -pulī, -pulsum, *I drive out* or *away.*

explōrātor, -tōris (m.), *scout.*

explōro, 1, *I reconnoitre, examine.*

expōno, -ere, -posuī, -positum (trans.), *I disembark.*

expugno, 1, *I storm.*

exsilium, -ī (n.), *exile.*

exspecto, 1, *I wait for.*

exsto, -stāre, *I stand out.*

externus, -a, -um, *foreign.*

extrēmus, -a, -um, *last;* extrēmī, *the hindmost.*

Faber, fabrī (m.), *workman, carpenter.*

fābula, -ae (f.), *story.*

facile, *easily.*

facilis, -e, *easy.*

facio, facere, fēcī, factum, *I make, do.*

factum, -ī (n.), *deed.*

fallo, -ere, fefellī, falsum, *I deceive, escape notice of.*

falsus, -a, -um, *false.*

famēs, famis, Abl. famē (f.), *hunger.*

fātālis, -e, *destined.*

fatīgo, 1 (trans.), *I tire.*

faveo, -ēre, fāvī, fautum (Dat.), *I favour.*

fēmina, -ae (f.). *woman, female.*

ferē, *almost, about.*

fermē, *about.*

fero, ferre, tulī, lātum, *I carry, bear, endure, propose* (*law*).

ferox, Gen. **ferōcis,** *fierce, high-spirited.*

ferreus, -a, -um, *of iron.*

ferrum, -ī (n.), *iron.*

ferveo, -ēre, ferbuī, *I burn, glow.*

fessus, -a, -um, *tired.*

festīno, 1, *I hasten.*

festus, -a, -um, *festival.*

fidēlis, -e, *faithful.*

fidēs, -eī (f.), *belief.*

fīlia, -ae (f.), *daughter.*

fīlius, -ī (m.), *son.*

fīnis, fīnis (m.), *end;* **fīnes** (pl.), *boundaries, territories.*

fingo, -ere, finxī, fictum, *I imagine, pretend.*

fīo, fierī, factus sum, *I become, am made* or *done.*

fleo, flēre, flēvī, flētum, *I weep.*

flōreo, -ēre, flōruī, *I flourish.*

flūmen, flūminis (n.), *river.*

fluvius, -ī (m.), *river.*

foedus, -a, -um, *foul, shameful.*

forma, -ae (f.), *figure, shape.*

forte, *by chance.*

fortis, -e, *brave.*

fortiter, *bravely.*

fortūna, -ae (f.), *fortune.*

forum, -ī (n.), *forum, marketplace.*

fossa, -ae (f.), *ditch.*

fragor, fragōris (m.), *crash.*

frango, -ere, frēgī, fractum, *I break.*

frāter, frātris (m.), *brother.*

fraus, fraudis (f.), *deception, deceit.*

fremitus, -ūs (m.), *murmuring.*

frīgus, frīgoris (n.), *cold.*

frons, frontis (f.), *front.*

fructus, -ūs (m.), *fruit.*

frūmentum, -ī (n.), *corn.*

fruor, -ī, fructus sum (Abl.), *enjoy.*

frustrā, *in vain.*

fuga, -ae (f.), *flight.*

fugio, fugere, fūgī (fugitūrus), *I flee.*

fugo, 1, *I rout.*

fūmus, -ī (m.), *smoke.*

funditor, -tōris (m.), *slinger.*

fundo, -ere, fūdī, fūsum, *I pour, rout.*

fūnis, fūnis (m.), *rope.*

furtim, *stealthily.*

Gallia, -ae (f.), *Gaul.*

Gallicus, -a, -um, *of the Gauls.*

Gallus, -ī (m.), *a Gaul.*

gaudeo, -ēre, gāvīsus sum, *I rejoice.*

gaudium, -ī (n.), *joy.*

gemo, -ere, gemuī, gemitum, *I groan.*

gens, gentis (f.), *tribe.*

genus, generis (n.), *kind, class.*

gero, -ere, gessī, gestum, *I carry, wage* (*war*), *wear.*

gladius, -ī (m.), *sword.*

glōria, -ae (f.), *glory, renown.*
Graecia, -ae (f.), *Greece.*
Graecus, -a, -um, *Greek;* **Graecus, -ī** (m.), *a Greek.*
grātus, -a, -um, *pleasing, welcome.*
gravis, -e, *heavy, of weight, important, serious.*
gravitās, -tātis (f.), *weight.*
grex, gregis (m.), *herd.*
gubernātor, -tōris (m.), *helmsman.*

Habeo, 2, *I have, hold, consider.*
habitus, -ūs (m.), *clothing.*
Hannibal, -balis (m.), *Hannibal.*
Hasdrubal,-balis (m.), *Hasdrubal.*
hasta, -ae (f.), *spear.*
haud, *not.*
herbidus, -a, -um, *grassy.*
Herculēs, -is (m.), *Hercules.*
herī, *yesterday.*
hīberna, -ōrum (n. pl.), *winter-quarters.*
hīc, haec, hōc (Pron. and Adj.), *this; the latter.*
hīc (Advb.), *here.*
hiemo, 1, *I spend the winter.*
hiems, hiemis (f.), *winter.*
hinc, *hence;* **hinc et illinc,** *on this side and on that.*
Hispānia, -ae (f.), *Spain.*
Hispānus, -a, -um, *Spanish;* **Hispānus, -ī** (m.), *a Spaniard.*
hodiē, *today.*
homō, hominis (m.), *man* (opposed to *animal*).
honestus, -a, -um, *honourable.*

honōs, honōris (m.), *honour, office.*
hōra, -ae (f.), *hour.*
horridus, -a, -um, *terrible, awe-inspiring.*
hortor, -ārī, hortātus sum, *I encourage, exhort.*
hostis, hostis (c.), *enemy* (*of country*).
hūmānus, -a, -um, *of man, human.*
humilis, -e, *low.*
humus, -ī (f.), *earth, soil.*

Iaceo, -ēre, iacuī, *I lie.*
iacio, iacere, iēcī, iactum, *I throw, heap up* (*rampart*).
iaculum, -ī (n.), *javelin.*
iam, *already, now;* **nōn iam,** *no longer.*
ibi, *there.*
ictus, -ūs (m.), *blow.*
īdem, eadem, idem (Pron. and Adj.), *the same.*
idōneus, -a, -um, *suitable.*
igitur, *therefore.*
ignārus, -a, -um, *ignorant.*
ignis, ignis (m.), *fire.*
ignōminia, -ae (f.), *disgrace.*
ignōro, 1, *I do not know.*
ille, illa, illud (Pron. and Adj.), *that* (*yonder*); *the famous; the former.*
imber, imbris (m.), *rain-storm.*
immensus, -a, -um, *huge.*
immitto, -ere, -mīsī, -missum, *I send into;* **mē immitto,** *I launch myself.*
immōbilis, -e, *motionless.*

impedīmenta, -ōrum (n. pl.), *baggage.*

impedio, 4, *I hinder, prevent.*

impendeo, -ēre, *I overhang.*

imperātor, -tōris (m.), *commander, general.*

imperium, -ī (n.), *order, command, power, empire.*

impero, 1 (Dat.), *I command.*

impetro, 1 (trans.), *I gain (by request).*

impetus, -ūs (m.), *attack, rush.*

impleo, -ēre, -plēvī, -plētum, *I fill.*

imprōvidē, *incautiously.*

īmus, -a, -um, *lowest, bottom.*

in (Acc.), *into, on to, against.*

in (Abl.), *in, on.*

inānis, -e, *empty.*

incēdo, -ere, -cessī, -cessum, *I advance.*

incendium, -ī (n.), *conflagration.*

incendo, -ere, -cendī, -census, *I set on fire, kindle.*

incido, -ere, -cidī, **in** with Acc., *I fall into* or *on to.*

incipio, -cipere, -cēpī, -ceptum, *I begin.*

incito, 1, *I rouse, encourage.*

incola, -ae (c.), *inhabitant.*

incolo, -ere, -coluī (trans. and intrans.), *I live in, dwell.*

incolumis, -e, *safe.*

incommodum, -ī (n.), *damage.*

inde, *thence, then.*

indignus, -a, -um, *unworthy.*

induo, -ere, induī, indūtum, *I put on.*

industria, -ae (f.), *diligence;* **dē industriā,** *on purpose.*

ineo, -īre, -iī, -itum, *I enter.*

inermis, -e, *unarmed.*

inferī, -ōrum (m. pl.), *the inhabitants of the Lower World,* and so, *the dead.*

infero, -ferre, -tulī, illātum, **bellum in** with Acc., *I wage war against.*

infestus, -a, -um, *hostile.*

infimus, -a, -um, *lowest.*

infundo, -ere, -fūdī, -fūsum, *I pour upon, into.*

ingenium, -ī (n.), *talents, ability.*

ingens, Gen. **ingentis,** *huge.*

ingrātus, -a, -um, *displeasing.*

ingredior, -gredī, -gressus sum, *enter.*

iniūria, -ae (f.), *wrongdoing.*

iniustus, -a, -um, *unjust.*

innumerābilis, -e, *countless.*

inquit, inquiunt (from defective **inquam,** *say I*), *says he, say they.*

insidiae, -ārum (f. pl.), *ambush.*

insignis, -e, *conspicuous.*

instituo, -ere, -stituī -stitūtum, *I begin.*

instruo, -ere, -struxī -structum, *I draw up, equip.*

insula, -ae (f.), *island.*

insuperābilis, -e, *insurmountable.*

integer, integra, integrum, *untouched, fresh.*

intellego, -ere, -lexī, -lectum *understand, realize.*

intento, 1, *I stretch towards, point.*

intentus, -a, -um (with Dat.), *busy with.*

inter (Acc.), *between, among.*

intercipio, -cipere, -cēpī, -ceptum, *I intercept.*

interdiū, *in the daytime.*

interdum, *sometimes.*

intereā, *meanwhile.*

interficio, -ficere, -fēcī, -fectum, *I kill.*

interim, *meanwhile.*

intermitto, -ere, -mīsī, -missum, *I leave off, interrupt.*

interrogo, 1, *I question, cross-examine.*

interrumpo, -ere, -rūpī, -ruptum, *I cut in two.*

intervallum, -ī (n.), *space, interval, distance.*

intrā (Acc.), *within.*

intro, 1, *I enter.*

intrōdūco, -ere, -duxī, -ductum, *I lead into, introduce.*

inūtilis, -e, *useless.*

invādo, -ere, -vāsī, -vāsum, *I attack, invade.*

invalidus, -a, -um, *weak.*

invenio, -īre, -vēnī, -ventum, *I find, invent.*

inventor, -tōris (m.), *contriver, inventor.*

invideo, -ēre, -vīdī, -vīsum (Dat.), *I envy.*

invidia, -ae (f.), *envy, jealousy.*

inviolātus, -a, -um, *untouched, unharmed.*

invīto, 1, *I invite.*

invius, -a, -um, *impassable.*

ipse, ipsa, ipsum, *self, very.*

īra, -ae (f.), *anger.*

īrascor, -ī, īrātus sum, *I am angry.*

irrīto, 1, *I goad, provoke.*

is, ea, id (Pron. and Adj.), *he, she, it; this, that.*

iste, ista, istud (Pron. and Adj.), *that (near you).*

ita, *thus, so, in this way;* **ita ut** (with indic.), *just as;* **ita . . . ut** (with subj.), *in such a way that.*

Ītalia, -ae (f.), *Italy.*

Ītalicus, -a, -um, *of Italy.*

itaque, *therefore.*

iter, itineris (n.), *journey, march, route, way.*

iterum, *again, a second time, once more.*

iubeo, -ēre, iussī, iussum, *I order, command.*

iūcundus, -a, -um, *pleasant.*

iugum, -ī (n.), *yoke.*

iūmentum, -ī (n.), *pack-animal, mule.*

Iuppiter, Iovis (m.), *Jupiter.*

iūro, 1, *I swear.*

iūs, iūris (n.), *right.*

iussū, *by order.*

iustus, -a, -um, *just.*

iuvo, -āre, iūvī, iūtum, *I help.*

Lābor, -ī, lapsus sum, *I slip, fall.*

labor, labōris (m.), *work, toil, labour.*

labōro, 1, *I work.*

lacesso, -ere, lacessīvī, lacessītum, *I provoke.*

lacrima, -ae (f.), *tear.*

lacus, -ūs (m.), *lake.*

laetitia, -ae (f.), *joy.*

laetus, -a, -um, *joyful, glad, happy.*

lancea, -ae (f.), *lance, spear.*

lapis, lapidis (m.), *stone.*

lapsus, -ūs (m.), *fall.*

lassitūdō, -dinis (f.), *weariness.*

Latīnē, *in Latin.*

Latīnus, -a, -um, *Latin.*

latus, lateris (n.), *side.*

lātus, -a, -um, *wide.*

laudo, 1, *I praise.*

laus, laudis (f.), *praise.*

lēgātus, -ī (m.), *ambassador, lieutenant.*

legiō, -ōnis (f.), *legion.*

lego, -ere, lēgī, lectum, *I read.*

lēnis, -e, *gentle.*

lentē, *slowly.*

leō, leōnis (m.), *lion.*

levis, -e, *light.*

levo, 1, *I raise.*

lex, lēgis (f.), *law.*

liber, librī (m.), *book.*

līberī, -ōrum (m. pl.), *children.*

lībero, 1, *I free.*

lībertās, -tātis (f.), *freedom.*

lignum, -ī (n.), *log.*

lingua, -ae (f.), *tongue, language.*

littera, -ae (f.), *letter (of alphabet);* litterae (pl.), *letter, despatch.*

lītus, lītoris (n.), *shore.*

loco, 1, *I place, station.*

locus, -ī (m.), *place, position* (Nom. and Acc. pl., also neuter, loca).

longē, *far.*

longus, -a, -um, *long.*

loquor, -ī, locūtus sum, *I speak.*

lūbricus, -a, -um, *slippery.*

Lūcerīnī, -ōrum (m. pl.), *inhabitants of Luceria.*

lūdus, -ī (m.), *school.*

lupa, -ae (f.), *she-wolf.*

lux, lūcis (f.), *light, daylight.*

luxuria, -ae (f.), *luxury.*

Macedones, -um (m. pl.), *the Macedonians.*

maestitia, -ae (f.), *sadness.*

magis (Advb.), *more.*

magister, magistrī (m.), *master (of school).*

magistrātus, -ūs (m.), *magistrate.*

magnopere, *greatly.*

magnus, -a, -um, *great, large, loud* (voice).

māior, māius, *greater, bigger.*

male, *badly.*

mālo, malle, māluī, *I prefer.*

malum, -ī (n.), *trouble, calamity.*

mando, 1, *I entrust;* mē fugae mando, *I take flight.*

māne, *in the morning.*

maneo, -ēre, mansī (mansūrus), *I remain.*

manus, -ūs (f.), *hand;* in manū (with Gen.), *subject (to).*

mare, maris (n.), *sea.*

maritimus, -a, -um, *on the coast.*

marītus, -ī (m.), *husband.*

mātrōna, -ae (f.), *lady*.

maximē, *very greatly, especially*.

maximus, -a, -um, *very big, greatest*.

mediōcris, -e, *ordinary, of moderate size*.

medius, -a, -um, *middle*.

melior, melius, *better*.

membrum, -ī (n.), *limb*.

memor, Gen. **memoris**, *mindful, remembering*.

memoria, -ae (f.), *memory, account*.

mereor, -ērī, meritus sum, *I deserve*.

merīdiānus, -a, -um, *of noon*.

merīdiēs, merīdiēī (m.), *noon*.

metuo, -ere, metuī, *I fear*.

meus, -a, -um, *my*.

migro, 1, *I move, depart*.

mīles, mīlitis (c.), *soldier*.

mille, *a thousand;* **mīlia, -ium** (n. pl., followed by Gen.), *thousands;* **mille passūs**, *one mile*.

minimus, -a, -um, *very little*.

minor, minus, *smaller, less*.

minuo, -ere, minuī, minūtum, *I lessen*.

minus (Advb.), *less*.

mīrābilis, -e, *wonderful*.

mīror, -ārī, mīrātus sum, *I wonder (at)*.

miser, misera, miserum, *wretched*.

miserābilis, -e, *wretched, pitiable*.

misereor, -ērī, miseritus sum (Gen.), *I pity*.

misericordia, -ae (f.), *pity*.

mitto, -ere, mīsī, missum, *I send; I hurl*.

modo, *only*.

modus, -ī (m.), *way, method*.

moenia, -ium (n. pl.), *walls*.

mōlēs, mōlis (f.), *mass*.

mollio, 4, *I soften*.

moneo, 2, *I advise, warn*.

mons, montis (m.), *hill, mountain*.

monstro, 1, *I show*.

montānus, -a, -um, *mountain-dwelling*.

mora, -ae (f.), *delay*.

moribundus, -a, -um, *dying*.

morior, morī, mortuus sum, *I die*.

moror, -ārī, morātus sum, *I delay*.

mors, mortis (f.), *death*.

mōs, mōris (m.), *custom*.

mōtus, -ūs (m.), *sudden rising, tumult*.

moveo, -ēre, mōvī, mōtum (trans.), *I move*.

mox, *soon*.

mulier, mulieris (f.), *woman*.

multitūdō, -dinis (f.), *large number, crowd*.

multum (Advb.), *much, far*.

multus, -a, -um, *much* (in pl., *many*).

mūnio, 4, *I fortify, build (road)*.

mūnītiō, -ōnis (f.), *fortification*.

mūrus, -ī (m.), *wall*.

Nam, *for*.

nanciscor, -ī, nactus sum, *I obtain*.

narro, 1, *I relate*.

nascor, -ī, nātus sum, *I am born.*

nato, 1, *I swim.*

nātūra, -ae (f.), *nature.*

nauta, -ae (m.), *sailor.*

nāvālis, -e, *of ships;* **castra nāv.,** *camp to protect the ships.*

nāvigātiō, -ōnis (f.), *voyage.*

nāvigium, -ī (n.), *boat.*

nāvis, nāvis (f.), *ship;* **nāvis longa,** *ship of war.*

nē (Advb. with subj.), *not;* (conj.), *in order that . . . not, that . . . not.*

nē . . . quidem, *not even.*

nec, neque, *and not, nor;* **nec . . . nec, neque . . . neque,** *neither . . . nor.*

necessārius, -a, -um, *necessary, essential.*

necne (in indir. question), *or not.*

neco, 1, *I kill.*

neglegenter (Advb. of **neglegens**), *carelessly.*

neglego, -ere, neglexī, neglectum, *I neglect.*

nego, 1, *I deny, say . . . not; I refuse.*

nēmō, Acc. **nēminem** (no Gen. or Abl.), *no one.*

neque, see **nec.**

nescio, 4, *I do not know.*

neuter, neutra, neutrum, *neither.*

nēve (in final clause and indir. command), *and not.*

nihil, *nothing.*

nihilōminus, *nevertheless.*

nisi, *unless, except.*

nix, nivis (f.), *snow.*

noceo, 2 (Dat.), *harm, injure.*

noctū, *by night.*

nōlo, nolle, nōluī, *I am unwilling;* **nōlī, nōlīte** (imperative, followed by infinitive), *do not.*

nōmen, nōminis (n.), *name.*

nōn, *not.*

nōndum, *not yet.*

nōniam, *no longer.*

nonne? *not* in question of which the expected answer is *yes.*

nonnullī, -ae, -a, *some.*

nōnus, -a, -um, *ninth.*

noster, nostra, nostrum, *our.*

nōtus, -a, -um, *well-known.*

novem, *nine.*

novus, -a, -um, *new, strange;* **novae cōpiae,** *reinforcements.*

nox, noctis (f.), *night.*

nullus, -a, -um, *no, none.*

num? *surely not* in direct question of which the answer is already felt to be *no;* **num** (in indir. question), *whether.*

numero, 1, *I count.*

numerus, -ī (m.), *number, quantity.*

Numidae, -ārum (m. pl.), *the Numidians.*

nunc, *now.*

nunquam, *never.*

nuntio, 1, *I announce, report.*

nuntius, -ī (m.), *messenger; message.*

Ō (exclamation sometimes used with Voc. or Acc.), *O.*

ob (Acc.), *on account of.*

obliviscor, -ī, oblītus sum (Gen.), *I forget.*

obses, obsidis (c.), *hostage.*

obsideo, -ēre, -sēdī, -sessum, *I besiege.*

obsidiō, -ōnis (f.), *siege.*

obstinātus, -a, -um, *steadfast, resolute.*

obstruo, -ere, -struxī, -structum, *I block.*

occāsus, -ūs (m.), *setting;* **sōlis occ.,** *sunset.*

occīdo, -ere, -cīdī, -cīsum, *I kill.*

occupātus, -a, -um, *busied.*

occupo, 1, *I seize.*

octingentī, -ae, -a, *eight hundred.*

octō, *eight.*

octōgintā, *eighty.*

oculus, -ī (m.), *eye.*

oleum, -ī (n.), *oil.*

ōlim, *once, formerly.*

omitto, -ere, -mīsī, -missum, *I give up.*

omnīnō, *altogether.*

omnis, -e, *all, every.*

oppidānus, -ī (m.), *townsman.*

oppidum, -ī (n.), *town.*

opprimo, -ere, -pressī, -pressum, *I overwhelm.*

oppugnātiō, -ōnis (f.), *attack.*

oppugno, 1, *I attack.*

optimus, -a, -um, *best.*

opus, operis (n.), *work.*

ōra, -ae (f.), *coast.*

ōrātiō, -ōnis (f.), *speech.*

orior, orīrī, ortus sum, *I rise.*

ornāmentum, -ī (n.), *ornament, jewel.*

ornātus, -ūs (m.), *adornment.*

orno, 1, *I adorn.*

ōro, 1, *I beg* or *ask* (*for*), *beseech.*

ostendo, -ere, ostendī, ostensum or **ostentum,** *I show.*

ostento, 1, *I show.*

Pābulātor, -tōris (m.), *forager.*

pābulum, -ī (n.), *fodder.*

paene, *almost.*

palūs, palūdis (f.), *marsh.*

pār, Gen. **paris,** *equal.*

parātus, -a, -um, *ready.*

parco, -ere, pepercī, parsum (Dat.), *I spare.*

parens, parentis (c.), *parent.*

pāreo, 2 (Dat.), *I obey.*

paro, 1, *I prepare, get ready.*

pars, partis (f.), *part, direction;* *some.*

partim, *partly.*

parum, *too little, not enough.*

parvus, -a, -um, *small.*

pasco, -ere, pāvī, pastum (trans.), *I feed.*

passus, -ūs (m.), *pace, yard.*

pastōrālis, -e, *of shepherds.*

pateo, -ēre, patuī, *I am open.*

pater, patris (m.), *father.*

patior, patī, passus sum, *I suffer, endure, allow.*

patria, -ae (f.), *native land, country.*

patrius, -a, -um, *of one's forefathers.*

paucī, -ae, -a, *few.*

paulisper, *for a short time.*

paulum (Advb.), *a little.*

pauper, Gen. **pauperis**, *poor*.

pavidus, -a, -um, *fearful, alarmed*.

pax, pācis (f.), *peace*.

pectus, pectoris (n.), *chest*.

pecūnia, -ae (f.), *money*.

pecus, pecoris (n.), *flock, herd, cattle*.

pedes, peditis (m.), *infantryman;* **peditēs**, *infantry*.

penātēs, -ium (m. pl.), *household gods*.

per (Acc.), *through, throughout, by means of*.

perangustus, -a, -um, *very narrow*.

percutio, -cutere, -cussī, -cussum, *I strike*.

perdūco, -ere, -duxī, -ductum, *I bring over*.

pereo, -īre, periī, peritum, *I perish*.

perficio, -ficere, -fēcī, -fectum, *I finish*.

perfuga, -ae (m.), *deserter*.

pergo, -ere, perrexī, perrectum, *I proceed*.

perīculum, -ī (n.), *danger*.

perlego, -ere, -lēgī, -lectum, *I read through*.

permitto, -ere, -mīsī, -missum, *I allow*.

permoveo, -ēre, -mōvī, -mōtum, *I move deeply, stir, disturb*.

permultī, -ae, -a, *very many*.

perpaucī, -ae, -a, *very few*.

perpetuus, -a, -um, *continuous*.

perrumpo, -ere, -rūpī, -ruptum, *I break through*.

Persae, -ārum (m. pl.), *the Persians*.

persequor, -ī, -secūtus sum, *I pursue*.

perspicio, -spicere, -spexī, -spectum, *I perceive*.

persuādeo, -ēre, -suāsī, -suāsum (Dat.), *I persuade*.

perterreo, 2, *I thoroughly frighten*.

pertraho, -ere, -traxī, -tractum, *I draw (entice)*.

perturbo, 1, *I confuse, upset*.

pervenio, -īre, -vēnī, -ventum, ad, *I arrive at, reach*.

pēs, pedis (m.), *foot*.

pessimus, -a, -um, *worst*.

pestilentia, -ae (f.), *plague, disease*.

pestis, pestis (f.), *plague*.

peto, -ere, petīvī, petītum, *I seek, make for, attack*.

pīlum, -ī (n.), *javelin*.

placeo, 2 (Dat.), *I please*.

plānus, -a, -um, *level, flat*.

plebs, plēbis (f.), *people*.

plēnus, -a, -um, *full*.

plūrimī, -ae, -a, *very many*.

plūs, Gen. **plūris**, *more;* pl. **plūrēs, plūra**.

Poenus, -a, -um, *Carthaginian;* **Poenī, -ōrum** (m. pl.), *the Carthaginians*.

polliceor, -ērī, pollicitus sum, *I promise*.

pondus, ponderis (n.), *weight*.

pōne (Acc.), *behind*.

pōno, -ere, posuī, positum, *I place, put, pitch (camp)*.

pons pontis (m.), *bridge*.

populor, -ārī, populātus sum, *I ravage.*

populus, -ī (m.), *people.*

porrigo, -ere, porrexī, porrectum, *I stretch.*

porta, -ae (f.), *gate.*

porto, 1, *carry.*

portus, -ūs (m.), *harbour.*

posco, -ere, poposcī, *I demand.*

possessiō, -ōnis (f.), *occupation.*

possessor, possessōris (m.), *owner.*

possum, posse, potuī, *I am able, can.*

post (Prep. with Acc.), *after, behind;* (Advb.), *behind.*

posteā, *afterwards.*

posterus, -a, -um, *next.*

postrēmō, *finally, at last.*

postrīdiē, *on the next day.*

postulo, 1, *I demand.*

potestās, -tātis (f.), *power.*

potius, *rather.*

praebeo, 2, *I supply.*

praecēdo, -ere, -cessī, -cessum, *I go before.*

praeceps, Gen. **praecipitis,** *headlong.*

praecipito, 1, *I hurl headlong.*

praeclārus, -a, -um, *glorious, famous.*

praecō, -ōnis (m.), *herald, auctioneer.*

praeda, -ae (f.), *booty.*

praefectus, -ī (m.), *commander.*

praeficio, -ficere, -fēcī, -fectum, *I put in command.*

praefīgo, -ere, -fixī, -fixum, *I fix in front.*

praemitto, -ere, -mīsī, -missum, *send forward.*

praemium, -ī (n.), *reward.*

praesidium, -ī (n.), *protection, garrison.*

praesto, -stāre, -stitī, -stitum, *I show.*

praesum, -esse, -fuī (Dat.), *I am in command of, have rule over.*

praeter (Acc.), *except.*

praistereā, *besides.*

praeter̄eā, besides.

prandeo, -ēre, prandī, pransum, *I have breakfast.*

precor, -ārī, precātus sum, *I pray.*

pretium, -ī (n.), *price.*

prīdiē, *on the day before.*

prīmō, *at first.*

prīmum, *for the first time.*

prīmus, -a, -um, *first;* **prīma lux,** *dawn.*

princeps, principis (c.), *chief;* also as Adj., *first, chief.*

prior, prius, *former, previous, last.*

pristinus, -a, -um, *former.*

prīvātus, -a, -um, *private;* in **prīvātō,** *in private;* also as Noun, **prīvātus, -ī** (m.), *private citizen.*

prō (Abl.), *in front of, on behalf of, in return for.*

prōcēdo, -ere, -cessī, -cessum, *I go forward, advance.*

procul, *far, afar.*

prōcurro, -ere, -currī or **-cucurrī, -cursum,** *I run forward.*

prōdo, -ere, -didī, -ditum, *I betray.*

proelium, -ī (n.), *battle.*

proficiscor, -ī, profectus sum, *I set out, start.*

prōgredior, -gredī, -gressus sum, *I advance.*

prohibeo, 2, *I keep off, prevent.*

prōmitto, -ere, -mīsī, -missum, *I promise.*

prope (Prep. with Acc.), *near;* (Advb.), *nearly.*

propero, 1, *I hasten.*

propinquus, -a, -um, *near;* ex **propinquō,** *from near at hand.*

propior, -ius, *nearer.*

prōpōno, -ere, -posuī, -positum, *I set forth, propose.*

propter (Acc.), *on account of.*

prōra, -ae (f.), *prow.*

prōsequor, -ī, prōsecūtus sum, *I pursue.*

prōveho, -ere, -vexī, -vectum, *I carry forward.*

prōvideo, -ēre, -vīdī, -vīsum, *I foresee.*

prōvincia, -ae (f.), *province.*

prōvolvo, -ere, -volvī, -volūtum, *I roll forward.*

proximus, -a, -um, *nearest, next.*

prūdens, Gen. **prūdentis,** *wise.*

publicus, -a, -um, *public;* **publicum, -ī** (n.), (1) *public treasury, public use,* e.g. in **publicum,** *for public use,* (2) *a public place,* e.g. in **publicō,** *in public.*

puer, puerī (m.), *boy*

pugna, -ae (f.), *fight, battle, combat.*

pugno, 1 (intrans.), *I fight.*

pulcher, pulchra, pulchrum, *beautiful.*

pulchrē, *beautifully.*

pulchritūdō, -dinis (f.), *beauty.*

pulvis, pulveris (m.), *dust.*

Pūnicus, -a, -um, *Carthaginian.*

puppis, puppis (f.), *stern.*

purpura, -ae (f.), *purple.*

puter, putris, putre, *crumbling.*

puto, 1, *I think.*

Pȳrēnaeī montēs (m. pl.), *the Pyrenees.*

Quadrāgintā, *forty.*

quaero, -ere, quaesīvī, quaesītum, *I seek.*

quaestor, -tōris (m.), *quaestor.*

quālis, -e? *of what sort?*

quam (Advb.), (in questions, with Adj. or Advb.) *how;* (after comparative) *than;* (before superlative) *as—as possible.*

quamdīu? *how long?*

quandō? *when?*

quanquam, *although.*

quantus, -a, -um? *how big?*

quartus, -a, -um, *fourth.*

quattuor, *four.*

queror, -ī, questus sum, *I complain.*

quī, quae, quod (rel. Pron.), *who, which;* (interrog. Adj.) *which, what?*

quia, *because.*

**quīdam, quaedam, quiddam (quod-
dam),** (indef. Pron. and Adj.),
a certain person, a certain.

quidem, *indeed;* **nē . . . quidem,** *not
even.*

quiēs, quiētis (f.), *rest.*

quindecim, *fifteen.*

quinque, *five.*

quinquerēmis, -rēmis (f.), *quin-
quereme, ship with five banks
of oars.*

quis? quid? (interrog. Pron.),
who? what?

quis, qua, quid (indef. Pron.
after **nē** and **num**), *anyone,
anything.*

quisquam, quidquam or **quicquam**
(indef. Pron. after negative),
anyone, anything.

quisque, quaeque, quidque or
quicque (quodque), (indef.
Pron. and Adj.) *each one, each.*

quō? *whither?*

quod (conj.), *because.*

quōmodo? *how, in what way?*

quondam, *once (upon a time).*

quoque, *also.*

quotiēs? *how often?*

Rārus, -a, -um, *scattered, far
apart.*

ratis, ratis (f.), *raft.*

recenseo, -ēre, -censuī, -censum,
I review.

recipio, -cipere, -cēpī, -ceptum, *I
take back, accept;* **mē recipio,**
I retreat.

recito, 1, *I repeat, read out.*

rector, -tōris (m.), *driver.*

reddo, -ere, reddidī, redditum, *I
give back, restore.*

redeo, -īre, -iī, -itum, *I return.*

redigo, -ere, -ēgī, -actum, *I re-
duce.*

redintegro, 1, *I renew.*

reditus, -ūs (m.), *return.*

redūco, -ere, -duxī, -ductum, *I
lead back.*

refero, -ferre, rettulī, relātum, *I
carry back;* **pedem ref.,** *I retreat.*

reficio, -ficere, -fēcī, -fectum, *I
repair.*

regiō, -ōnis (f.), *district.*

regno, 1, *I reign.*

regredior, -gredī, -gressus sum, *I
go back, return.*

religo, 1, *I fasten.*

relinquo, -ere, -līquī, -lictum, *I
leave behind, leave, abandon.*

reliquus, -a, -um, *remaining,
rest.*

remitto, -ere, -mīsī, -missum, *I
send back, let go.*

removeo, -ēre, -mōvī, -mōtum
(trans.), *I withdraw.*

rēmus, -ī (m.), *oar;* so **rēmīs,** *by
rowing.*

renovo, 1, *I renew.*

renuntio, 1, *I report.*

repello, -ere, reppulī, repulsum, *I
drive back.*

repente, *suddenly.*

repentīnus, -a, -um, *sudden.*

reperio, -īre, repperī, repertum, *I
find, discover.*

repeto, -ere, -petīvī, -petītum, *I seek again, retrace.*

reporto, 1, *I carry back.*

repudio, 1, *I reject.*

res, reī (f.), *thing, matter.*

resisto, -ere, restitī (Dat.), *I resist.*

resolvo, -ere, -solvī, -solūtum, *I unloose, untie.*

respicio, -spicere, -spexī, -spectum, *I look back at.*

respondeo, -ēre, -spondī, -sponsum, *I reply, answer.*

rēspublica, reīpublicae (f.), *state, commonwealth.*

retineo, -ēre, -tinuī, -tentum, *I keep back, keep, hold on to.*

revoco, 1, *I recall.*

rex, rēgis (m.), *king.*

Rhodanus, -ī (m.), *the Rhone.*

rīdeo, -ēre, rīsī, rīsum, *I laugh, smile.*

rigeo, -ēre, *I am stiff.*

rīpa, -ae (f.), *bank.*

rōbur, rōboris (n.), *strength, flower (of army).*

rogo, 1, *I ask.*

Rōma, -ae (f.), *Rome.*

Rōmānus, -a, -um, *Roman;* Rōmānus, -ī (m.), *a Roman.*

rubor, rubōris (m.), *blush.*

rūmor, rūmōris (m.), *rumour.*

ruo, -ere, ruī, (ruitūrus), *I rush.*

rūpēs, rūpis (f.), *rock.*

rursus, *again.*

Sabīnī, -ōrum, (m. pl.), *the Sabines.*

sacrifico, 1, *I sacrifice.*

sacrum, -ī (n.), *sacrifice.*

saepe, *often.*

saepio, -īre, saepsī, saeptum, *I enclose.*

sagittārius, -ī (m.), *archer.*

salio, -īre, saluī, *I jump.*

saltus, -ūs (m.), *pass.*

salūs, salūtis (f.), *safety.*

salūto, 1, *I greet.*

Samnītēs, -ium (m. pl.), *the Samnites.*

sapiens, Gen. sapientis, *wise.*

sapientia, -ae (f.), *wisdom.*

satis, *enough.*

saxum, -ī (n.), *stone, rock.*

scāla, -ae (f.), *ladder.*

scio, 4, *I know.*

Scīpiō, -ōnis (m.), *Scipio.*

scrībo, -ere, scripsī, scriptum, *I write.*

scriptor, -tōris (m.), *writer.*

scūtum, -ī (n.), *shield.*

sē (reflexive Pronoun), *himself, herself, itself, themselves.*

secundum (Acc.), *according to.*

secundus, -a, -um, *second; favourable;* rēs secundae (f. pl.), *prosperity.*

sed, *but.*

sēminūdus, -a, -um, *half-naked.*

semper, *always.*

senātus, -ūs (m.), *senate.*

senectūs, -tūtis (f.), *old age.*

senex, senis (m.), *old man.*

sensim, *gradually.*

sententia, -ae (f.), *opinion.*

sentio, -īre, sensī, sensum, *I feel, perceive.*

sepelio, -īre, sepelīvī, sepultum, *I bury.*

septem, *seven.*

septimus, -a, -um, *seventh.*

sepultūra, -ae (f.), *burial.*

sequor, -ī, secūtus sum, *I follow.*

servo, 1, *I save.*

sescentī, -ae, -a, *six hundred.*

sex, *six.*

sexāgintā, *sixty.*

sī, *if.*

Sicilia, -ae (f.), *Sicily.*

signum, -ī (n.), *signal, standard, statue.*

silentium, -ī (n.), *silence.*

sileo, -ēre, siluī, *I am silent.*

silva, -ae (f.), *wood.*

silvestris, -e, *woody.*

silvōsus, -a, -um, *woody.*

similis, -e (with Gen. or Dat.), *like.*

simpliciter (Advb. of **simplex**), *simply.*

simul, *at the same time, together.*

simulo, 1, *I pretend.*

sine (Abl.), *without.*

singulī, -ae, -a, *one each.*

sinister, sinistra, sinistrum, *left;* **sinistra, -ae** (f.), *the left;* **ā sin.,** *on the left.*

sino, -ere, sīvī, situm, *I allow.*

socius, -ī (m.), *ally.*

sōl, sōlis (m.), *sun.*

soleo, -ēre, solitus sum, *I am accustomed, am wont.*

solitus, -a, -um, *usual.*

sollicitus, -a, -um, *anxious.*

sōlum, *only.*

sōlus, -a, -um, *alone.*

solvo, -ere, solvī, solūtum, *I loose;* **nāvem s.,** or simply **solvo,** *I set sail.*

somnus, -ī (m.), *sleep.*

sonitus, -ūs (m.), *sound.*

sōpio, 4, *I lull to sleep.*

soror, sorōris (f.), *sister.*

spectāculum, -ī (n.), *show.*

spectātor, -tōris (m.), *observer.*

specto, 1, *I look at, examine;* **specto ad,** *I face.*

speculātor, -tōris (m.), *scout.*

sperno, -ere, sprēvī, sprētum, *I despise.*

spēro, 1, *I hope.*

spēs, speī (f.), *hope.*

spolia, -ōrum (n. pl.), *spoils.*

stabilis, -e, *standing firm, fixed, steady.*

statim, *at once, immediately.*

statiō, -ōnis (f.), *post;* **in statiōne,** *on guard.*

statua, -ae (f.), *statue.*

strāmentum, -ī (n.), *straw;* in pl., *thatch.*

strepitus, -ūs (m.), *noise.*

stultitia, -ae (f.), *folly.*

stultus, -a, -um, *foolish.*

stupor, stupōris (m.), *amazement.*

suādeo, -ēre, suāsī, suāsum (Dat.), *I advise, urge.*

sub (Acc.), *under* (motion *to*); (Abl.), *under* (rest).

subdūco, -ere, -duxī, -ductum, *I draw up, beach* (*ship*).

subitō, *suddenly.*

subitus, -a, -um, *sudden.*

submitto, -ere, -mīsī, -missum, *I send up.*

subsidium, -ī (n.), *support.*

succīdo, -ere, succīdī, succīsum, *I cut through, fell.*

succurro, -ere, succurrī, succursum (Dat.), *I help.*

sudis, sudis (f.), *stake.*

suffrāgium, -ī (n.), *vote.*

sum, esse, fuī, *I am.*

summus, -a, -um, *highest, utmost;* s. mons, *the top of the mountain.*

sūmo, -ere, sumpsī, sumptum, *I take, take up.*

sumptus, -ūs (m.), *expense.*

superābilis, -e, *surmountable.*

superbia, -ae (f.), *pride.*

superbus, -a, -um, *proud.*

superior, -ius, *higher, earlier, previous, superior.*

supero, 1, *I overcome, conquer, climb, cross* (*mountain*).

supersum, -esse, -fuī, *I am left, survive.*

suprā (Acc.), *above, beyond.*

surgo, -ere, surrexī, surrectum, *I rise.*

suscipio, -cipere, -cēpī, -ceptum, *I undertake.*

suspendo, -ere, -pendī, -pensum (trans.), *I hang.*

sustineo, -ēre, -tinuī, -tentum, *I withstand, resist.*

suus, -a, -um (reflexive Adj.), *his, her, its, their, own.*

Syrācūsae, -ārum (f. pl.), *Syracuse.*

Syrācūsānī, -ōrum (m. pl.), *the Syracusans.*

Taberna, -ae (f.), *shop.*

tabernāculum, -ī (n.), *tent.*

tacitus, -a, -um, *silent.*

talentum, -ī (n.), *talent* (sum of money).

tālis, -e, *such.*

tam (with Adj. and Advbs.), *so.*

tamen, *yet, however.*

Tamesis, Tamesis (m.), *the Thames.*

tandem, *at last.*

tango, -ere, tetigī, tactum, *I touch, reach to.*

tantus, -a, -um, *so big, so great.*

tego, -ere, texī, tectum, *I cover.*

tēlum, -ī (n.), *weapon.*

temerē, *rashly.*

tempestās, -tātis (f.), *weather, storm.*

templum, -ī (n.), *temple.*

tempus, temporis (n.), *time, season.*

teneo, -ēre, tenuī, tentum, *I hold.*

tenus (after Abl.), *as far as, up to.*

tergum, -ī (n.), *back, rear.*

terra, -ae (f.), *land.*

terreo, 2, *I frighten.*

terror, terrōris (m.), *dread, terror.*

tertius, -a, -um, *third.*

testūdō, -dinis (f.), *tortoise.*

theātrum, -ī (n.), *theatre.*

timeo, -ēre, timuī, *I fear.*

toga, -ae (f.), *toga, gown.*

tormentum, -ī (n.), *engine* (*for hurling missiles*); pl., *artillery.*

tot, *so many.*

totiēs, *so often.*

tōtus, -a, -um, *whole.*

trādo, -ere, trādidī, trāditum, *I hand over, hand down.*

traho, -ere, traxī, tractum, *I drag, draw, attract.*

trans (Acc.), *across.*

transeo, -īre, -iī, -itum, *I cross.*

transgredior, -gredī, -gressus sum, *I cross.*

transmitto, -ere, -mīsī, -missum, *I send across.*

transporto, 1, *I transport, carry across.*

transveho, -ere, -vexī, -vectum, *I carry across.*

trepidātiō, -ōnis (f.), *panic.*

trepido, 1, *I am in a panic, bustle.*

trēs, tria, *three.*

tribūnus, -ī (m.), *tribune.*

tristis, -e, *sad.*

triumphus, -ī (m.), *triumph.*

tuba, -ae (f.), *trumpet.*

tueor, -ērī, *I defend, protect.*

tum, *then.*

tumultus, -ūs (m.), *confusion.*

tumulus, -ī (m.), *mound, hillock.*

tunc, *then, at that time.*

turba, -ae (f.), *crowd.*

turma, -ae (f.), *squadron.*

turpis, -e, *disgraceful.*

turris, turris, Abl. **turrī** (f.), *tower.*

tūtus, -a, -um, *safe.*

tuus, -a, -um, *your* (sing.).

Ubi, *where, when.*

ubi? *where?*

ullus, -a, -um (after negative), *any.*

ulterior, -ius, *further.*

ultimus, -a, -um, *last.*

umerus, -ī (m.), *shoulder.*

ūnā, *together.*

unda, -ae (f.), *wave.*

unde, *whence, from which.*

undique, *from all sides, on all sides.*

ūniversus, -a, -um, *all together.*

unquam (after negative), *ever.*

ūnus, -a, -um, *one.*

urbs, urbis (f.), *city.*

usque ad (Acc.), *right up to.*

ūsus, -ūs (m.), *use.*

ut (with indic.), *as, when;* (with subj.), *so that; in order that.*

uter, utra, utrum? *which of two?*

uterque, utraque, utrumque, *each of two.*

ūtilis, -e, *useful.*

ūtor, -ī, ūsus sum (Abl.), *I use.*

utrinque, *on both sides.*

utrum (in double indir. quest.), *whether.*

uxor, uxōris (f.), *wife.*

Vadum, -ī (n.), *shallow.*

vagor, -ārī, vagātus sum, *I wander.*

validus, -a, -um, *strong.*

vallum, -ī (n.), *rampart.*

vānus, -a, -um, *useless.*

vario, 1, *I differ.*

vasto, 1, *I ravage, lay waste.*

vectīgal, vectīgālis (n.), *tribute.*

vectis, vectis (m.), *lever.*

veho, -ere, vexī, vectum, *I carry;*
 vehor, *I ride, drive.*
vel, *even.*
velut, *as if.*
vendito, 1, *I offer for sale.*
venio, -īre, vēnī, ventum, *I come.*
ventus, -ī (m.), *wind.*
verbum, -ī (n.), *word.*
vereor, -ērī, veritus sum, *I fear,*
 reverence.
vērō, *indeed.*
vērus, -a, -um, *true.*
vester, vestra, vestrum, *your*
 (plur.).
vestīmentum, -ī (n.), *garment.*
vestis, vestis (f.), *clothing.*
veto, -āre, vetuī, vetitum, *I forbid,*
 order . . . not.
via, -ae (f.), *way, road.*
victōria, -ae (f.), *victory.*
video, -ēre, vīdī, vīsum, *I see;*
 videor, *I seem.*
vigeo, -ēre, *I am strong, flourish.*
vigil, vigilis (m.), *sentry.*
vigilia, -ae (f.), *watch.*
vīgintī, *twenty.*
villa, -ae (f.), *country-house, farm.*

vincio, -īre, vinxī, vinctum, *I*
 bind.
vinco, -ere, vīcī, victum, *I conquer.*
vinculum, -ī (n.), *chain.*
vīnum, -ī (n.), *wine.*
vir, virī (m.), *man, husband.*
virgō, virginis (f.), *maiden.*
virtūs, -tūtis (f.), *courage.*
vīs, Acc. vim, Abl. vī (f.), *force,*
 vigour, violence; pl. **vīrēs,**
 vīrium, *strength.*
vīso, -ere, vīsī, vīsum, *I visit.*
vīta, -ae (f.), *life.*
vitium, -ī (n.), *fault, failing.*
vīto, 1, *I avoid.*
vitrum, -ī (n.), *woad.*
vīvo, -ere, vixī, victum, *I live.*
vix, *hardly, scarcely, with difficulty.*
vixdum, *scarcely yet.*
volo, velle, voluī, *I am willing,
 wish.*
vox, vōcis (f.), *voice.*
vulgo, 1, *I publish.*
vulnero, 1, *I wound.*
vulnus, vulneris (n.), *wound.*
vultus, -ūs (m.), *expression, looks.*

English–Latin Vocabulary

Verbs which are followed by 1 *or* 2 *or* 4, *to show the number of their Conjugation, are conjugated regularly.*

Proper Nouns are usually not given, if they are the same in Latin as in English.

The long quantity of the final -o *of Verbs has been omitted.*

Able, I am, **possum, posse, potuī.**

about (*concerning*), **dē** (Abl.); (*time*), **ferē.**

about to. Future participle, Ch. 23.

account of, on, **ob, propter** (Acc.).

accuse, I, **accūso,** 1.

across, **trans** (Acc.).

adopt a plan, I, **consilium capio, capere, cēpī, captum.**

adornment, **ornātus, -ūs** (m.).

advance, I, **prōcēdo, incēdo, -ere, -cessī, -cessum; prōgredior, -gredī, -gressus sum.**

advice, **consilium, -ī** (n.),

advise, I, **moneo,** 2.

afford, I, **praebeo,** 2.

afraid (*of*), *I am,* **timeo, -ēre, timuī.**

after (Prep.), **post** (Acc.).

afterwards, **posteā.**

again, **rursus;** (*a second time*), **iterum.**

against (*enemy*), **adversus** (Acc.); (*danger, law, etc.*), **contrā** (Acc.).

alert, **ācer, ācris, ācre.**

Alexander, **Alexander, Alexandrī** (m.).

all, **omnis, omne.**

allow (*someone to*), *I,* **sino, -ere, sīvī, situm; patior, patī, passus sum;** *allow something to someone,* **permitto, -ere, -mīsī, -missum.**

ally, **socius, -ī** (m.).

almost, **prope, paene.**

along, **praeter** (Acc.).

Alps, the, **Alpēs, -ium** (f.).

already, **iam.**

also, **etiam, quoque.**

although, **quanquam.**

always, **semper.**

am, I, **sum, esse, fuī;** *am* (*a distance*) *from,* **absum, -esse, -fuī.**

ambassador, **lēgātus, -ī** (m.).

ambush, **insidiae, -ārum** (f. pl.).

among, **inter, apud** (Acc.).

ancestors, **māiōrēs, -um** (m. pl.).

anchor, **ancora, -ae** (f.).

ancient, **vetus,** Gen. **veteris.**

and, **et, ac** (before consonant), **atque, -que;** *and not,* **nec, neque;** (in final and indir. command clauses), **nēve, neu.**

angry, **īrātus, -a, -um.**

angry, I am, **īrascor, -ī, īrātus sum.**

animal, **animal, animālis** (n.).

226

announce, I, **nuntio**, 1.

another, **alius, alia, aliud.**

any (after negative), **ullus, ulla, ullum.**

anyone (after word with negative meaning), **quisquam**; (after **nē** in final clauses and indir. commands), **quis** (indef. Pron.).

appear, I, **appāreo**, 2.

appoint, I, **creo**, 1.

approach, I, **appropinquo**, 1 (intrans.), **ad**; (*a person*), **adeo, -īre, -iī, -itum** (trans. or with **ad**).

Archimedes, **Archimēdēs, Archimēdis** (m.).

armed, **armātus, -a, -um.**

arms (*weapons*), **arma, -ōrum** (n. pl.).

army, **exercitus, -ūs** (m.).

around, **circā** (Acc.).

arrival, **adventus, -ūs** (m.).

arrive, I, **pervenio, -īre, -vēnī, -ventum, ad.**

artillery, **tormenta, -ōrum** (n. pl.).

as (*because*), **quia, quod; cum** (with subj.).

as (*just as, according as*), **ut.**

as (*while*). Present participle is often used, Ch. 23.

as—as possible, **quam**, with superlative; *as soon as possible*, **quam prīmum.**

as far as, **usque ad** (Acc.).

ask, I (*question*), **rogo**, 1.

ask, I (*request*), **rogo**, 1; **ōro**, 1.

ask for, I, **ōro**, 1 (with two Acc.); **rogo**, 1.

assemble, I (intrans.), **convenio, -īre, -vēnī, -ventum.**

Athenians, the, **Athēniensēs, -ium** (m. pl.).

attack, I, **oppugno**, 1; **impetum facio in** (Acc.).

attack (*charge*), **impetus, -ūs** (m.); (*siege*), **oppugnātiō, -ōnis** (f.).

auctioneer, **praecō, -ōnis** (m.).

avoid, I, **vīto**, 1.

await, I, **exspecto**, 1.

awake, I (trans.), **excito**, 1.

Bad, very, **pessimus, -a, -um.**

baggage, **impedīmenta, -ōrum** (n. pl.).

bank, **rīpa, -ae** (f.).

battle, **proelium, -ī** (n.).

beach, I, **subdūco, -ere, -duxī, -ductum.**

bear, I, **fero, ferre, tulī, lātum.**

beast of burden, **iūmentum, -ī** (n.).

beautiful, **pulcher, pulchra, pulchrum.**

beautifully, **pulchrē.**

because, **quia, quod.**

because of, **ob, propter** (Acc.).

become, I; **fīo, fierī, factus sum.**

before (Prep.), **ante** (Acc.); (Advb.), **anteā**; *on the day before*, **prīdiē.**

beg, I, **ōro**, 1; *I beg for*, **ōro** (with two Acc.).

begin, I, **incipio, -cipere, -cēpī, -ceptum;** also, *I began*, **coepī.** Note also the use of imperf. tense for *began to.*

believe, I, crēdo, -ere, crēdidī, crēditum (Dat.).

benefit, for the public, in ūsum publicum.

beseech, I, ōro, 1.

besides, praetereā.

besiege, I, obsideo, -ēre, -sēdī, -sessum.

best, optimus, -a, -um.

betake myself, I, mē confero, -ferre, -tulī, collātum.

betray, I, prōdo, -ere, -didī, -ditum.

better, melior, melius.

between, inter (Acc.).

bidding, at the, iussū.

big, magnus, -a, -um; *bigger*, māior, māius; *biggest*, maximus, -a, -um.

bind, I, vincio, -īre, vinxī, vinctum.

bitter, e.g. *of words*, asper, aspera, asperum.

blame, I, culpo, 1.

blind, caecus, -a, -um.

block, I, obstruo, -ere, -struxī, -structum.

Boadicea, Boudicca, -ae (f.).

body, corpus, corporis (n.).

boldly, audacter.

boldness, audācia, -ae (f.).

book, liber, librī (m.).

booty, praeda, -ae (f.).

both (Adj.), ambō, ambae, ambō.

both . . . and, et . . . et.

bottom of, the, use īmus, -a, -um.

boy, puer, puerī (m.).

brave, fortis, -e.

bravely, fortiter.

bravery, fortitūdō, -dinis (f.).

break, I, frango, -ere, frēgī, fractum; *break a way*, viam rumpo, -ere, rūpī, ruptum; *break away* (trans.), abrumpo.

breakfast, I have, prandeo, -ēre, prandī, pransum.

breakfast, prandium, -ī (n.).

bridge, pons, pontis (m.).

bring, I, fero, ferre, tulī, lātum; (*away*), aufero, -ferre, abstulī, ablātum; (*back*), refero, -ferre, rettulī, relātum; *I am brought* (*by tide*), dēferor, dēferrī, dēlātus sum.

bring (*ship*), *I*, appello, -ere, appulī, appulsum.

Britain, Britannia, -ae (f.).

Britons, the, Britannī, -ōrum (m. pl.).

brother, frāter, frātris (m.).

build, I, aedifico, 1; (*road*), mūnio, 4.

busied in, occupātus, -a, -um, in (Abl.).

busy on, intentus, -a, -um, with Dat.

but, sed; *but not*, nec tamen.

but (*except*) *after negative*, nisi.

buy, I, emo, -ere, ēmī, emptum.

by (agent), ā, ab before vowel (Abl.).

Caesar, Caesar, Caesaris (m.).

call, I (*by name*), appello, 1; voco, 1; (*back*), revoco, 1; (*together*), convoco, 1.

camp, **castra, -ōrum** (n. pl.).

can, *I*, **possum, posse, potuī.**

Capitol, **Capitōlium, -ī** (n.).

capture, *I*, **capio, capere, cēpī, captum.**

carefully, **dīligenter.**

carry, *I*, **porto**, 1 ; **fero, ferre, tulī, lātum;** (*across*), **transporto**, 1 ; (*away*), **aufero, -ferre, abstulī, ablātum;** (*deliver*), **dēfero;** (*forward*), **prōveho, -ere, -vexī, -vectum.**

Carthage, **Carthāgō, -ginis** (f.).

Carthaginian, **Carthāginiensis, -e;** *Carthaginians, the*, **Poenī, -ōrum** (m. pl.).

catch, *I*, **capio, capere, cēpī, captum.**

catch sight of, *I*, **conspicio, -ere, -spexī, -spectum; conspicor, -ārī, conspicātus sum.**

Cato, **Catō, -ōnis** (m.).

cause, **causa, -ae** (f.).

cautious, **cautus, -a, -um.**

cavalryman, **eques, equitis** (m.); *cavalry*, **equitēs, -um** (m. pl.).

celebrate, *I*, **celebro**, 1.

certain, a, **quīdam, quaedam, quoddam.**

certain (*reliable*), **certus, -a, -um.**

chain, **vinculum, -ī** (n.).

challenge, *I*, **lacesso, -ere, lacessīvī, lacessītum.**

chance, by, **forte.**

change, *I* (trans.), **mūto**, 1.

character (*letter of alphabet*), **littera, -ae** (f.).

chariot (*war*), **esseda, -ae** (f.).

charioteer, **essedārius, -ī** (m.).

check, *I*, **cohibeo**, 2.

chest, **pectus, pectoris** (n.).

chief (Noun), **princeps, principis** (c.); (Adj.), **princeps, Gen. principis.**

children, **līberī, -ōrum** (m. pl.).

choose, *I*, **dēligo, -ere, -lēgī, -lectum;** (*site*), **capio.**

Cicero, **Cicerō, -ōnis** (m.).

circus, **circus, -ī** (m.).

citadel, **arx, arcis** (f.).

citizen, **cīvis, cīvis** (c.).

city, **urbs, urbis** (f.).

climb, *I*, **supero**, 1 ; **ascendo, -ere, -scendī, -scensum;** *climb up* (intrans.), **ascendo.**

club, **clāva, -ae** (f.).

coast, **ōra, -ae** (f.).

cohort, **cohors, cohortis** (f.).

cold (Noun), **frīgus, frīgoris** (n.).

colleague, **collēga, -ae** (m.).

collect, *I*, **colligo, -ere, collēgī, collectum.**

column, **agmen, agminis** (n.).

combat, **pugna, -ae** (f.).

come, *I*, **venio, -īre, vēnī, ventum;** (*back*), **redeo, -īre, rediī, reditum; regredior, -gredī, -gressus sum.**

command, *I put in*, **praeficio, -ficere, -fēcī, -fectum** (Acc. of dir. object, followed by Dat.).

command (*authority*), **imperium, -ī** (n.).

commander, **praefectus, -ī** (m.); (*c. in chief*), **imperātor, -tōris** (m.).

compel, I, cōgo, -ere, coēgī, coactum.

complain, I, queror, -ī, questus sum.

complete, I, perficio, -ficere, -fēcī, -fectum.

compose, I, compōno, -ere, -posuī, -positum.

condition (of peace), condiciō, -ōnis (f.).

confess, I, confiteor, -ērī, -fessus sum.

conflagration, incendium, -ī (n.).

conquer, I, supero, 1 ; vinco, -ere, vīcī, victum.

conqueror, victor, victōris (m.).

consider, I (someone as), habeo, 2.

consul, consul, consulis (m.).

continued (to), I. Imperfect tense.

contrary to, praeter (Acc.).

contribute, I, confero, -ferre, -tulī, collātum.

converse, I, colloquor, -ī, collocūtus sum.

convey, I, dēfero, -ferre, -tulī, -lātum.

corn, frūmentum, -ī (n.).

count, I, numero, 1.

country, a, terra, -ae (f.) ; (native land), patria, -ae (f.).

country-house, villa, -ae (f.).

courage, virtūs, -tūtis (f.).

course, cursus, -ūs (m.).

cover, I, tego, -ere, texī, tectum.

crisis, discrīmen, -minis (n.).

cross, I (mountain), supero, 1 ; (mountain or river), transeo, -īre, -iī, -itum (trans.) ; transgredior, -gredī, -gressus sum.

crowd, turba, -ae (f.).

cry, I, clāmo, 1 ; (out), exclāmo.

Damage, I, laedo, -ere, laesī, laesum.

danger, perīculum, -ī (n.).

dare, I, audeo, -ēre, ausus sum.

daughter, fīlia, -ae (f.).

dawn, prīma lux, prīmae lūcis (f.).

day, diēs, diēī (m.).

death, mors, mortis (f.).

deceive, I, fallo, -ere, fefellī, falsum; dēcipio, -cipere, -cēpī, -ceptum.

decide, I, constituo, -ere, -stituī, -stitūtum.

deep, altus, -a, -um.

defeat, I, supero, 1 ; vinco, -ere, vīcī, victum.

defend, I, dēfendo, -ere, -fendī, -fensum.

delay, I (trans.), tardo, 1 ; (intrans.), moror, -ārī, morātus sum; cunctor, -ārī, cunctātus sum.

delay, mora, -ae (f.).

deliberate, I, dēlībero, 1.

delight, I, dēlecto, 1.

demand, I, postulo, 1 ; posco, -ere, poposcī.

denarius (silver coin), dēnārius, -ī (m.).

deny, I refuse something to someone), nego, 1.

depart, I, discēdo, -ere, -cessī, -cessum.

depth, **altitūdō, -dinis** (f.).

descend, *I*, **dēscendo, -ere, -scendī, -scensum.**

desert from, *I*, **dēficio, -ficere, -fēcī, -fectum, ab.**

deserter, **perfuga, -ae** (m.).

deserve, *I*, **mereor, -ērī, meritus sum.**

desire, *I*, **cupio, cupere, cupīvī, cupītum.**

despair, *I*, **dēspēro**, 1.

despatch, **litterae, -ārum** (f. pl.).

despise, *I*, **contemno, -ere, -tempsī, -temptum.**

destroy, *I*, **dēleo, -ēre, dēlēvī, dēlētum**; (*by illness*), **absūmo, -ere, -sumpsī, -sumptum.**

determine, *I*, **constituo, -ere, -stituī, -stitūtum.**

dictator, **dictātor, -tōris** (m.).

die, *I*, **morior, morī, mortuus sum.**

difficult, **difficilis, -e.**

difficulty, **difficultās, -tātis** (f.); *with d.*, **vix, aegrē.**

disaster, **clādēs, clādis** (f.).

disband, *I*, **dīmitto, -ere, -mīsī, -missum.**

discover, *I*, **reperio, -īre, repperī, repertum**; (*find out*), **cognosco, -ere, -nōvī, -nitum.**

disembark, *I* (trans.), **expōno, -ere, -posuī, -positum.**

disgrace, **ignōminia, -ae** (f.).

disgraceful, **turpis, -e.**

displease, *I*, **displiceo**, 2 (Dat.).

ditch, **fossa, -ae** (f.).

divide (*from*), *I*, **dīvido, -ere, dīvīsī, dīvīsum, (ab).**

do, *I*, **facio, facere, fēcī, factum.**

do not, **nōlī, nōlīte** (with infin.).

dog, **canis, canis** (c.).

doubt, *I*, **dubito**, 1.

doubt, *without*, **sine dubiō.**

down from, **dē** (Abl.).

draw (*entice*) *I*, **pertraho, -ere, -traxī, -tractum.**

draw up, *I*, **instruo, -ere, -struxī, -structum.**

draw (*figure*), *I*, **dēscrībo, -ere, -scripsī, -scriptum.**

dread, *I*, **reformīdo**, 1 (no perf.).

drink, *I*, **bibo, -ere, bibī.**

drive, *I*, **compello, -ere, -pulī, -pulsum**; (*back*), **repello, -ere, reppulī, repulsum**; (*out*), **expello, -ere, -pulī, -pulsum.**

drive (*in carriage*), *I*, **vehor, -ī, vectus sum.**

driver, **rector, rectōris** (m.).

Each, **quisque, quaeque, quidque** or **quicque** (**quodque**); *each of two*, **uterque, utraque, utrumque.**

each other, *with each other*, **inter sē.**

eager, **alacer, alacris, alacre.**

eagerly, use Adjective.

ear, **auris, auris** (f.).

earth, **terra, -ae** (f.).

easily, **facile.**

easy, **facilis, -e.**

eight, **octō.**

elephant, **elephantus, -ī** (m.).

employ, *I*, **ūtor, -ī, ūsus sum** (Abl.).

encourage, I, confirmo, 1; *(to)* hortor, -ārī, hortātus sum (ut).

end, I, conficio, -ficere, -fēcī, -fectum.

endure, I, fero, ferre, tulī, lātum.

enemy, hostis, hostis (c.), mostly used in pl. for *the enemy.*

enjoy, I, fruor, -ī, fructus sum (Abl.).

enter, I, intro, 1; ineo, -īre, -iī, -itum (both trans.).

entirely, omnīnō.

entrance, aditus, -ūs (m.).

entrust, I, mando, 1.

envy, I, invideo, -ēre, -vīdī, -vīsum (Dat.).

equal, pār, Gen. paris.

equip, I, instruo, -ere, -struxī, -structum.

escape, I, ēvādo, -ere, -vāsī, -vāsum; effugio, -fugere, -fūgī.

escape, fuga, -ae (f.).

establish, I, firmo, 1.

Etruscans, the, Etruscī, -ōrum (m. pl.).

even, etiam, et.

ever (after negative), unquam.

everlasting, perpetuus, -a, -um.

every, omnis, omne.

everywhere, ubīque.

examine, I, explōro, 1.

example, exemplum, -ī (n.).

except for, praeter (Acc.).

excessive, nimius, -a, -um.

expect, I, exspecto, 1.

expectation, opīniō, -ōnis (f.).

expedient, ūtilis, -e.

explain, I, expōno, -ere, -posuī, -positum.

eye, oculus, -ī (m.).

Fail, I, dēficio, -ficere, -fēcī, -fectum.

fair (*beautiful*), pulcher, pulchra, pulchrum.

fair (*just*), aequus, -a, -um.

faithful, fidēlis, -e; fīdus, -a, -um.

fall, I, cado, -ere, cecidī, cāsum; lābor, -ī, lapsus sum; (*into*), incido, -ere, -cidī, with in and Acc.

fall, cāsus, -ūs (m.).

false, falsus, -a, -um.

famous, praeclārus, -a, -um; sometimes ille (Ch. 10).

far, longē, procul; *too far,* longius.

far away, I am, longē or multum absum.

fasten (*to*), *I,* deligo, 1 (ad).

fatal, fātālis, -e.

father, pater, patris (m.).

favourable, secundus, -a, -um.

fear, I, timeo, -ēre, timuī.

festival (Adj.), festus, -a, -um.

few, paucī, -ae, -a.

field, ager, agrī (m.).

fiercely, ācriter.

fifteen, quindecim.

fight, I, pugno, 1.

fight, proelium, -ī (n.).

figure, forma, -ae (f.).

fill, I, impleo, compleo, -ēre, -plēvī, -plētum.

finally, postrēmō.

find, I, invenio, -īre, -vēnī, -ventum.

find out (*from*), *I,* cognosco, -ere, -nōvī, -nitum (ex).

finish (*end*), *I*, **conficio, -ficere -fēcī, -fectum**; (*complete*), **perficio.**

fire, **ignis, ignis** (m.).

firmly, **constanter.**

first, **prīmus, -a, -um.**

first, at first, **prīmum, prīmō**; *for the first time*, **prīmum.**

fitly, **ēleganter.**

five, **quinque.**

fix, I, **dēfīgo, -ere, -fixī, -fixum.**

flank, **latus, lateris** (n.); *on the flanks*, **ā lateribus.**

flee, I, **fugio, fugere, fūgī, (fugitūrus).**

fleet, **classis, classis** (f.).

flight, **fuga, -ae** (f.).

flock, **grex, gregis** (m.).

flourish, I, **flōreo, -ēre, flōruī.**

fly out, I, **ēvolo, 1.**

fodder, **pābulum, -ī** (n.).

follow, I, **sequor, -ī, secūtus sum.**

folly, **stultitia, -ae** (f.).

foolish, **stultus, -a, -um.**

foot, **pēs, pedis** (m.); *on foot*, **pedibus.**

footprint, **vestīgium, -ī** (n.).

for (Conjunction), **nam** (1st word); **enim** (2nd word).

for (*because of*), **propter** (Acc.).

for (*on behalf of*), **prō** (Abl.), but often, Dat. of Advantage.

for (*the purpose of*), **ad** (Acc.).

forager, **pābulātor, -tōris** (m.).

forbid, I, **veto, -āre, vetuī, vetitum.**

forces, **cōpiae, -ārum** (f. pl.).

foreigners, **barbarī, -ōrum** (m. pl.).

forget, I, **oblīviscor, -ī, oblītus sum** (Gen.).

former, **prior, prius; superior, -ius;** of *qualities*, e.g. *courage*, **prior;** *the former* (opposed to *the latter*), **ille, illa, illud.**

fortification, **mūnītiō, -ōnis** (f.).

fortify, I, **mūnio, 4.**

fortunate, **fēlix**, Gen. **fēlīcis.**

fortune, **fortūna, -ae** (f.).

forum, **forum, -ī** (n.).

four, **quattuor.**

free (*from*), *I*, **lībero, 1 (ab).**

friend, **amīcus, -ī** (m.).

friendship, **amīcitia, -ae** (f.).

frighten, I, **terreo, 2.**

from, **ā, ab** before vowel (Abl.); (*out of* and after verbs of *finding out*), **ē, ex** before vowel.

from here, **hinc**; *from there*, **inde** *from where*, **unde.**

front, in, **ā fronte.**

front of, in, **ante** (Acc.); **prō** (Abl.).

fruits, **fructus, -ūs** (m.) (used in sing.).

full, **plēnus, -a, -um.**

further (Adj.), **ulterior, -ius.**

further (Advb.), **longius.**

Gallic, **Gallicus, -a, -um.**

game, **lūdus, -ī** (m.).

garrison, **praesidium, -ī** (n.).

gate, **porta, -ae** (f.).

Gaul, **Gallia, -ae** (f.).

Gaul, a, **Gallus, -ī** (m.).

general, **dux, ducis** (c.); **imperātor, -tōris** (m.).

get ready, I, **paro, 1.**

gift, dōnum, -ī (n.).

give, I, do, dare, dedī, datum.

give way, I, cēdo, -ere, cessī, cessum.

go, I, eo, īre, iī, itum; (*away*), abeo; (*down*), dēscendo, -ere, -scendī, -scensum; (*into*), ineo (trans.); (*out*), exeo; (*up to*), subeo ad.

goad, I, irrīto, 1.

god, deus, -ī (m.).

gold, aurum, -ī (n.).

good, bonus, -a, -um.

goose, anser, anseris (m.).

grappling-hook, manus, -ūs (f.).

grassy, herbidus, -a, -um.

great, magnus, -a, -um.

greatest, very great, maximus, -a, -um.

greatly, magnopere.

Greece, Graecia, -ae (f.).

Greek (Adj.), Graecus, -a, -um; *Greeks, the,* Graecī, -ōrum (m. pl.).

Greek (*language*), lingua Graeca (f.).

greet, I, salūto, 1.

groan, I, gemo, -ere, gemuī, gemitum.

ground, often locus, -ī (m.).

grow, I, cresco, -ere, crēvī, crētum.

grow old, I, see under *old.*

guard, I, custōdio, 4.

guard, custōs, -tōdis (c.).

guide, dux, ducis (c.).

Hail, I, salūto, 1.

halt, I, consisto, -ere, -stitī, -stitum.

hand, manus, -ūs (f.).

hand down, I, trādo, -ere, -didī, -ditum.

hand over, I, trādo.

Hannibal, Hannibal, -balis (m.).

happens, it, accidit, perf. accidit.

harbour, portus, -ūs (m.).

harm, I, laedo, -ere, laesī, laesum (Acc.); noceo, 2 (Dat.).

Hasdrubal, Hasdrubal, -balis (m.).

hatred, odium, -ī (n.).

have, I, habeo, 2; often expressed by sum with Dat. of possessor.

he, is, ille.

heap together, I, congero, -ere, -gessī, -gestum.

hear, I, audio, 4.

heat, aestus, -ūs (m.).

heavy, gravis, -e.

height, altitūdō, -dinis (f.).

help, I, iuvo, -āre, iūvī, iūtum; so also adiuvo.

help, auxilium, -ī (n.).

Hercules, Herculēs, Herculis (m.).

herd, pecus, pecoris (n.).

here, hīc; *from here,* hinc.

hesitate, I, dubito, 1.

hide, I, abdo, -ere, -didī, -ditum.

high, altus, -a, -um; *higher* (*ground*), superior.

highly (*at a high price*), magnī; *very highly,* maximī.

hill, collis, collis (m.).

hillock, tumulus, -ī (m.).

himself (reflexive Pron.), sē.

hinder, I, **impedio,** 4.

his, **ēius;** *his own* (reflexive), **suus, -a, -um.**

hold, I, **teneo, -ēre, tenuī, tentum;** *I hold back* (*check*), **prohibeo,** 2.

home (*homewards*), **domum;** *at home,* **domī.**

Homer, **Homērus, -ī** (m.).

hope, I, **spēro,** 1.

hope, **spēs, speī** (f.).

horse, **equus, -ī** (m.).

hostage, **obses, obsidis** (c.).

hot, **calidus, -a, -um.**

hour, **hōra, -ae** (f.).

how (*in what way*)? **quōmodo?**

how big? **quantus, -a, -um?**

how many? **quot?**

how often? **quotiēs?**

however, **tamen** (2nd word).

huge, **ingens,** Gen. **ingentis.**

human, **hūmānus, -a, -um.**

hunger, **famēs, famis,** Abl. **famē** (f.).

hurl, I, **iacto,** 1; **iacio, iacere, iēcī, iactum; cōnicio, -icere, -iēcī, -iectum; mitto, -ere, mīsī, missum;** (*forth*), **ēmitto;** (*forward*), **prōicio;** (*headlong*), **praecipito,** 1.

hurry, I, **propero,** 1.

husband, **vir, virī** (m.); **marītus, -ī** (m.).

hut, **casa, -ae** (f.).

I, **ego.**

ice, **glaciēs, glaciēī** (f.).

if, **sī;** (*whether,* in indir. question), **num.**

ignorance, in, **ignārus, -a, -um.**

impassable, **invius, -a, -um.**

import, I, **importo,** 1.

impose, I, **impōno, -ere, -posuī, -positum.**

in, **in** (Abl.).

incautiously, use Adj., **incautus, -a, -um.**

increase, I (trans.), **augeo, -ēre, auxī, auctum.**

indeed, **quidem** (2nd word).

infantry, **peditēs, -um** (m. pl.).

inform, I, **certiōrem facio,** with person *informed* in Acc.; *I am informed,* **certior fīo.**

inhabitant, **incola, -ae** (c.).

injure, I, **laedo, -ere, laesī, laesum** (Acc.); **noceo,** 2 (Dat.).

inside (Prep.), **intrā** (Acc.).

instrument, **instrūmentum, -ī** (n.).

into, **in** (Acc.).

invent, I, **invenio, -īre, -vēnī, -ventum.**

invite (*to*), *I,* **invīto,** 1 (ad).

iron, **ferrum, -ī** (n.).

iron (Adj.), **ferreus, -a, -um.**

Italy, **Ītalia, -ae** (f.).

Italy, of, **Ītalicus, -a, -um.**

Javelin, **iaculum, -ī** (n.); **telum, -ī** (n.).

jealousy, **invidia, -ae** (f.).

join (*tie together*), *I,* **cōpulo,** 1; (*forces*), **coniungo, -ere, -iunxī, -iunctum;** (*battle*), **committo, -ere, -mīsī, -missum.**

journey, **iter, itineris** (n.).

joyfully, use Adj., **laetus, -a, -um.**
just, **iustus, -a, -um.**

Keep (*retain*), *I*, **retineo, -ēre, -tinuī, -tentum.**
keep hands off, *I*, **manūs abstineo, -ēre, -tinuī, -tentum, ab.**
Kent, **Cantium, -ī** (n.).
kill, *I*, **neco,** 1; **occīdo, -ere, occīdī, occīsum; interficio, -ficere, -fecī, -fectum.**
kind, **genus, generis** (n.).
kind of man to, **is quī** with subjunctive.
kindness (*act*), **beneficium, -ī** (n.).
king, **rex, rēgis** (m.).
know, *I*, **scio,** 4.
know, *I do not*, **ignōro,** 1; **nescio,** 4; (*how to*), **nescio,** 4, with infin.

Ladder, **scāla, -ae** (f.).
lady, **mātrōna, -ae** (f.).
lament, *I*, **dēplōro,** 1.
land, **terra, -ae** (f.); *lands* (*territory*), **fīnēs, fīnium** (m. pl.).
land, *I* (trans.), **expōno, -ere, -posuī, -positum.**
landing-place, **ēgressus, -ūs** (m.).
large, **magnus, -a, -um.**
last, **ultimus, -a, -um.**
last, at, **postrēmō, tandem.**
lately, **nūper.**
Latin, in, **Latīnē.**
latter, the, **hīc, haec, hōc.**
laugh, *I*, **rīdeo, -ēre, rīsī, rīsum.**
laughter, **rīsus, -ūs** (m.).

law, **lex, lēgis** (f.).
lay aside, *I*, **dēpōno, -ere, -posuī, -positum.**
lay waste, *I*, **vasto,** 1.
lead, *I*, **dūco, -ere, duxī, ductum;** (*back*), **redūco;** (*down*), **dēdūco;** (*out*), **ēdūco.**
leader, **dux, ducis** (c.).
leap down, *I*, **dēsilio, -īre, -siluī, -sultum;** *I leap over*, **transilio, -īre, transiluī.**
learn (*find out*), *I*, **cognosco, -ere, -nōvī, -nitum.**
learn (*by study*), *I*, **disco, -ere, didicī.**
leave (*depart*), *I*, **discēdo, -ere, -cessī, -cessum, ab.**
leave (*behind*), *I*, **relinquo, -ere, -līquī, -lictum.**
left, I am, **supersum, -esse, -fuī.**
legion, **legiō, -ōnis** (f.).
length, **longitūdō, -dinis** (f.).
length, at, **tandem.**
less (Advb.), **minus.**
lest, **nē.**
let down, *I*, **dēmitto, -ere, -mīsī, -missum.**
let go (*dismiss*), *I*, **dīmitto;** *I let* (*something*) *go*, **remitto.**
letter, **epistola, -ae** (f.); **litterae, -ārum** (f. pl.).
levy, **dīlectus, -ūs** (m.); *I hold a levy*, **dīlectum habeo,** 2.
lie, *I*, **iaceo, -ēre, iacuī.**
lie, *I* (*tell a lie*), **mentior, -īrī, mentītus sum.**
light (Adj.), **levis, -e.**
like, **similis, -e.**

line (of battle), **aciēs, aciēī** (f.).
line of march, **iter, itineris** (n.).
lion, **leō, leōnis** (m.).
listen to, I, **audio, 4**.
little, a (Advb.), **paulum**.
little (value), at very, **minimī**.
live, I, **vīvo, -ere, vixī, victum**.
log, **lignum, -ī** (n.).
long, **longus, -a, -um**.
long time, for a, **diū**.
longer (Advb.), **diūtius**.
look at, I, **specto, 1; aspicio, -spicere, -spexī, -spectum; (back at)**, **respicio**.
look after, I, **cūro, 1.**
loose, I, **resolvo, -ere, -solvī, -solūtum**.
lose, I, **āmitto, -ere, -mīsī, -missum;** *I lose hope*, **spem dēpōno, -ere, -posuī, -positum**.
loss, **dētrīmentum, -ī** (n.).
love, **amor, amōris** (m.).
low, **humilis, -e;** *lower (ground)*, **inferior**.
loyalty, **fidēs, fideī** (f.).
luxury, **luxuria, -ae** (f.).

Magistrate, **magistrātus, -ūs** (m.).
maiden, **virgō, virginis** (f.).
make, I, **facio, facere, fēcī, factum; (road)**, **mūnio, 4; (speech)**, **habeo, 2.**
make for, I, **peto, -ere, petīvī, petītum**.
man (opposed to woman), **vir, virī** (m.); *(opposed to animal)*, **homō, hominis** (m.).
many, see *much*.

march, I, **contendo, -ere, -tendī, -tentum; iter facio**.
march, **iter, itineris** (n.).
market-place, **forum, -ī** (n.).
master (of school), **magister, magistrī** (m.).
matter, **rēs, reī** (f.).
means of, by, **per** (Acc.).
means, by every, **omnī modō**.
meanwhile, **interim**.
meeting, **contiō, -ōnis** (f.).
message, **nuntius, -ī** (m.).
messenger, **nuntius, -ī** (m.).
mid-day, **merīdiēs, merīdiēī** (m.).
mid-night, **media nox, mediae noctis** (f.).
middle, **medius, -a, -um**.
mile, **mille passūs** (m. pl.); pl. **mīlia passuum**.
mind, **mens, mentis** (f.).
mind to, I turn my, **animum applico, 1, ad.**
miserable, **miser, misera, miserum**.
miserably, **miserē**.
moderate, **modestus, -a, -um**.
moment, (at that), use **tempus, temporis** (n.).
money, **pecūnia, -ae** (f.).
month, **mensis, mensis** (m.).
more, **plūs**, Gen. **plūris** (Noun in sing.); pl. **plūrēs, plūra** (Adj.).
morning, in the, **māne**.
most (Adj.), **plūrimī, -ae, -a**.
mound, **tumulus, -ī** (m.).
mountain, **mons, montis** (m.).
mountain (Adj.), **montānus, -a, -um**.

move (*camp*), *I*, **moveo, -ēre, mōvī, mōtum;** (of *feeling*), **commoveo.**

much, **multus, -a, -um;** *many,* **multī, -ae, -a;** *very many,* **plūrimī, -ae, -a.**

much (Advb.), **multum;** *so much,* **tantum;** *too much,* **nimium, nimis.**

my, **meus, -a, -um.**

Name, **nōmen, nōminis** (n.).
narrow, **angustus, -a, -um.**
native, **incola, -ae** (c.).
nature, **nātūra, -ae** (f.).
near, **prope** (Acc.).
nearer (Adj.), **propior, -ius.**
nearest, **proximus, -a, -um.**
nearly, **prope.**
neglect, I, **neglego, -ere, neglexī, neglectum.**
neighbouring, **proximus, -a, -um.**
neither (Adj.), **neuter, neutra, neutrum.**
never, **nunquam.**
nevertheless, **nihilōminus.**
new, **novus, -a, -um.**
news, **nuntius, -ī** (m.).
next (Adj.), **proximus, -a, -um;** *on the next day,* **postrīdiē.**
next (Advb.), **deīnde.**
night, **nox, noctis** (f.); *by night,* **noctū.**
no one, **nēmō,** Acc. **nēminem** (no Gen. or Abl.); *that no one* (in final clauses and indir. commands), **nē quis.**
no, none, **nullus, -a, -um.**

noise, **strepitus, -ūs** (m.).
noon, **merīdiēs, merīdiēī** (m.).
nor, **nec, neque.**
not, **nōn;** (with pres. subj. expressing exhortation, wish, or command), **nē;** *in order that . . . not,* **nē;** (in indir. commands and petitions), **nē.**
not even, **nē . . . quidem.**
not only . . . but also, **nōn modo . . . sed etiam.**
not yet, **nōndum.**
note, I, **noto,** 1.
nothing, **nihil.**
novel, **novus, -a, -um.**
now, **nunc, iam.**
number, large, **multitūdō, -dinis** (f.).
Numidians, the, **Numidae, -ārum** (m. pl.).

Obey, I, **pāreo,** 2 (Dat.).
obtain, I, **nanciscor, -ī, nactus sum.**
offer, I, **offero, offerre, obtulī, oblātum.**
offer for sale, I, **vendito,** 1.
officer, **praefectus, -ī** (m.).
often, **saepe;** *very often,* **saepissimē.**
oil, **oleum, -ī** (n.).
old, I grow, **consenesco, -ere, -senuī.**
on, in (Abl.); (after *attack*), **in** with Acc.
on to, in (Acc.).
once (*upon a time*), **quondam, ōlim.**

once, at, **statim.**

one, **ūnus, -a, -um;** *one . . ., another . . .,* **alius . . ., alius . . .**

one (of two), the one, **alter, altera, alterum.**

only, **sōlum, modo.**

open, I, **aperio, -īre, aperuī, apertum.**

opinion, **sententia, -ae** (f.).

Oppian, **Oppius, -a, -um.**

opportunity, **occāsiō, -ōnis** (f.).

oppress, I, **opprimo, -ere, -pressī, -pressum.**

or, **aut;** (in questions), **an;** *or not* (in dir. question), **annōn;** (in indir. question), **necne.**

order, I, **iubeo, -ēre, iussī, iussum** (infin.); **impero,** 1 (Dat. and **ut** with subj.).

order (command), **imperium, -ī** (n.); *by order,* **iussū.**

order (rank), **ordō, ordinis** (m.).

order that, in, **ut;** *in order that . . . not,* **nē.**

other, **alius, alia, aliud.**

other, the (of two), **alter, altera, alterum.**

ought, I, **dēbeo,** 2.

our, our own, **noster, nostra, nostrum.**

outpost, **statiō, -ōnis** (f.).

out of, **ē, ex** before vowel (Abl.).

outside (Prep), **extrā** (Acc.).

over, **trans** (Acc.).

overcome, I, **supero,** 1.

overwhelm, I, **opprimo** (see *oppress*).

owing to, **ob, propter** (Acc.).

Parent, **parens, parentis** (c.).

part, **pars, partis** (f.).

pass, **saltus, -ūs** (m.); **angustiae, -ārum** (f. pl.).

past, **praeter** (Acc.).

peace, **pax, pācis** (f.).

penetrate, I, **penetro,** 1.

people, **populus, -ī** (m.).

perceive, I, **sentio, -īre, sensī, sensum.**

perhaps, **fortasse.**

perish, I, **pereo, -īre, -iī, -itum.**

persuade, I, **persuādeo, -ēre, -suāsī, suāsum** (Dat.).

pestilence, **pestilentia, -ae** (f.).

pile, **cumulus, -ī** (m.).

pile together, I, **congero, -ere, -gessī, -gestum.**

pitch camp, I, **castra pōno, -ere, posuī, positum.**

pity, I, **misereor, -ērī, miseritus sum** (Gen.).

place, I, **loco,** 1; **pōno, -ere, posuī, positum.**

place, **locus, -ī** (m.).

plague, **pestilentia, -ae** (f.).

plain, **campus, -ī** (m.).

plan, **consilium, -ī** (n.).

play, I, **lūdo, -ere, lūsī, lūsum.**

pleasant, **iūcundus, -a, -um; grātus, -a, -um.**

please, I, **placeo,** 2 (Dat.).

pleasing, see *pleasant.*

plunder, **praeda, -ae** (f.).

poem, **carmen, carminis** (n.).

point of, on the. Future participle, Ch. 23.

pointed, **acūtus, -a, -um.**

poor, **pauper**, Gen. **pauperis.**

portcullis, **cataracta, -ae** (f.).

position, **locus, -ī** (m.).

pour, *I*, **fundo, -ere, fūdī, fūsum;**
   I pour on to, **infundo** in with
   Acc.

power (*of king, magistrate, state,
   general*), **imperium, -ī** (n.);
   (*control*), **potestās -tātis** (f.).

praise, *I*, **laudo,** 1.

pray, *I*, **precor, -ārī, precātus sum.**

prefer, *I*, **mālo, malle, māluī.**

prepare, *I*, **paro,** 1.

pretend, *I*, **simulo,** 1.

prevent, *I*, **prohibeo,** 2.

previous, **superior, -ius;** (*time*),
   prior, prius.

price, **pretium, -ī** (n.).

prisoner, **captīvus, -ī** (m.).

private citizen, **prīvātus, -ī** (m.).

private, in, **in prīvātō.**

promise, *I*, **prōmitto, -ere, -mīsī,
   -missum; polliceor, -ērī, pollicitus sum.**

propose (*law*) *I*, **fero, ferre, tulī,
   lātum.**

prosperity, **rēs secundae** (f. pl.).

protect, *I*, **dēfendo, -ere, -fendī,
   -fensum.**

proud, **superbus, -a, -um.**

provisions, **commeātus, -ūs** (m.),
   used in sing.

provoke, *I*, **lacesso, -ere, lacessīvī, lacessītum.**

public, in, **in publicō.**

public benefit, for the, see under
   benefit.

publish, *I*, **vulgo,** 1.

purple, **purpura, -ae** (f.).

purpose, on, **dē industriā.**

pursue, *I*, **persequor, -ī, persecū-
   tus sum.**

put, *I*, **pōno, -ere, posuī, positum.**

put in command, *I*, see under
   command.

put on, *I*, **induo, -ere, induī, indūtum.**

put to flight, *I*, **fugo,** 1.

Pyrenees, the, **montēs Pȳrēnaeī**
   (m. pl.).

Question, *I*, **interrogo,** 1.

quickly, **celeriter.**

Rabble, **turba, -ae** (f.).

raft, **ratis, ratis** (f.).

rainstorm, **imber, imbris** (m.).

raise, *I*, **ērigo, -ere, -rexī, -rec-
   tum; levo,** 1.

rampart, **agger, aggeris** (m.);
   vallum, -ī (n.).

ranks (*battle-line*), **aciēs, aciēī**
   (f.), in sing.

rashly, **temerē.**

rashness, **temeritās, -tātis** (f.).

rather, I would, **mālo, malle,
   māluī.**

rather (with Adj.), use comparative.

ravage, *I*, **populor, -ārī, populātus
   sum.**

reach, *I*, **pervenio, -īre, -vēnī,
   -ventum, ad.**

read, *I*, **lego, -ere, lēgī, lectum.**

ready, I get, **paro,** 1.

ready (*for*), **parātus (ad).**

realize, I, **intellego, -ere, -lexī, -lectum; sentio, -īre, sensī, sensum.**

rear, **tergum, -ī** (n.); *in the rear*, **ā tergō.**

reason, **causa, -ae** (f.).

recall, I, **revoco,** 1.

receive, I, **accipio, -cipere, -cēpī, -ceptum.**

recent, **recens,** Gen. **recentis.**

recently, **nūper.**

reckon, I, **aestimo,** 1.

reconnoitre, I, **explōro,** 1.

red-hot, **fervens,** Gen. **ferventis.**

refresh myself, I, **corpus cūro;** *they refresh themselves*, **corpora cūrant.**

refuse (*something*), I, **recūso,** 1.

refuse (*to*), I, **nōlo, nolle, nōluī.**

reinforcements, **novae cōpiae** (f. pl.).

reject, I, **repudio,** 1.

rejoice, I, **gaudeo, -ēre, gāvīsus sum.**

relate, I, **narro,** 1.

remain (*survive*), I, **supersum, -esse, -fuī;** (*stay*), **maneo, -ēre, mansī, (mansūrus).**

remainder, the, **reliquī, -ae, -a.**

remove, I (trans.), **removeo, -ēre, -mōvī, -mōtum.**

renew, I, **redintegro,** 1.

repair, I, **reficio, -ere, -fēcī, -fectum.**

repeal, I, **abrogo,** 1.

repeatedly, **identidem.**

reply, I, **respondeo, -ēre, -spondī, -sponsum.**

reply, **responsum, -ī** (n.).

report, I, **nuntio,** 1.

resist, I, **resisto, -ere, restitī** (Dat.).

resolve, I, **constituo, -ere, -stituī, -stitūtum.**

rest, **quiēs, quiētis** (f.).

rest, the, **reliquī, -ae, -a; cēterī, -ae, -a.**

restore, I, **reddo, -ere, reddidī, redditum.**

retain, I, **retineo, -ēre, -tinuī, -tentum.**

retreat, I, **pedem refero, -ferre, rettulī, relātum; mē recipio, -cipere, -cēpī, -ceptum.**

return, I (intrans.), **regredior, -gredī, -gressus sum; redeo, -īre, -iī, -itum.**

return, **reditus, -ūs** (m.).

return for, in, **prō** (Abl.).

reverence, I, **vereor, -ērī, veritus sum.**

revolt from, I, **dēficio, -ficere, -fēcī, -fectum, ab.**

reward, **praemium, -ī** (n.).

Rhone, the, **Rhodanus, -ī** (m.).

rich, **dīves,** Gen. **dīvitis.**

riches, **opēs, opum** (f. pl.).

ride, I, **vehor, -ī, vectus sum.**

right, **iūs, iūris** (n.).

right up to, **usque ad** (Acc.).

ring, **ānulus, -ī** (m.).

rise, I, **surgo, -ere, surrexī, surrectum; orior, orīrī, ortus sum;** (*up*), **exorior.**

river, **flūmen, flūminis** (n.).

road, **via, viae** (f.).

rock, **saxum, -ī** (n.).

roll down, I, dēvolvo, -ere, -volvī, -volūtum.

Roman, Rōmānus, -a, -um; *Romans, the,* Rōmānī, -ōrum (m. pl.).

Rome, Rōma, -ae (f.).

round (Prep.), circā (Acc.).

rouse, I, excito, 1.

rout, I, fugo, 1.

route, iter, itineris (n.).

rowing, by means of, rēmīs (*by oars*).

royal, rēgius, -a, -um.

rule, I, rego, -ere, rexī, rectum.

rumour, rūmor, rūmōris (m.).

run, I, curro, -ere, cucurrī, cursum; (*down*), dēcurro.

rush, impetus, -ūs (m.).

Sabine, Sabīnus, -a, -um; *Sabines, the,* Sabīnī, -ōrum (m. pl.).

sad, tristis, -e.

sadly, use Adjective.

safe, tūtus, -a, -um.

safety, salūs, salūtis (f.).

said (*says*) *he* (with actual words of speech), inquit; *said* (*say*) *they,* inquiunt.

sail, I, nāvigo, 1.

sail, I set, nāvem solvo, -ere, solvī, solūtum.

sale, I offer for, see under *offer.*

sally out, I, ēruptiōnem facio, facere, fēcī, factum.

same, īdem, eadem, idem.

Samnites, the, Samnītēs, -ium (m. pl.).

save, I, conservo, 1.

say, I, dīco, -ere, dixī, dictum; (*speak*), loquor, -ī, locūtus sum; *I say that ... not,* nego, 1.

says he, say they, see under *said.*

scarcely, vix, aegrē.

scarcity, inopia, -ae (f.).

scatter, I, fugo, 1.

schoolmaster, magister, magistrī (m.).

Scipio, Scīpiō, -ōnis (m.).

scout, explōrātor, -tōris (m.); so also speculātor.

sea, mare, maris (n.).

search of, in, use causā (after Gen.).

second, secundus, -a, -um.

secretly, clam.

see, I, video, -ēre, vīdī, vīsum.

seek, I, peto, -ere, petīvī, petītum.

seem, I, videor, -ērī, vīsus sum.

seize, I, occupo, 1.

self, ipse, ipsa, ipsum.

sell, I, vendo, -ere, -didī, -ditum.

senate, senātus, -ūs (m.).

senator, senātor, -tōris (m.).

send, I, mitto, -ere, mīsī, missum; (*across*), transmitto (trans); (*back*), remitto; (*forward*), praemitto; (*out*), ēmitto; (*over*), transmitto.

send for, I, arcesso, -ere, arcessīvī, arcessītum.

sentry, vigil, vigilis (m.).

serious, gravis, -e.

set free, I, lībero, 1.

set on fire, I, incendo, -ere, -cendī, -censum.

set out, I, proficiscor, -ī, profectus sum.

set sail, I, see under *sail.*

seven, **septem.**

severe, **gravis, -e.**

share, I, **commūnico, 1.**

sharp (ear), **ācer, ācris, ācre.**

shield, **scūtum, -ī** (n.).

ship, **nāvis, nāvis** (f.).

shop, **taberna, -ae** (f.).

shore, **lītus, lītoris** (n.).

short, **brevis, -e.**

short time, for a, **parumper.**

should (ought), I, **dēbeo, 2.**

shout, I, **clāmo, 1.**

show (a quality or *myself as being something), I,* **praesto, -stāre, -stitī, -stitum.**

show, **spectāculum, -ī** (n.).

shut, I, **claudo, -ere, clausī, clausum.**

Sicily, **Sicilia, -ae** (f.).

sick, **aeger, aegra, aegrum.**

side (direction), **pars, partis** (f.), e.g. **ex eā parte,** *on this side;* *on* or *from all sides, every side,* **undique.**

side (flank), **latus, lateris** (n.); *from a side,* **ā latere.**

sight, **conspectus, -ūs** (m.).

sign, **signum, -ī** (n.).

signal, **signum, -ī** (n.).

signet-ring, **ānulus, -ī** (m.).

silence, in, use Adj., **tacitus, -a, -um.**

silent, I am, **taceo, 2; sileo, -ēre, siluī.**

silently, use Adj., **tacitus.**

silver, **argentum, -ī** (n.).

simply, **simpliciter.**

since (because), **cum** (with subj.).

sister, **soror, sorōris** (f.).

site, **locus, -ī** (m.).

six, **sex.**

skilful, **perītus, -a, -um.**

skill, **ars, artis** (f.); **perītia, -ae** (f.).

sky, **caelum, -ī** (n.).

sleep, **somnus, -ī** (m.).

slowly, **lentē.**

small, very, **minimus, -a, -um.**

snow, **nix, nivis** (f.).

so (in this way), **ita.**

so (with Adj. and Advbs.), **tam;** (with Verbs), **adeō.**

so big, great, large, **tantus, -a, -um.**

so many, **tot.**

so much (of), **tantum** (with Gen.).

so often, **totiēs.**

so that (in final clauses), **ut;** *so that . . . not,* **nē.**

Socrates, **Sōcratēs, Sōcratis** (m.).

soften, I, **mollio, 4.**

soil, **humus, -ī** (f.).

soldier, **mīles, mīlitis** (c.).

some, **nonnullī, -ae, -a; aliquot;** *some . . . , others . . . ,* **aliī . . . , aliī . . . .**

sometimes, **interdum.**

son, **fīlius, -ī** (m.).

soon, **mox.**

Spanish, **Hispānus, -a, -um.**

spare, I, **parco, -ere, pepercī, parsum** (Dat.).

speak, I, **loquor, -ī, locūtus sum.**

spear, **hasta, -ae** (f.).

speech, **ōrātiō, -ōnis** (f.); **contiō,**

-ōnis (f.); *I make a speech*, ōr. habeo, 2.

speed, celeritās, -tātis (f.).

spend (*time*), *I*, ago, -ere, ēgī, actum.

spoils, spolia, -ōrum (n. pl.).

spring, vēr, vēris (n.).

squadron, turma, -ae (f.).

stake, sudis, sudis (f.).

stand, *I*, sto, stāre, stetī, statum.

standard, signum, -ī (n.).

star, stella, -ae (f.).

start, *I*, proficiscor, -ī, profectus sum.

state, cīvitās, -tātis; the Roman *commonwealth*, rēspublica, reīpublicae (f.).

station, *I*, pōno, -ere, posuī, positum.

statue, statua, -ae (f.).

stay, *I*, maneo, -ēre, mansī, (mansūrus).

stick to, *I*, adhaereo, -ēre, -haesī, -haesum, ad.

still, adhūc.

stone, saxum, -ī (n.); (*in a wall*), lapis, lapidis (m.).

storm, *I*, expugno, 1.

storm, tempestās, -tātis (f.).

story, fābula, -ae (f.).

street, via, -ae (f.).

strength, vīrēs, vīrium (f. pl.).

stretch, *I*, porrigo, -ere, porrexī, porrectum.

strike camp, *I*, castra moveo, -ēre, mōvī, mōtum.

strong (*person*), valens, Gen. valentis; (*place*), validus, -a, -um.

stronghold, oppidum, -ī (n.).

struggle, *I*, certo, 1.

struggle, certāmen, certāminis (n.).

such, tālis, -e; *in such a way*, ita.

sudden, subitus, -a, -um.

suddenly, subitō.

suffer, *I*, patior, patī, passus sum; (*loss*), accipio, -cipere, -cēpī, -ceptum.

suitable (*for*), aptus, -a, -um (with Dat.); (*weather*), idōneus, -a, -um.

summon, *I*, arcesso, -ere, arcessīvī, arcessītum.

superior, superior, -ius.

supply, cōpia, -ae (f.).

surely . . . not? num?

surrender, *I* (intrans.), mē dēdo, -ere, -didī, -ditum.

surrender, dēditiō, -ōnis (f.).

surround, *I*, circumdo, -dare, -dedī, -datum; circumvenio, -īre, -vēnī, -ventum.

survive, *I*, supersum, -esse, -fuī.

swear, *I*, iūro, 1.

swim, *I*, nato, 1.

sword, gladius, -ī (m.).

Syracusan, Syrācūsānus, -a, -um; *Syracusans, the*, Syrācūsānī, -ōrum (m. pl.).

Syracuse, Syrācūsae, -ārum (f. pl.).

Take across, *I*, transporto, 1.

take by storm, *I*, expugno, 1.

take over, *I*, transporto, 1.

teach, *I*, **doceo, -ēre, docuī, doctum.**

tell (*inform*), *I*, see *inform*.

tell (*order*), *I*, see *order*.

tell (*a story*), *I*, **narro,** 1.

temple, **templum, -ī** (n.).

ten, **decem.**

term, **condiciō, -ōnis** (f.).

terrify, *I*, **terreo,** 2.

Thames, the, **Tamesis, Tamesis** (m.).

than, **quam.**

that (demonstr. Pron. and Adj.), **is, ea, id** (unemphatic); *that* (*over there*), **ille, illa, illud;** *that* (*near you*), **iste, ista, istud.**

that (in consecutive clauses), **ut;** *that . . . not*, **ut nōn;** *in order that, so that* (in final clauses), **ut;** *in order that . . . not*, **nē;** *that* (in indir. commands and petitions), **ut;** *that . . . not*, **nē.**

thatch, **strāmenta, -ōrum** (n. pl.).

their, **eōrum, eārum, eōrum;** *their own* (reflexive), **suus, -a, -um.**

themselves (reflexive Pron.), **sē.**

then (*next*), **dēinde, tum.**

there, **ibi;** *from there*, **inde.**

therefore, **itaque** (1st word); **igitur** (2nd word).

thing, **rēs, reī** (f.).

think, *I*, **puto,** 1; **reor, rērī, ratus sum.**

thirty, **trīgintā.**

this (*near me*), **hīc, haec, hōc;** (unemphatic), **is, ea, id;** *this* (*of yours*), **iste, ista, istud.**

thither, **eō, illūc.**

thousand, **mille;** pl. **mīlia, mīlium** (with Gen.).

three, **trēs, tria.**

through, throughout, **per** (Acc.).

throw, *I*, **iacio, iacere, iēcī, iactum; mitto, -ere, mīsī, missum;** (*away*), **abicio, -icere, -iēcī, -iectum;** (*down*), **dēicio.**

thus, **ita.**

Tiber, the, **Tiberis, Tiberis** (m.).

tide, **aestus, -ūs** (m.).

tightly, **angustē.**

time, **tempus, temporis** (n.).

tired, **fessus, -a, -um.**

to, towards, **ad** (Acc.).

today, **hodiē.**

together, **ūnā.**

toil, **labor, labōris** (m.).

too (*also*), **quoque.**

too (with Adj. or Advb.), use comparative.

too much (*of*), **nimium** or **nimis** (with Gen.).

top of, the, use **summus, -a, -um.**

tortoise, **testūdō, -dinis** (f.).

towards (*place*), **ad** (Acc.); (*persons*), **ergā** (Acc.).

tower, **turris, turris** (f.).

town, **oppidum, -ī** (n.).

track, **vestīgium, -ī** (n.).

train, *I*, **exerceo,** 2.

transport, *I*, **transporto,** 1.

trap, **insidiae, -ārum** (f. pl.).

treachery, **perfidia, -ae** (f.).

treasure, **gāza, -ae** (f.).

treasury, **aerārium, -ī** (n.).

tree, **arbor, arboris** (f.).

trial of, I make, experior, -īrī, expertus sum.

tribe, populus, -ī (m.); gens, gentis (f.).

trick, dolus, -ī; *tricks,* artēs, artium (f. pl.).

Trinobantes, the, Trinobantēs, -um (m. pl.).

troops, cōpiae, -ārum (f. pl.).

true, vērus, -a, -um.

trust, I, crēdo, -ere, -didī, -ditum (Dat.); confīdo, -ere, -fīsus sum (Dat.).

try, I, cōnor, -ārī, cōnātus sum.

turn my mind to, I, see under *mind.*

twenty, vīgintī.

two, duo, duae, duo.

Unarmed, inermis, -e.

unawares, incautus, -a, -um; imprōvidus, -a, -um.

uncertain, incertus, -a, -um.

under (motion *to*), sub (Acc.); (rest), sub (Abl.).

undergo, I, subeo, -īre, -iī, -itum (trans.).

understand, I, intellego, -ere, -lexī, -lectum.

undertake, I, suscipio, -cipere, -cēpī, -ceptum.

unfair, inīquus, -a, -um.

unjust, iniustus, -a, -um.

unless, nisi.

until, usque ad (Acc.).

unwary, incautus, -a, -um.

unwilling, I am, nōlo, nolle, nōluī.

unworthy of, indignus, -a, -um, with Abl.

up to (*place*), usque ad; (*parts of body*), tenus (after Abl.).

urge, I, suādeo, -ēre, suāsī, suāsum (Dat.).

use, I, ūtor, -ī, ūsus sum (Abl.).

used to, I. Imperfect of soleo, -ēre, solitus sum, with infin.

useful, ūtilis, -e.

useless, inūtilis, -e.

usual, solitus, -a, -um.

Vain, in, frustrā.

value, I, aestimo, 1.

vanguard, prīmum agmen, prīmī agminis (n.).

various, varius, -a, -um.

Veii, Vēiī, -ōrum (m. pl.).

very, the, ipse, ipsa, ipsum.

victory, victōria, -ae (f.); *I win a victory,* vinco, -ere, vīcī, victum.

vinegar, acētum, -ī (n.).

violent, violentus, -a, -um.

voice, vox, vōcis (f.).

voyage nāvigātiō, -ōnis (f.).

Wage war against, I bellum infero, -ferre, -tulī, illātum, in (Acc.).

wait for, I, exspecto, 1.

wall, mūrus, -ī (m.); *city walls,* moenia, -ium (n. pl.).

wander, I, erro, 1; vagor, -ārī, vagātus sum.

want, I, volo, velle, voluī; *I do not want,* nōlo, nolle, nōluī.

war, bellum, -ī (n.).

warn, *I*, **moneo**, 2.

watch, *I*, **specto**, 1.

watch, **vigilia, -ae** (f.).

water, **aqua, -ae** (f.).

wave, **unda, -ae** (f.).

way (*manner*) **modus, -ī** (m.); (*road*), **via, -ae** (f.).

we, **nōs.**

wealth, **dīvitiae, -ārum** (f. pl.); **opēs, opum** (f. pl.).

weapon, **tēlum, -ī** (n.).

weary, **fessus, -a, -um.**

weather, **tempestās, -tātis** (f.).

weep, *I*, **fleo, flēre, flēvī, flētum.**

well, **bene.**

well-known, **nōtus, -a, -um.**

what? (interrog. Pron.), see under *who?*

what? which? (interrog. Adj.), **quī, quae, quod?**

what kind of? **quālis, -e?**

when, **ubi** (with indic.); **cum** (with past tense of subj.).

when? **quandō?** (in dir. and indir. questions).

whence, **unde.**

where, **ubi**; *from where*, **unde.**

where? **ubi?** *where to?* **quō?**

whether (in single indir. question), **num;** (in double indir. question), **utrum.**

which? (interrog. Adj.), see under *what?*

which of two? **uter, utra, utrum?**

while. Sometimes a present participle may be used (Ch. 23).

who, which (rel. Pron.), **quī, quae, quod.**

who? what? (interrog. Pron.) **quis, (quis), quid?**

whole, **tōtus, -a, -um.**

why? **cūr?**

wide, **lātus, -a, -um.**

wife, **uxor, uxōris** (f.); **coniux, -iugis** (f.).

willing, *I am*, **volo, velle, voluī.**

win, win a victory, *I*, **vinco, -ere, vīcī, victum.**

win over, *I*, **concilio**, 1.

wind, **ventus, -ī** (m.).

wine, **vīnum, -ī** (n.).

winter-quarters, **hīberna, -ōrum** (n. pl.).

wisdom, **sapientia, -ae** (f.).

wise, **sapiens**, Gen. **sapientis.**

wish, *I*, **volo, velle, voluī;** *I do not wish*, **nōlo, nolle, nōluī.**

with, (*in company*), **cum** (Abl.); **cum** is also used for *with* (*against*) after verbs of *fighting*.

withdraw, *I* (trans.), **removeo, -ēre, -mōvī, -mōtum.**

within (*time*), use Abl.

without, **sine** (Abl.).

woman, **fēmina, -ae** (f.); **mulier, mulieris** (f.).

wonder at, *I*, **mīror, -ārī, mīrātus sum.**

wont, *I am*, **soleo, -ēre, solitus sum.**

wood, **silva, -ae** (f.).

woody, **silvestris, -e.**

word, **verbum, -ī** (n.).

work, *I*, **labōro**, 1.

work (*toil*), **labor, labōris** (m.); (*task*), **opus, operis** (n.).

worse, **pēior, pēius.**

worthy (*of*), **dignus, -a, -um** (with Abl.).

wound, I, **vulnero,** 1.

wound, **vulnus, vulneris** (n.).

wretched, **miser, misera, miserum.**

write (*to*), **scrībo, -ere, scripsī, scriptum** (**ad**).

writer, **scriptor, -tōris** (m.)

wrong, **iniūria, -ae** (f.).

Year, **annus, -ī** (m.).

yet, not, **nōndum.**

yield, I, **cēdo, -ere, cessī, cessum.**

yoke, **iugum, -ī** (n.).

you (s.), **tū;** (pl.), **vōs.**

young man, **iuvenis, iuvenis** (m.).

your (s.), **tuus, -a, -um;** (pl.), **vester, vestra, vestrum.**

Additional Exercises

Relative Pronoun

EXERCISE 165.
1. Epistola, quam scripsisti, brevissima est.
2. Pauci sunt agricolae, quorum agros milites non vastaverunt.
3. Hannibal in insidias, quas Galli paraverant, subito incidit.
4. Is, cui Romani imperium mandaverant, appellatus est Fabius.
5. Feminae, quarum mariti pugnabant, maxime anxiae erant.
6. Difficile est muros superare quos spectas.
7. Hic est locus, in quo castra ponemus.
8. Ei, quos Hannibal ad insidias delegerat, erant Numidae.
9. Milites, quibuscum Marcellus processit, facile muros ascenderunt.
10. Litterae, quas Caesar legebat, ab Atrio scriptae erant.

EXERCISE 166.
1. Archimedes, who helped the Syracusans, was very skilful.
2. The book which you gave me is beautiful.
3. The city which Hannibal had determined to overcome was not far away.
4. The river whose banks they saw was the Anio.
5. The guides with whom the column was marching were false.
6. Those who entered the river held their arms with difficulty.
7. The lion to whom Androclus gave help was transported to Rome.
8. The soldiers at last saw the booty that had been promised.
9. The walls you see are those of the city of Rome.
10. The sailors who were approaching the wall were driven back by javelins.

EXERCISE 167.

1. Hannibal dixit victoriam esse certam.
2. Milites putabant bellum futurum esse longissimum.
3. Speculator vidit Romanos mox perventuros esse.
4. Puer dixit se ad patrem epistolam scripsisse.
5. Pater negat se ullam epistolam accepisse.
6. Romani senserunt se in hoc proelio victum iri.
7. Caesar cognoverat Britannos adiuvare Gallos.
8. Caesar audivit Britannos multitudine navium perterritos esse et discessisse.
9. Nuntii Caesarem certiorem fecerunt omnes naves iam instructas esse.
10. Romani senserunt se propter ventum adversum aliquamdiu impeditum iri.
11. Romani non poterant credere elephantos Alpes transisse.
12. Putasne hostes hodie in nostros impetum facturos esse?

EXERCISE 168.

1. The messenger says that the fleet is ready.
2. Hannibal said that everything would be easy.
3. The Romans heard that the city had been captured.
4. Do you think that the ships will arrive before noon?
5. The general said that such men would never be conquered.
6. Caesar perceived that no enemy had been drawn up on the shore.
7. Hannibal promised to give his soldiers rewards.
8. Caesar said that the wind was not favourable.
9. We hope to capture the city.
10. The cavalry did not think that they would be seen by the enemy.
11. Hannibal thought that the citizens had been deceived by the trick.
12. It was announced that the Romans had at last won a victory.

EXERCISE 169.

1. Dux erat tam fortis, ut omnes eum laudarent.
2. Tam validi sunt muri, ut eos expugnare non possimus.
3. Tot naves aderant, ut nullus hostis in litore maneret.
4. Tam grave vulnus acceperat Marcellus, ut mortuus sit.
5. Tanta erat audacia hostium, ut nostros perterrerent.
6. Caesar nuntio adeo perturbatus est, ut statim regressus sit.
7. Tales erant Romani, ut omnes eis inviderent.
8. Britanni primo ita pugnabant, ut nostri non resistere possent.
9. Haec urbs est tam pulchra, ut nemo ab ea discedere velit.
10. Tot litteras heri scripsi, ut hodie defessus sim.
11. Adeo gaudebamus propter victoriam, ut statim ad templum rueremus.
12. Romani toties superati erant, ut iam desperarent.

EXERCISE 170.

1. The enemy fought so fiercely that our men retreated.
2. The elephants were so frightened that some fell into the river.
3. This mountain is so high that we cannot climb it.
4. So often have you learnt these words that you ought to know them.
5. The difficulties were so great that the soldiers were unwilling to advance.
6. I have taught so many boys that I sometimes forget their names.
7. The law was so unjust that few were willing to obey it.
8. So many books are written that we cannot read them all.
9. So sudden was the attack that no reinforcements could be sent.
10. Such is his bravery that all men are willing to follow him.
11. The soldiers were so wretched that no one replied.
12. The road had been broken in such a way that we could not advance.

EXERCISE 171.

1. Ut hiemem vitaret, copias reduxit.
2. Equites emissi sunt, qui locum explorarent.
3. Caesar munitionem aedificat, ut naves defendat.
4. Ne se recipere cogeretur, novas copias arcessivit.
5. Caesar tres legiones emisit, quae frumentum comparent.
6. Scribe litteras, ut Caesarem de his rebus certiorem facias.
7. Hannibal agmen consistere iussit, ut milites hortaretur.
8. Ne Caesar transiret, Britanni ripam fluminis muniverant.
9. Perfice hoc opus statim, ne magister te culpet.
10. Marcellus, ut urbem spectaret, in locum altum ascendit.
11. Nuntius venit, ut hanc cladem nuntiaret.
12. Sepelite pecuniam, ne quis eam diripiat.

EXERCISE 172.

1. Many seek the gates in order to escape.
2. The enemy flew out to attack the foragers.
3. Hannibal has written a letter to deceive the citizens.
4. We will stay in the column, so that we may not be caught by an ambush.
5. Messengers were sent to inform Caesar about the storm.
6. The enemy remained in the wood that no one might see them.
7. Caesar advanced with his legions to capture the stronghold.
8. A good general should send out scouts that he may never be caught unawares.
9. The soldier had approached the wall to count the stones.
10. Send cavalry to help us.
11. Do not write to ask for money.
12. In order not to be killed or captured, Horatius leapt down into the river.

EXERCISE 173.

1. Quattuor reges profecti sunt, ut castra Romanorum oppugnarent.
2. Tot milites interfecti sunt, ut reges se reciperent.
3. Talis est ille, ut ei semper credam.
4. Ad illum locum contendamus, ut flumen pedibus transeamus.
5. Legatos ad Caesarem mittemus, ne plures e nostris frustra interficiantur.
6. Oppidum non satis est validum ut resistat.
7. Mitte puerum qui cibum nobis emat.
8. Oppidum erat tam invalidum ut non resisteret.
9. Subducite naves, ne quam amittatis.
10. Cives ita urbem muniverant, ut Romani intrare non possent.
11. Exploratoribus semper utere, ne quis te subito oppugnet.
12. Tam celeriter contendit, ut nemo eum capere possit.

EXERCISE 174.

1. They left behind their heavy arms, so that no one might hinder them.
2. Caesar waited for ships to transport his men to Gaul.
3. The Gauls were so silent that no one could hear them.
4. Hannibal waited so long for reinforcements that he began to despair.
5. The scout was placed there so as to catch sight of the Romans.
6. Send out some scouts to reconnoitre that road.
7. Fabius was delaying so that he might never be defeated in battle.
8. So quickly did our men drive back the enemy that they could not halt or resist.
9. The Carthaginians sent cavalry to draw the Romans across the river.
10. Read good books so that you may become a good writer.
11. So great was Roman power that no people could resist it for long.
12. The citizens so rejoiced that they could scarcely speak.

EXERCISE 175.

1. Praefectus suis imperavit ut castra oppugnarent.
2. Caesar nostris imperat ne hostes longius prosequantur.
3. Dux postulavit ut ea gens obsides sibi daret.
4. Consul exercitum hortabatur ne spem abiceret.
5. Caesarem oravimus ut captivo parceret.
6. Nonne te iussi epistolam hodie scribere?
7. Magister puerum monebat ut librum legeret neve opus neglegeret.
8. Amico meo persuasi ut hunc librum legat.
9. Cives moniti erant ne quem in urbem admitterent.
10. Cur lex ista mulieres pulchre ornari vetat?
11. Hannibal patri persuasit ut se ad Hispaniam ire sineret.
12. Caesar Cassivellauno imperavit ne illi populo unquam noceret.

EXERCISE 176.

1. Hannibal ordered his men to advance towards the river.
2. The leader told the Gauls not to speak.
3. Caesar begged one of the Gauls to convey a message.
4. I was asked to come as quickly as possible.
5. The master encouraged the boy to learn Greek.
6. In vain will you urge such a soldier to retreat.
7. The citizens have begged Marcellus not to harm them.
8. Why did Sempronius order his forces to follow the enemy's cavalry?
9. We were advised to read well-written books.
10. Lentulus persuaded the Romans not to try to resist.
11. Fabius urged that the Romans should delay and not join battle.
12. I beseech you to write to me soon.

EXERCISE 177.

1. Roga eum quis sit et quid faciat.
2. Captivum rogavimus ubi hostes essent.
3. Nescimus quo Britanni se receperint.
4. Romani rogabant cur Fabius moraretur.
5. Caesar ignorabat quando naves rediturae essent.
6. Caesar certior factus est quomodo Britanni ripam fluminis munivissent.
7. Audivistine num Caesar mox perventurus sit?
8. Hannibal intellexit cur Carthaginem revocatus esset.
9. Nescio utrum hunc librum legeris necne.
10. Caesar voluit reperire qualis esset munitio.
11. Imperator equites rogavit num silvam exploravissent.
12. Volo scire utrum imperatorem meliorem fuisse credas.

EXERCISE 178.

1. The commander asked the prisoner how many men were in the wood.
2. They told us who they were and where they had come from.
3. Caesar wanted to discover why the cavalry had not arrived.
4. Have you heard whether he has been made consul?
5. Tell me the size of the country.
6. Let us see what kind of leader he will be.
7. Do you know when your sister will come back?
8. It is difficult to say whether this advice is foolish or not.
9. The Romans did not know what Archimedes was now inventing.
10. Ask the cavalry whether they have received the corn or not.
11. I could not see from the top of the hill what the enemy were doing.
12. I want to know which of these three horses you think to be best.

EXERCISE 179.

1. Aliud est polliceri, aliud facere.
2. Hoc opus mihi difficilius est nec quisquam adest qui me adiuvet.
3. Certiores facti sumus copias hostium maiores esse nostris.
4. Mitte quam plurimos in mediam silvam.
5. Caesar ea, quae fecerat, ipse narravit ; Alexander secum scriptores habebat.
6. Alter puer miles fiet, alter nauta.
7. Non is erat cui persuaderetur hoc esse verum.
8. Romani Fabium tanti aestimabant, ut eum dictatorem creaverint.
9. Milites quisque in suo loco manere constituerant.
10. Hannibal proelium primus inibat, ex proelio ultimus excedebat.
11. Putasne exercitum Romanum vicisse annon?
12. Nonne optimus quisque reipublicae succurrere cupit?

EXERCISE 180.

1. Which of the two boys was the first to reach the bottom of the mountain?
2. Do you value his advice highly or not?
3. To please all men is very difficult.
4. I bought this corn for eight denarii.
5. I know you are not the kind of man to despair.
6. After reading the new book, she gave it to a friend.
7. The general advanced six miles and ordered his men to pitch camp.
8. All the bravest men followed the example of the consuls.
9. The Britons fortified the bank of the river and waited for the enemy.
10. What the general has decided to do is uncertain.
11. The snow was so deep that the elephant fell.
12. The general had few troops left and could not expect any reinforcements.